The Upper Room
Disciplines
2005

UPPER ROOM BOOKS®
NASHVILLE

An Outline for Small-Group Use of Disciplines

Here is a simple plan for a one-hour, weekly group meeting based on reading *Disciplines*. One person may act as convener every week, or the role can rotate among group members. You may want to light a white Christ candle each week to signal the beginning of your time together.

Opening

Convener: Let us come into the presence of God.
Others: Lord Jesus Christ, thank you for being with us. Let us hear your word to us as we speak to one another.

Scripture

Convener reads the scripture suggested for that day in *Disciplines*. After a one- or two-minute silence, convener asks: What did you hear God saying to you in this passage? What response does this call for? (*Group members respond in turn or as led.*)

Reflection

- What scripture passage(s) and meditation(s) from this week was (were) particularly meaningful for you? Why? (*Group members respond in turn or as led.*)
- What actions were you nudged to take in response to the week's meditations? (*Group members respond in turn or as led.*)
- Where were you challenged in your discipleship this week? How did you respond to the challenge? (*Group members respond in turn or as led.*)

Praying together

Convener says: Based on today's discussion, what people and situations do you want us to pray for now and in the coming week?
Convener or other volunteer then prays about the concerns named.

Departing

Convener says: Let us go in peace to serve God and our neighbors in all that we do.

Adapted from *The Upper Room Daily Devotional Guide*, January–February 2001. ©2000 The Upper Room. Used by permission.

Cover design: Ed Maksimowicz
First Printing: 2004

Lectionary texts from *The Revised Common Lectionary* copyright © 1992 by The Consultation on Common Texts (CCT), P. O. Box 340003, Room 381, Nashville, TN 37203-0003 USA. All rights reserved. Reprinted with permission.

Scripture quotations not otherwise identified are from the *New Revised Standard Version Bible* © 1989, Division of Christian Education of the National Council of the Churches of Christ in the United States of America. Used by permission. All rights reserved.

Scripture quotations designated RSV are from the *Revised Standard Version Bible*, copyright 1952 (2nd edition, 1971) by the Division of Christian Education of the National Council of the Churches of Christ in the United States of America. Used by permission. All rights reserved.

Scripture quotations designated NIV are from the *Holy Bible, New International Version*. NIV. Copyright © 1973, 1978, 1984 International Bible Society. Used by permission of Zondervan Publishing House. All rights reserved.

Scripture quotations designated KJV are from the King James Version of the Bible.

Scripture quotations designated REB are taken from the Revised English Bible, copyright © Oxford University Press and Cambridge University Press 1989. All rights reserved.

Verses marked GNT are taken from the Good News Translation—Second Edition; Today's English Version © 1992 American Bible Society. Used by permission.

ISBN: 0-8358-9870-9
Printed in the United States of America

Contents

Foreword

For the past fifteen years, I've been a "road warrior." I've spoken in all forty-eight contiguous states, Hawaii, Puerto Rico, and all ten provinces of Canada. I've crossed the ocean to England and Scotland and flown halfway around the world to the Philippines. As a professional speaker, I've stood before audiences in London, Manila, New York, and Fargo, North Dakota.

Most Sundays saw me not in church but heading for the airport, since my working week always began with a flight from my small airport to a major U.S. or Canadian city. From there, I would continue on to my final destination. Five days and five cities later, I'd board a plane and return home. Often bad weather, bad connections, or bad traffic kept me from getting home until Saturday.

Between those Sundays and Fridays, I was alone on the road, living in hotel rooms, flying or driving between cities every night, and speaking to hundreds of strangers. In the tradition of "the show must go on," I worked through blizzards, riots, power failures, airline strikes, earthquakes, hurricanes, raging fevers, mind-numbing head colds, laryngitis, migraines, and bomb threats. I never missed an engagement.

What kept me going? A small book that I picked up shortly after I embarked on this career, *A Guide to Prayer for Ministers and Other Servants* published by Upper Room Books became the basis of my lifeline on the road. Each morning, whether in the Hyatt Regency in New York City or the Holiday Inn in Wausau, Wisconsin, I would make a cup of tea (often hot tap water and a tea bag), settle down in the armchair or prop myself up on the bed, and begin my daily time of devotions and prayer.

It wasn't a long time. Usually, I spent only fifteen to twenty minutes with the devotional passages. However, I soon learned that a day begun in this way became a day in which I could face "all things." On the rare occasions when I was running late and decided to eschew the devotional time, I felt the loss keenly for the rest of the day.

A few years later, I began to carry sticky notes with me. When a thought or insight jumped out from the pages during my devotion time, I'd write it on the note and post it on my lectern where I could see it throughout the day as I spoke to my audience.

Then I began to use hotel notepads to write down particular verses from the Bible selection each day; by the end of the week, a pattern of God's word would emerge. Not only did I perceive a strong sense of God's speaking to me personally, but often these patterns would indicate a leading or an answer to prayer that I had been seeking.

~

I retired three months ago. It's a funny feeling not to rush off to the airport on a Sunday but leisurely to make my way to church. Each morning I wake up in my own bed, pursue my own interests during the day, and crawl back into the same bed at night. However, one thing has remained from my "road warrior" days, and that is my daily time with God.

Here in my quiet at-home life, I may not face the same challenges that met me on the road. I may not have the same fears, worries, or daily hurdles to cross that came with the job. However, I still need that quiet time, that moment of centering that brings me to the foot of the Cross and reminds me that I am never alone. Without the daily time with God, I feel as if I've forgotten to turn off the coffeepot or lock the door before leaving the house. The nagging feeling of having forgotten something important overshadows my day.

In the end, it's very simple. Daily devotions are no more and no less than a deliberate meeting with your God. In that brief time, you come together as Father and child, Guide and follower. You give your reports, confirm your direction, receive instructions, and affirm your faith in the concept of God with us.

—PATRICIA WILSON
Author and speaker

Living for the Praise of God's Glory

January 1–2, 2005 • *Beth Porter*[‡]

SATURDAY, JANUARY 1 • Read Ecclesiastes 3:1-13; Revelation 21:1-6a

Today's readings invite us to be aware of ourselves and of our call in the here and now—a good way to start the New Year! The heavenly vision from the book of Revelation reassures us that God is at the beginning and end of all history, including the coming year. The pace of the much-loved reading from Ecclesiastes suggests a measured, reflective, and holy living throughout the span of our lives.

Roy left an institution at age sixty-nine to live in L'Arche Daybreak community. He was one of the last to leave the institution because people thought he could not make the adjustment. Actually he adjusted well, seemingly seizing his time at L'Arche as a new season of his life. He lived it to the full until his heart finally stopped at age eighty-five.

After the institutional environment of locked doors, dormitories, and few options, Roy reveled in his life's variety in our community. An exuberant and warmhearted man, he soon had numerous friends eager to take him fishing, bowling, on country drives, or out for coffee. He delighted in the unlocked kitchen refrigerator, stashing various treats in his pillowcase at night. At the Seniors' Club he painted with a passion, saving his most colorful artwork for special friends. Roy didn't spend time lamenting what hadn't been in his life but lived this season with all his heart and brought much joy to others.

PRAYER: Loving God, in the coming year help me recognize the seasons of life that I am invited to live. May I live them fully, trusting your gracious presence in all of my history. Amen.

[‡]Member and interfaith chair, L'Arche Daybreak community, Toronto, Canada; editor of the "thought sheet," *A Human Future*, for L'Arche Canada; writer on spirituality and disability issues.

EPIPHANY SUNDAY

Openness to the unexpected is key to spiritual vitality. The wise men in Matthew's infancy narrative probably come from Persia, yet they ably grasp that God's revelation is coming to a different religious and ethnic group than their own. Do they know that the royal child they will worship will be born into material circumstances far beneath theirs? Not likely! Others might have said, "There must be some mistake here!" But undeterred, the magi bow in obeisance and offer their gifts.

The beloved spiritual writer Henri J. M. Nouwen, in his early book *The Wounded Healer,* expressed an important spiritual insight—that the person who seems most in need of healing may himself or herself be a healer. But his insight acquired a new and transformative personal reality for him when he came to know Adam Arnett. When Henri moved to L'Arche, one of his tasks was to help Adam get ready in the morning. Adam could not talk and had many physical needs; he was as slow as Henri was fast. But Adam radiated a deep peacefulness. Bathing and dressing Adam, fixing his breakfast and sitting with him as he awkwardly ate it, Henri, whose brilliant inner being was driven by a constant anguish and sense of urgency, was opened up to discover Adam as his healer and teacher in a more centered and profoundly life-giving way of being.

Rabbi Abraham Joshua Heschel wrote, "To meet a human being is a major challenge to mind and heart [for] the human is a disclosure of the divine."★ Sometimes God's self-disclosure comes not in a form we desire, let alone expect; but it is always gracious and life-giving.

PRAYER: Loving God, help me to be open to the unexpected, to treasure moments of revelation, and to live out of the energy and insight they give. Amen.

★"No Religion Is an Island" in *Moral Grandeur and Spiritual Audacity,* by Susannah Heschel (New York: Farrar, Straus and Giroux, 1997), 238.

Servants of the Lord

January 3–9, 2005 • Norval I. Brown[‡]

MONDAY, JANUARY 3 • Read Isaiah 42:1-4

I grew up watching a television show called *Family Affair*. One of its main characters was Mr. French, a gentleman's gentleman (a butler, although he detested that appellation). This kind of work was part of his lineage, and he proudly upheld the family tradition. His ancestors had served some of the great nobles of the British Empire, and Mr. French attended to the needs of a rather well-to-do New Yorker. However, few of us would choose to be a servant. In fact, we would rather *have* servants than *be* servants! But God's servant redefines the role and breaks the mold. God delights in God's servant. Rather than serving the elite and powerful, this servant bends to the downtrodden and the oppressed.

God calls forth and creates a new servant with a different mind-set. This servant crusades for justice, unlike Mr. French. Rather than bringing dainty pastries to the rich and famous, this servant seeks to bring bread to the world's hungry. With unceasing energy, this servant works until all is accomplished. Our spiritual legacy places us in this lineage of servants! To be fiercely proud of upholding a work ethic dedicated to the dispossessed and disenfranchised is the calling of those named Christian.

SUGGESTION FOR REFLECTION: Go to a soup kitchen or homeless shelter and spend some time serving the residents. Try to discover the cause of the plight of one of the patrons, and ponder what you might do to ease his or her condition.

PRAYER: Lord, always let me your servant be.
       Lead me, O Lord, lead me. Amen.

[‡]Director of Chicago Southern District Campus Ministry, Chicago, Illinois; elder in the Northern Illinois Conference of The United Methodist Church; certified spiritual director; active participant in the Emmaus community and The Upper Room Academy for Spiritual Formation.

Opening the Eyes of the Blind

My favorite uncle was my Uncle Thurman, my father's mother's brother. He was the closest thing to a grandfather that I had growing up. I loved him dearly. Now I must tell you, Uncle Thurman was blind. Well, at least he couldn't see with his eyes. He constantly amazed me with the things he could do—helping to raise a crop of tobacco from sowing to getting it to market, walking the five miles from his home to my home without missing a step or trailing off into the woods. Uncle Thurman served as the superintendent of our church school, as a lay speaker and as the church's lay member to the annual conference. He could sing, preach, and pray. Oh, could he pray—long conversations with God that never seemed to end. In fact, "amen" never seemed to be a part of his vocabulary when he was praying. His faith shone through all that he did.

But from stories I have heard, that wasn't always the case, just as Uncle Thurman wasn't always blind. Apparently, as a sighted person, he tended to be rather self-centered. But when Uncle Thurman lost his ability to see the world through his image-forming organs of sight, his inward eyes were opened. He began really to "see" the world, becoming a servant in that world.

God will open the eyes of the blind, which does not necessarily refer to those who are unable to see the world with their eyes. Each of us lives with some degree of blindness, thereby missing some, most, or all that God has in store for us. Opening the eyes of the blind means that we will see the glory of the Lord in our inward being and be drawn to that glory.

Suggestion for meditation: Throughout the day, use this phrase as a breath prayer: O God, what blindness in me do I refuse to see?

Prayer: God of eye-opening surprises, "open my eyes, illumine me, Spirit divine." Amen.

The voice of the Lord

I entered the church chancel to begin the service of death and resurrection for George. Somewhere within the packed sanctuary sat my wife and children. As I began to read the words of the liturgy, a voice called out from among the worshipers, "Daddy! Daddy!" Members of George's family smiled as they recognized the voice of my fifteen-month-old daughter, Crystal, responding to a voice she knew.

The psalmist affirms that all of nature and the heavenly beings recognize the voice of God and yield to the power and authority displayed in that voice. The psalmist testifies to ways in which the earth resounds with the voice of the Lord. The voice comes over the waters and thunders over the sound of mighty waters. The voice flashes and shakes and, notes the psalmist, causes the oaks to whirl. Mighty is the voice of the Lord! The biblical witness speaks also to the still small, loving voice of God. As my daughter Crystal responded to the familiar sound of my voice, so the psalmist reminds us that all nature and heavenly beings respond to God's familiar voice. As God speaks, they all cry "glory."

When I listen prayerfully, I hear that voice. I hear anew that the primary aim of all creation, humanity included, is to glorify God. And so we join in a hymn of praise that echoes Psalm 29:

> This is my Father's world.
> O let me ne'er forget that though the wrong
>   seems oft so strong,
> God is the ruler yet.

> This is my Father's world: why should my heart be sad?
> The Lord is King; let the heavens ring!
> God reigns; let the earth be glad!

SUGGESTION FOR MEDITATION: Slowly read again Psalm 29. Call to mind the ways that you have experienced God in nature. Compose a breath prayer thanking God for divine revelation through nature to you.

THURSDAY, JANUARY 6 • Read Psalm 29:10-11

The quest for peace

When I served as the pastor of a suburban Chicago congregation, the impetus for a war with Iraq gained momentum. To bear witness against such an action, the church members observed a season of nonviolence, which began with a candlelight vigil on January 30, the anniversary of the assassination of Mahatma Gandhi, through April 4, the anniversary of the assassination of Martin Luther King Jr. During this time, we prayed daily for peace in the world—the natural world, the nurturing community, the social community, the economic community, the political community, and the world community. We focused on becoming an instrument of God's peace.

The church's observance culminated on April 4 with the dedication and planting of a Peace Pole and a Peace Garden, declaring that the sacred area around the church was safe for all of creation. The Peace Pole included four plaques with the words *May Peace Prevail on Earth* written in English, American sign language, paw print, and leaf print. The church members planted in the garden a capsule that contained prayers for peace.

The psalmist has declared the great power of the voice of God. Notice the upheaval and fury of nature as God speaks— forests are stripped bare, the wilderness shakes, flames flash forth! Yet this God who rules over wind and sea can and does will peace for creation. The psalmist prays that the people of God will be blessed with peace. And peace will come when we, the people of God, are yielded and still in order to be recreated to enjoy the fullness of life that God has purposed for us.

SUGGESTION FOR MEDITATION: Use as a breath prayer today these words attributed to Saint Francis, "Lord, make me an instrument of thy peace."

Understanding that God shows no partiality

I am often reminded that I am a black man in America. Security guards in department stores have watched me. Police officers have followed my car and pulled me over for no apparent reason. I am old enough to remember when some people thought my name was "Boy." And the church often reminds me that I am a black man in the church. Our conference journal with its notation of BM (Black Male) next to my name in committee listings reminds me. When I attend workshops and seminars as the only black in attendance, people ask me, "Where are the blacks?" or "Norval, what do the blacks think or feel about this issue?" I am reminded. My appointment as the first black pastor of a predominantly Anglo congregation served as a definite reminder. These memories make me realize that human beings do show partiality.

Peter declares, "I truly understand that God shows no partiality." This is evident in God's call to Cornelius—an uncircumcised Gentile. We cannot imagine ourselves as God's elect without considering why God would exclusively choose us and not others. We know who the others are—those who are not like us. The labels we use—single, divorced, deaf, mute, gay—indicate the partiality we exhibit in the church and in the world. Our ad slogan in The United Methodist Church for the past several years has been "Open Hearts, Open Minds, Open Doors." If Peter's perception is to become the church's reality, then we must pray that God will change our hearts.

SUGGESTION FOR MEDITATION: Call to mind a time when you have been the victim of prejudice because of age, gender, nationality, sexual orientation, or other reason. How did it feel? Now ask yourself, "Would I want to make others feel that way?"

PRAYER: O God, let me see you in everyone I meet today. O God, let others see you in me today. Amen.

Role reversal

Easter Sunday 1986 was an extra special day for my family and me. Crystal, our daughter, was to be baptized. She had been welcomed into a family in which both parents served as ordained pastors. Everything stood in readiness at my wife's church—gathered family and congregation, the bowl of water on the altar, the elements to celebrate Eucharist. We came to the time for the celebration of the sacrament of baptism, but there was a problem. The pastor who was to officiate at the baptism hadn't arrived! Finally my wife looked at me and said, "Well, I guess you are just going to have to do this." With some hesitancy, I stepped behind the altar and proceeded to lead the liturgy of the baptismal covenant. I had anticipated my role as parent on that day, but circumstances precipitated another action for me.

John hesitates to baptize Jesus. John's baptism is a baptism of repentance for those who acknowledge their sin. He recognizes the absence of such a condition in Jesus. In fact, a few verses earlier he had preached about the one who was to come of whom he was unworthy. He really feels that Jesus should be baptizing him. But now John is called on to serve in a capacity that he does not feel is his right—yet, it is all in God's hand. While John does not understand God's will, Jesus' declaration that righteousness must be fulfilled causes him to join Jesus in God's plan for salvation. Jesus' first words in Matthew's Gospel are direct and filled with authority. So John consents, and the baptism proceeds.

SUGGESTION FOR MEDITATION: Consider those who often minister to you—your pastor, a parent, a colleague—and look for a way to minister to them today. Consider praying with and for your pastor or tending to the need of a parent. Be creative.

Precious and beloved child

I am the father of four children, although I am not biologically related to any of them. I believe each one is God's special gift to me and each is precious and beloved. I can call to mind a special moment in each of their lives when my heart swelled with pride. Christopher, my oldest, once asked why I always helped the homeless people who rang the bell at the church or knocked on the parsonage door. I replied that whenever someone sought assistance and I had the resources to meet that need, I was acting as Christ would. One day, while heading back to school after his lunch break Christopher stopped by the church office. He wanted to talk; I wanted my change back from the lunch money I had given him. He explained that a girl at the sandwich shop was hungry and didn't have any money. Remembering our earlier conversation, he used the change from his lunch to buy a meal for this girl. I looked at him and smiled. This was my son, the beloved.

At Jesus' baptism, a voice from heaven speaks, saying, "This is my Son, the Beloved, with whom I am well pleased." Jesus has responded positively to the clarion call of John that the time is now at hand to begin the ministry for which he came. Possessing free will, Jesus could have easily turned from this moment, ignoring it. God does not orchestrate his movements—the choice is his. As Jesus begins the ministry for which he divested himself of divinity and clothed himself in humanity, it becomes clear that he is the Messiah, the chosen one of God, the Anointed One who has come to save.

PRAYER: O God, Loving Parent that you are, love me as your child and be pleased with me today. Amen.

Waiting in Faith, Serving by Grace

January 10–16, 2005 • John W. Bryant[‡]

MONDAY, JANUARY 10 • Read Isaiah 49:1-7

Few of us have not occasionally doubted our individual significance or despaired of finding a meaningful purpose for our lives. Some struggle continually with doubt and despair; others are overwhelmed by those emotions in the aftermath of failure or great personal loss.

Isaiah proclaims that each of us is not only significant but of *divine* significance. Known to the living God before our birth, our destiny takes shape in God's loving purposes for us: "The LORD called me before I was born, while I was in my mother's womb he named me. . . . And he said to me, "You are my servant, Israel, in whom I will be glorified.""

These words reflect an eternal truth for all of us, not just the characters in the Bible, the rich and famous, or the neighbors who seem to have it all together. This present knowledge about the nature of life and human existence gives us a foundation and a starting point for understanding our lives.

We seek personal meaning and direction through regular study, prayer, and meditation. But even these God-given tools are hindered unless we ground our prayers in scriptural confidence: Our individual lives have divine significance, and God has a purpose for our lives that we can know. Confidence in this truth expresses itself as faith, which lightens the burden of our quest and gives us assurance and patience as we wait upon the Lord. It allows our prayers for personal direction to take flight.

PRAYER: Eternal God, you are the source of our existence, the substance of which we are made, the fountain of life from which we come and to which we return. Breathe the wisdom of Isaiah deep into our being, that it may become our starting place as we attempt to live meaningful lives in you. Amen.

[‡]Lawyer; member of First United Methodist Church, Dallas, Texas.

I fondly recall a devotional group in which I participated several years ago. Each week good-hearted colleagues became closer and closer as we learned, shared, and grew spiritually together. I never wanted the meeting to end and couldn't wait for the next one.

We may derive much comfort in being present in a community of Christian fellowship. Whether worshiping, studying as a group, or working together on a service project, the sharing, goodwill, and spirit of cooperation we experience opens us to God's presence. We can be ourselves, receive comfort from hearing others' experiences, and pray with depth and meaning. Christian fellowship can raise our spirits and inspire us to witness, to deepen our spiritual life, and to offer ourselves in further service to our church.

But Isaiah calls us to move beyond our familiar community to a greater role and a greater blessing: "It is too light a thing that you should be my servant to raise up the tribes of Jacob and to restore the survivors of Israel; I will give you as a light to the nations, that my salvation may reach to the end of the earth."

The richest blessing comes not only in experiencing the expression of faith within our own community of believers. We also free ourselves to be fully in the world, in the midst of all God's people, living lives transformed by a Christ-centered openness to the needs of others and a faithful sense of purpose. When we live our lives in the world in glad service and availability to the word of God, we become a "light unto the nations," beaming a way of "salvation" to a world of people watching, hoping, and searching for meaning for their own lives.

PRAYER: Open us to a wider world of brothers and sisters, O Lord, that your love might be manifest in us and your salvation may reach "the end of the earth." Amen.

Being able to wait in faith for God-given insight or action in our lives at a time of challenge or crisis is the fruit of spiritual growth. Yet how often in the hard times we at first forget the most important lessons of our faith.

We want immediate relief and quick answers. Conditioned to manage our way out of everything, we rely entirely on our intellect and talent to engineer a good result. We despair when the solution does not come easily, often looking to strong personalities for deliverance. Yet, if we marginalize important faith lessons in times of crisis and forget the only source of true wisdom, our spiritual life becomes little more than a Sunday ritual.

The psalmist proclaims the reality of the Lord's work in our lives; he exults in his rescue from the desolate pit by "waiting patiently for the LORD." He assures us that we can wait with confidence: "Happy are those who make the LORD their trust, who do not turn to the proud, to those who go astray after false gods." He then goes on to remind us that while we wait, our prayers are heard: "You have given me an open ear."

And the psalmist calls upon us to give ourselves over to God completely while we wait: "Then I said, 'Here I am. . . . I delight to do your will, O my God.'" Waiting patiently and praying confidently after giving ourselves entirely to God is the most basic exercise of our faith. God waits for us. The psalmist exhorts us always to wait for the Lord.

PRAYER: **Teach us to wait upon you, O God, and to seek first your guidance and wisdom. Amen.**

Early Christian communities, such as the one in Corinth to which Paul writes, were islands of faith in a hostile environment. Their tenacity is more than most Christians today can imagine. Social ridicule, physical hardship, and threats were compounded by doubts, uncertainties, false doctrines, and the challenges of getting along with one another. Surely the temptation to abandon the new faith and return to old ways constantly pulled at the fabric of the community.

Paul, acutely aware of these difficulties, emphasizes his own call to be an apostle as he writes as one with authority to church members in Corinth, describing them as called to be saints, thereby in every way having been enriched in Christ "so that you are not lacking in any spiritual gift." Having been called, he writes, they have been given all they need to face every difficulty.

Are we not called to be saints as well? Paul's assurance that the Corinthians have the resources to deal with every challenge is the same assurance offered to all of us who try to live in Christian community.

Are we modern Christians really so different from the Corinthians? Most of us (but not all) live in a safer physical and political environment. But aren't we and our faith communities assaulted daily by vivid and numerous temptations from articulate challenges to scripture and faith to unrelenting pressure to conform to popular values?

Paul addresses his letter not only to the Corinthians but to those "who in every place call on the name of our Lord Jesus Christ." His letter is written to *us*. We welcome Paul's assurances that "God is faithful; by him you were called into the fellowship of his Son, Jesus Christ our Lord" and that we also have been given every spiritual gift to remain faithful Christian communities.

PRAYER: Help us to live in awareness of your spiritual gifts to us, Lord, and to rely on them in times of testing. Amen.

FRIDAY, JANUARY 14 • **Read 1 Corinthians 1:1-9**

Paul speaks often of being "called." He refers to himself as "Paul, called to be an apostle of Christ Jesus by the will of God." He says the members of the church in Corinth are "called to be saints." He writes, "God is faithful; by him you were called into the fellowship of his Son, Jesus Christ our Lord."

Christians are familiar with the concept of a divine calling. Sometimes its use implies instant messaging from on high to those with a special ability to receive divine inspiration. But Paul speaks of everyone in the church in Corinth as having been called, not just a special few.

We often hear the term *divine calling* in reference to those who have decided on a career in pastoral ministry or in mission work. But clearly not everyone can be a full-time minister or missionary. Who would grow our food, fight fires, or teach school? Most of us are called to other purposes and means of service. And for most of us, it is enough that we are simply called to our daily work, allowing the light of Christ to guide us in service and love. We let Christ shine through us as a means of grace for others.

How do we receive our calling? Must we be suddenly struck by a vision, like Paul on the road to Damascus? Even Paul, after his Damascus experience, needed a long period of prayer and reflection to understand the full meaning of his calling. For most of us, as in the great old hymn, our calling comes to us not all at once but day by day:

"Jesus calls us o'er the tumult of our life's wild, restless sea; day by day his sweet voice soundeth, saying, 'Christian, follow me!'" ("Jesus Calls Us," *United Methodist Hymnal*, No. 398).

PRAYER: Make us quiet and humble, Lord, that we may hear your call, even in the midst of tumult. Amen.

God offers us grace without precondition. Brothers and sisters in Christ can lead us into the path of God's grace, where we begin to understand and receive it. A conversation with someone, an article or book, or a chance encounter with a persuasive speaker can lead to a second step, drawing one to a closer examination of faith that leads to lifelong commitment. Discipleship often seems to begin casually. But the means of grace that touch us on the way to discipleship are the fruit of the availability, work, and commitment of others who went before.

John the Baptist's ministry was the means of grace through which the first two disciples, Andrew and Peter, encountered and followed Jesus. John also offered a means by which people could understand the coming of Jesus: "I came baptizing with water for this reason, that he might be revealed to Israel."

Through regular availability to the various means of grace, including scripture reading, prayer, the Eucharist, and worship, we continually grow in our understanding of God and our ability to let Christ be manifest in our lives. And we find ourselves continually enabled to use our unique gifts and our service as a means of grace to others.

The availability, love, and service of those who went before placed the first two disciples in the way of Jesus. So it is with us and every follower of Christ. Availability to the means of grace in our lives allows the work of God to be done, not only in ourselves but in others. How do we make ourselves available?

PRAYER: Open us to your purposes, O Lord. Lead us in your way, that we might give ourselves to you without reservation and prepare the way for others. Amen.

SUNDAY, JANUARY 16 • Read John 1:35-42

Though we are placed in the way of Christ by God's grace, manifest in unique events in our lives and in the works of others who have prepared the way, discipleship is sealed by the open invitation of Christ himself.

John the Baptist pointed Andrew and Peter to the path of discipleship. But Jesus' response to their question, "Where are you staying?" leads them into communion with his life and mission. He responds, "Come and see."

Jesus does not tell them, "Contact me later," "Make an appointment," or "Drop by day after tomorrow." Instead, in this moment of possibility for Andrew and Peter, Jesus evidences an immediate willingness to fulfill their desire to see where he is staying and to learn all about him.

So it is with us. Christ is ever present to us. When grace leads us to seek him, whether for the first time or the thousandth time, no ritual or formality precedes our approach. The mere stirring of our heart and the simple opening of our attention to him places us in his presence. He is available to us, as he was to Andrew and Peter, to help us "see."

The invitation of Christ is a standing invitation. It is an eternal and ever-present principle of life itself, a constant beckoning to communion. All who seek him find him.

With the confidence given to us by the Gospels, both the new arrival to Christ and the lifelong Christian may seek him during high moments of gratitude. We may seek him in low moments of doubt or despair or during daily pursuit of spiritual growth. We remain confident not only of his presence but of his standing invitation to "come and see."

PRAYER: Open us to a sense of ease and certainty in approaching you, O Lord. Instill in us the confident knowledge that you are immediately present whenever we turn our hearts to you. Amen.

Light Living

January 17–23, 2005 • Cheryl G. Bostrom[‡]

MONDAY, JANUARY 17 • Read Isaiah 9:1-4

Most Januarys we in northwest Washington state have been living in gloom for months. Murky clouds propagate like mold, occluding the sun's brilliance even as the tipping earth limits it. I feel my posture slouch with the dim days; my mood slumps. Winter here is an oppressive season; darkness is strong. Even when I turn on every light in the house, the days remain dark.

Similarly, dark seasons in relationships, health, employment, and culture can launch us into a climate of hopelessness and despair. The Israelites of Isaiah's day understood such distress, darkness, and fearful gloom. The presence of Assyrian invaders oppressed and disheartened them.

Isaiah writes to them and to us who know darkness too pervasive for medication, entertainment, and self-help to illuminate. He doesn't talk about temporary solutions, puddles of light that people can switch on and off like houselights. Instead he makes an amazing prediction: promised Light that will dispel the 3:00 AM blackness. "There will be no more gloom for those who were in distress. . . . The people walking in darkness have seen a great light; on those living in the land of the shadow of death a light has dawned" (NIV).

That light? Not an incandescent bulb or a halogen beam with a few hundred yards' reach. Not Botox and collagen, a six-figure salary, applause, or a gated community. Isaiah describes the one who will come as the Light of the world, shattering "the yoke that burdens them, the bar across their shoulders, the rod of their oppressor" (NIV), and the Son will shine for good.

PRAYER: Lord, keep us from depending upon mortal philosophies, procedures, or treasures to brighten our lives. Amen.

[‡]Author, educator, speaker; member of Sonlight Community Christian Reformed Church, Lynden, Washington.

Most days I visit my grandmother who, since her stroke last summer, has shared a room in our local care center with Jill, a twenty-six-year-old with dark hair, jade-colored eyes, and cerebral palsy. Both view life from wheelchairs. Both frail, vulnerable women depend on aides to move, eat, and bathe.

Both, like the psalmist, have enemies. Their bodies have betrayed them, becoming enemies of mobility and independence. Just the thought of being in their condition frightens many who meet them.

Yet also like the psalmist, neither woman is afraid. Either woman could have spoken the words of Psalm 27: "The LORD is my light and my salvation—whom shall I fear? The LORD is the stronghold of my life—of whom shall I be afraid?" (NIV)

I sense a direct correlation between the time they have spent seeking God's face, as did the psalmist, and their fearlessness. They have learned that when they praise and thank God, they "gaze upon the beauty of the LORD" (NIV) and "seek him in his temple" (NIV), God will place ordinary, limited people like them—and like us all—in God's safe dwelling.

Now, as they face days of trouble like those described in Psalm 27, the women are guarded from the enemy of fear that can assail them like floodwaters. The psalmist explains, "He will keep me safe in his dwelling; he will hide me in the shelter of his tabernacle and set me high upon a rock" (NIV). Gazing at God places us there. The results? Safety, peace, fearlessness.

When I sit with Gram and Jill, and they begin with "I'm so thankful for . . . ," I hear something akin to the psalmist's shouts of joy, as these two dear women "make music to the LORD" (NIV), even as enemies threaten.

PRAYER: Father, may we concentrate our minds and hearts on your beauty. And may enemies of discontent and fear stumble and fall. Amen.

For the sake of victory in an athletic contest, coaches admonish players to work together. For the sake of strength in battle, sergeants bark at new recruits to march in step with other soldiers. For the sake of peace, parents insist that children get along. Victory, strength, and peace—all worthwhile goals and good reasons for unity.

But when the apostle Paul appeals to believers to "agree with one another so that there may be no divisions among you" (NIV), he asks them to get along for the sake of the Lord Jesus. For those of us who love Christ, that reason alone ought to silence petty dissension. Because of God's desire for unity, we concentrate on common ground rather than disagreement. We let go of nonessential, divisive issues. All of our image promotions, opinions, and power plays lose their brilliance when exposed to God's light—kingdom light, eternal light.

Better yet, as we focus on Jesus and allow his Spirit to temper and direct us, divisions that create controversy and disputes between us may actually disappear! Differences may remain, but without divisiveness agreement can prevail. At that point, we experience a true unity that surpasses outward civility or cooperation: a unity of mind and thought with one another and with our Lord.

How much energy would Jesus spend on this conflict? In light of eternity, how weighty is the issue? Does pursuing the issue contribute to the act of loving God and loving people? How does pressing the issue contribute to someone's salvation?

PRAYER: Lord, make us agreeable people. Quiet the opinions and nit-picking that divide us and keep us from loving well. May we think, feel, and show grace and Light-mindedness that mimics yours and that perfectly unites us with other believers. Amen.

THURSDAY, JANUARY 20 • Read 1 Corinthians 1:11-13

When white light passes through a prism, it breaks into a series of colored light bands, each with a different wavelength. While colorful, the split-out bands of light lose the pure brilliance of undivided light.

People share similarities with light too—only the divided kind. We show various "colors" of personality, ability, and appearance. We certainly can operate on different wavelengths. Fortunately, when we come together in Christ, those divisions can disappear.

When Paul wrote to the Corinthians, he had to contend with people who lived in a sensual, materialistic culture not unlike our own. Many had held multiple allegiances to pagan gods, aligning themselves with cultural norms and practices.

So Paul's appeal for agreement among believers seemed an unfamiliar plea. The Corinthians, experienced quarrelers, carried their contentiousness into the church. Verses 11-12 tell us that instead of recognizing the ministries of Paul, Apollos, or Cephas as gifts from Christ himself, members of the Corinthian church tried to set their teachers up as leaders of competing factions. The one-upmanship degenerated into fighting over whose teacher was best.

In verse 13 Paul redirects them to Christ, the author of all they have learned through their various teachers and the one who died for them. He asks the piercing questions, "Has Christ been divided? Was Paul crucified for you?" The apostle implores them to avoid needless quarrels by looking straight at the undivided, true light, Jesus Christ. May we do likewise.

PRAYER: Father, excise the quarrelsome ways that divide us and fill us with unity in you. Amen.

Persuasive marketing: big business capitalizes on it; small business depends upon it; individuals trust it to convince others. But the apostle Paul refuses to use it. Though he had today's equivalent of a graduate degree in theology and credentials as a capable, intelligent, experienced missionary, he refuses to depend upon those qualifications to help him market Jesus Christ.

Instead, Paul depends totally on the power of the cross—on the Christ who conquered sin through his death and resurrection—to convince people to accept the gospel. Paul trusts neither human action (even the physical act of baptism) nor human wisdom to persuade. For he knows that human wisdom in any form will, at best, bring about temporary, superficial change in people rather than the radical, eternal, inner transformation that the indwelling Christ accomplishes.

How often do we hesitate to share the gospel because we doubt our ability to "say it right"? Or when we do share and our words fall on deaf ears, we assume that if we had only been more persuasive or if we had only offered a more convincing argument (or if we had just taken that class in evangelism!) the listener would have believed.

Paul's words can set our minds at rest as we speak up for Jesus. God does the convincing, not us! No amount of training, education, or experience can save those who are perishing. Only the power of God revealed in the cross can save from death's darkness and bring into God's light. No matter how eloquently we present the gospel, if someone is perishing, our words will sound foolish. But if that person is being saved, even the simplest language will hold the power of God!

PRAYER: Our loving Father, forgive us when we want to save people through our own wisdom rather than through your illuminating power. May we trust you, not ourselves. Amen.

A change in circumstances often spurs movement. Positive events like a new job or marriage, for example, can relocate us to a new town or lifestyle. Likewise, painful events regularly shift our direction or plant us in a new place. Clearly, adversity can play a role in advancing God's plans.

Imagine Jesus' pain when he learns of John's imprisonment by the violent, cowardly Herod Antipas (who would behead John soon thereafter). Surely the traumatic news jolts Jesus and seemingly prompts him to change locations. He leaves Nazareth and headquarters his ministry in Capernaum on the Galilean shore.

Centuries earlier, the prophet Isaiah had noted this move: "Land of Zebulun and land of Naphtali, the way to the sea, along the Jordan, Galilee of the Gentiles—the people living in darkness have seen a great light; on those living in the land of the shadow of death, a light has dawned" (NIV). Matthew's Gospel links Jesus' move to a crossroads of commerce with the painful situation of John's imprisonment. Jesus begins preaching in Capernaum, and those living in the darkness hear God's truth firsthand. John's adversity becomes a catalyst for spreading the light!

We live in a world filled with pain and upheaval. But our pain can become a useful tool in God's redemptive work. Our suffering can propel us into new places of growth and service. We too can carry God's light into the shadows.

PRAYER: Lord, help us trust that you will transform our painful circumstances and use them for good. When pain spurs us to action, help us move according to your purposes. May we spread your light even in the midst of hurtful events. Amen.

Lightning struck a two-hundred-year-old spruce tree near our home last summer. In a dazzling splinter of time, a bolt tore a top-to-bottom, four-inch-wide path through the entire length of the tree's bark—permanently marking it as one of several "lightning trees" that pepper our region. Thunder reverberated through the surrounding hills—announcing the branding, the forever change in the tree.

I don't usually equate Jesus' calling the first disciples with a lightning strike, but I could. When Jesus calls Peter and Andrew, James and John, his voice strikes them with a divine initiative that penetrates their routines and relationships and etches an invitation on their souls.

While Simon Peter and Andrew cast fishing nets, lightning struck: Jesus, the Light of the world, calls them. Ramifications thunder: immediately they release their nets, livelihood, and plans. Likewise, James and John, spending time with their dad, hear Jesus' call, and Light carves change into family priorities and the community framework. Without a moment's hesitation, they turn to Jesus and leave boat and father behind for his sake.

"Come, follow me," Jesus says, approaching his disciples much as Elijah had sought out Elisha as his future attendant in 1 Kings 19. Jesus finds fishermen working with nets; Elijah threw his cloak over Elisha's shoulders as he plowed a field behind yoked oxen. Both enter the lives of their disciples and summon them to holy tutelage. But there Jesus' purpose expands. When Jesus calls his disciples, he begins laying the foundation of believers upon which he will build his church. From the moment he extends those personal, individual invitations to join him, the disciples began sharing in his redemptive work on earth, drawing others to his eternal, Light-powered kingdom.

Jesus calls us to nothing less.

Prayer: Thank you, Lord Jesus, that you initiate Light-filled relationship with us. May we desire nothing less. Amen.

The Challenge of Divine Integrity

January 24–30, 2005 • *Larry Castillo-Wilson*[‡]

MONDAY, JANUARY 24 • **Read Matthew 5:1-6**

My wife and I were at wit's end. Our twelve-year-old daughter would not inform us of her after-school activities. We grounded her, took away privileges—tried a number of forms of discipline. As a last resort, we chose a form of discipline I had never needed to use with my daughter. I felt a twinge of emotional regret and hesitation, but my duty as a parent stared me in the face.

After enforcing the decided-upon discipline, I left my daughter in her bedroom, opened the front door of the house, and walked the streets. My effort to fulfill the demands of parenthood included an effort to fulfill the demands of *righteousness*. But what does this word mean and require? Righteousness is to fulfill the duties and requirements of a relationship according to divine love, justice, and integrity. We thereby live the love and nobility of God's will in all relationships. God envisions a sacred integrity that exists between soul and self, parent and child, wife and husband, relative and relative, employer and employee, race and race, government and people, nation and nation, human being and nature—every conceivable relationship. Righteousness represents life at its best.

The New English Bible translates the verse this way: "How blest are those who hunger and thirst to see right prevail." As in the disciplining of a beloved child, living so that right prevails is not easy. It takes courage and faith. But despite the risk and hardship, Jesus' words challenge us to be motivated, not by a drive for wealth, high position, or hollow happiness but rather by a passion to see righteousness realized in all relationships.

PRAYER: God, develop within us a passionate aspiration for righteousness. Amen.

[‡]Pastor, New Mexico Annual Conference; writer, poet, historian; living in Rio Rancho, New Mexico.

As my family hiked through a grove of aspen trees, I chose this opportunity to teach my children about my passion and love for God's creation. I said to my six-year-old son, "Casidy, these are aspen trees we are walking through." I noticed that he brooded deeply as we continued to walk. He finally asked, "Papa, do aspirins really grow on these trees?"

The relationship between tongue and ear can be one of mis-understanding. Less obvious is a moral dimension in the relationship of tongue and ear: that of righteousness. If righteousness means to act on the love and noble intention of God in all relationships, we have a duty to communicate the love and nobility of God's will to the ear of the hearer. Righteousness is not just something we do; it is something we speak.

Psalm 15 contrasts the righteous tongue and the toxic tongue. A toxic tongue poisons relationships by killing self-esteem, confidence, affection, hope. It brings to life hate, despair, malice, mistrust. Ragged, shredded, patched words of gossip habitually dribble off the toxic tongue.

It has been said that a leaf gives a tongue to the wind. A righteous tongue gives speech to the Spirit of God, which gives new life to hope, healing, consolation, confidence, love, loyalty, truth, and trust in all relationships.

In the beginning, God spoke the world into being. In a similar way, our words create the world of relationships in which we and others must live. God summons us to discipline our tongues, using them to create a world of beauty and integrity—to speak with aspen-leaf tongues to create hillsides of golden beauty amidst the darkened contours of the earth.

PRAYER: **Lord God, transform my tongue into righteous gold. Amen.**

Beautiful is Spain to visit, to see, to savor. I stood in awe and studied in detail one morning the Cubist painting that stretched across a large wall in the Reina Sofia museum in Madrid, Spain. It was a painting not of grand beauty but of agonizing pain. *Guernica*, painted by Pablo Picasso in 1937, expressed his outrage at the terror bombing of civilians in that defenseless town during the Spanish Civil War.

My eyes scanned the painting to see a wailing mother, dead child in her arms; a man screaming to the heavens, arms reaching for help; disjointed arms and legs; a horse in the throes of death; a contorted face desperately looking upward for some light of hope amidst the darkness.

None of us is a stranger to this world of cruelty painted by Picasso. While Picasso vividly depicted reactions to the world's ruthlessness, we participate in more subtle and less visible ways. We undermine and subvert the self-esteem of others by word and deed; we use power tyrannically to abuse and humiliate; our arrogance makes others feel worthless; we stubbornly ensure our ego's triumph even if it results in chaos and conflict.

Cruelty, a form of cowardice, kowtows and surrenders to impulses of enmity and anger, mindlessly conforming to pernicious precedents both past and present. But God abhors cruelty and envisions a world interwoven with lovingkindness and ruled by righteousness. God entreats us, yea, requires us to permeate all we do and say with lovingkindness and thus make such a world possible.

When we fail to discipline our lives after the example of Christ by acting with lovingkindness in all situations and all relationships, we breathe life into the world of *Guernica*.

PRAYER: God, inspire within me the courage to fight against cruelty in all its forms and to labor in building a world of lovingkindness. Amen.

In a small country church in west Texas, I stood behind the pulpit to prepare for Sunday morning worship. A member entered, sat in her usual pew, and then rose and walked past me to a small room behind the pulpit. Shortly, she returned to her seat.

After the service, the woman explained, "I dressed in the dark. When I sat down in my pew, I looked down to see my dress seams. I had put my dress on inside out, so I went back to the small room to change."

In today's reading, the apostle Paul subtly criticizes the Corinthians for acting in ways contrary to Christian principle. These poor, common folk act with elitism, spiritual pride, and hypocrisy, all rooted in blind allegiance to dynamic teachers with substandard theology.

In essence, the Corinthians were experiencing a time in their lives when the rough, worst side of their personalities were being seen rather than the polished, best side—something we all experience. And during these times, ragged seams of sin display our hypocrisy, the thread of falsehood in the human soul. Hypocrisy permeates not only religious life but all dimensions of life. Hypocrisy struts on two feet: deception of oneself and deception of others. It destroys trust and disillusions those who seek genuine faith and truth.

God beckons us to a life of righteousness: to live divine love, justice, and integrity in all relationships. We must courageously refute all pretense and strive for relationships of authenticity—total truthfulness between appearance and reality. As we struggle toward divine integrity in our Christian character, the small room behind the pulpit will beckon us less and less.

PRAYER: God, give us the divine daring to:
> **debunk beliefs of holy conceit,**
> **disdain the lie in self and soul,**
> **dispel the false from mind and heart,**
> **pursue the truth with love and grit,**
> **infuse and renew all of life with truth and trust.**
> **Amen.**

No one in the small church, not even the mother, denied it. The young boy was bratty. One Sunday morning in worship, the boy's annoying behavior reached a new height. The mother had had enough. In her fury, she grabbed him by the arm and dragged him from the sanctuary into the narthex. As she commenced to chew out the young urchin, an automobile passed by the church and backfired. In the sanctuary someone blurted out, "Oh no, she shot him!"

In Hebrew, the original word for mercy comes from a stem which means "womb"; hence mercy represents the love, sensitivity, and understanding of a mother for her child. This compassion always manifests itself in two circumstances: in the presence of power and in the enforcing of punishment or negative consequences.

In the absence of mercy, power becomes abusive both close at hand and in the forces and events of history. The immobilization of mercy can kill self-confidence, self-worth, good mood, hope for the future, marriage, family, government, and good relations between nations.

In the course of human life, a surge of rage can lead to punishing oneself or another person, a group, or nation. Mercy is the surge protector that keeps us from treating ourselves and others cruelly. God's kindhearted mercy, which flows through the power cord that stretches between the divine and the human heart, enables human mercy to function this way. Only the courageous can restrain destructive impulses that arise within.

Mercy is not weakness, but neither is it naïveté. Genuine mercy understands that corrective action is still needed. Gold-plated mercy has the strength to act with wisdom and good judgment. Plated with the Golden Rule, it does what is best for all with compassion and empathy. Jesus speaks to us of a sparkling new vision of mercy—one of the best hopes of human life.

PRAYER: Lord, nurture within us the capacity for gold-plated mercy. Amen.

I needed mercy; I had made a costly mistake. Thoughts filtered through my mind: *There is no way to cover this up; there is no one else to blame; I must own up to my mistake; I will lose the respect of my congregation.* At the administrative council meeting the next week, after gagging my ego and pride, I stood before the members and squeezed out the words: "It was my mistake to allow a fly-by-night paving company to pave the parking lot. My intentions were good, but my judgment was faulty. I take full responsibility for the incident."

Humility is hard—and hard working. (Jesus' meaning may best be conveyed by the word *humility* rather than *meekness*.) Brave humility works hard to admit mistakes; to develop awareness of personal faults; to speak words of forgiveness; to seek reconciliation in situations of enmity; to use power with wisdom and compassion; to restrain egotism, arrogance, conceit, and know-it-allism.

A biopsy of the human spirit might reveal an enlarged, diseased ego with resulting symptoms of a mean-spirited use of power and authority among many. But the humility of which Jesus speaks is highly potent. Just as high-potency vitamins work to produce physical health, high-potency humility labors to produce health, healing, and harmony in all relationships. The source of the potency, the divine presence, enables the human spirit to do the hard work of disciplining and healing the ego.

High-potency humility is bifocal. It sees limitations but also possibilities, thus being both honest and objective. This dynamic force restrains dysfunction and inspires the realization of righteousness—the higher and divine potentials of the human spirit.

God asks that we own up to our failure to discipline and heal our pompous and malignant ego, that we rededicate ourselves anew to live the world-transforming, high-potency humility envisioned by Jesus.

PRAYER: Lord, help us to be visionaries like Jesus. Amen.

Warm and close-knit were the pastor and his friend. They held in common many beliefs and values, and they conversed for hours about deep issues of life. Trust, honesty, and affection formed the bonds of their relationship.

After much prayer and deliberation about his duty to Christ's teachings, the pastor spoke to the congregation about the need to be more open and accepting of persons of a different race and economic class. His words angered some members who began to spread false and malicious rumors about the pastor. The friend listened.

The next time the pastor spoke with his friend, he sensed ice in the relationship. He persisted in his attempts to communicate with his friend, but his words met only permafrost. The pastor carried in his heart the pain of that lost and broken relationship to the end of his days.

Persecution points to the chasm that exists between the divine will and the human will, the gap between divine values and human values. It exposes the pain of efforts made to bridge the chasm and live the higher ways and wisdom of God.

We live in a matrix of conflicting values and ideas. When we refuse to be fickle in our fidelity to Christ and his cause, persecution can result. Paying a price is inevitable when we accept Jesus' challenge to be true and tenacious in our commitment to him, to live divine love in all relationships, to stand for what is right in every situation. Amid the turbulence of adversity, loyalty to Christ and the high standards of righteousness can bring pain and agony.

When we pay the price for righteousness and devotion to Christ, we have a clear conscience; we experience the restless contentment of Christian integrity. We cherish a friend whose loyalty is everlasting.

PRAYER: Lord, make us unafraid to pay the price for dedication to Christ and his righteousness. Amen.

Into God's Presence

January 31–February 6, 2005 • *Mark A. Tabb[‡]*

MONDAY, JANUARY 31 • Read Exodus 24:12-18

Moses walked right into the fire. The voice of the Lord called, and he walked right in—into the smoke, into the cloud, into the fire. Surely the leaders of Israel watch from below. From where the Israelites sit "the appearance of the glory of the LORD was like a devouring fire." And they see Moses climb higher and higher until the fire and cloud consume him.

No one volunteers to go with him, although Joshua accompanies him part of the way. Moses tells the elders to stay put, and they're glad to oblige. They know better than to play with fire, especially holy fire. Most are content to stay put and wait for the crazy man to return from the burning mountaintop. After the fall of Adam and Eve, distance has characterized the relationship between the Creator and the created. The Israelites believed that no one could enter the Lord's presence and survive. When days turn into weeks, many may assume that Moses must be dead.

But all that is about to change. Through Moses God reestablishes a face-to-face relationship with humanity. Forty days after walking into the fire, Moses comes down from the mountain with detailed instructions about how the children of Israel could enter into God's presence on a regular basis. That's God's desire, and we hear the divine call to come near to God's presence—into the devouring fire.

PRAYER: O Lord, teach me to dwell in your presence; consume me with your holy fire. Amen.

[‡]Author and fire department chaplain, Knightstown, Indiana.

TUESDAY, FEBRUARY 1 • **Read Psalm 99**

In today's reading, the psalmist celebrates the Lord's glory and sovereignty over all creation. He continues by praising God and recounting events throughout human history when the Holy One has drawn close to the people to hear and answer their cries. Therein lies the problem.

God is easy to deal with from a distance. From a distance this deity seems to be a safe God, a God who fills my life with happiness and makes me feel good about myself. From a distance all I see is what I want to see: God's love, forgiveness, unconditional acceptance of me.

But when God comes near, everything changes. "The LORD is king," the psalmist cries out, "let the peoples tremble!" The peoples don't tremble with excitement to see God but quite the opposite. When the Lord asserts divine reign upon the earth, those of us who live here tremble in fear. Suddenly I see God for who God really is. And I see myself for who I really am, which sends a cold chill of dread down my spine.

The psalmist calls God holy, mighty, the lover of justice who establishes fairness and who acts with justice and righteousness. God draws near to set things right, to do what is fair and just and righteous. And that's why the peoples tremble. We who are unholy quiver in the presence of the holy. When the righteous judge draws near, fear sweeps over those of us who want justice for others but only grace for ourselves.

Thankfully God is both a forgiving and transforming God. The lover of justice expects those who claim relationship with the divine to love justice as well. God calls me to set things right and to establish fairness in this world. I can ignore this claim as long as I remain at a distance. But when God draws near, revealing the essence of divine being, my only choice is to change.

PRAYER: Holy Lord, make me an instrument of your justice. Use me to establish fairness and righteousness in this seemingly unfair and unrighteous world. Amen.

Peter, the disciple, enjoyed an advantage over us. He lived the Transfiguration. His eyes watched as Jesus' appearance changed, and his ears heard the voice of God boom from the cloud. The impact of that day never left him; he had witnessed Jesus' majestic splendor, a confirmation of the prophets' message. Peter had the assurance of personal experience that Jesus was the Christ, not just another popular myth among many.

You and I haven't seen what Peter saw. We talk about drawing near to God; but our experience comes by faith, not by sight. Our ears may never hear the voice of God call down from a cloud. Our intimacy with the Lord may only be felt in our hearts. We don't have the tangible, physical evidence Peter enjoyed. And sometimes our confidence wavers.

Yet our confidence need not falter. Although our eyes may not see Jesus' garments shining like the sun, God offers us something even better. After the writer of Second Peter shares the details of the Transfiguration, he advises us to pay attention to the words of the prophets, the scriptures, "as to a lamp shining in a dark place, until the day dawns and the morning star rises in your hearts." The dazzling light on the mount of Transfiguration now shines in our hearts as we encounter Jesus through the word.

Our experience doesn't sound as spectacular without the clouds, lights, and visitors from the past; yet it is just as real. The glory and splendor of Christ continues to shine through his word as we meet with him there. And we can relive it as often as we open the Bible and peer deep inside.

PRAYER: O Lord, replace my doubt with the firm confidence that comes from your word. Amen.

THURSDAY, FEBRUARY 3 • Read Psalm 99

God's people are no strangers to hardship and suffering. Yet, the psalmist repeatedly praises the Lord's holiness, the very foundation of their hope. No one is exempt from life's bitterness and pain. When suffering falls down around our heads, we feel very distant from God. We cry out, but all we can hear is the sobbing that comes from deep within ourselves. The more we think about the pain, the greater our agony. How much more can we take?

The writer of Lamentations experienced his own strength slipping away. Thoughts of his affliction and wandering filled him with bitterness and gall. Yet something kept him going and gave him hope:

> This I call to mind,
>   and therefore I have hope:
> The steadfast love of the LORD never ceases,
>   his mercies never come to an end;
> they are new every morning;
>   great is your faithfulness. (3:21-23)

We often wait for God's revelation of self in a spectacular way. Yet divine glory often invades our space through the still, quiet voice of the promises given long ago. A voice doesn't have to boom from a cloud when we can hear God whisper through scripture. And God's voice is unmistakable. It turns a night of despair into an unforgettable moment of hope. Our situation may not immediately change, and our suffering may drag on for what seems like an eternity; yet, after God speaks, everything changes. Like the psalmist, we can be confident in the Lord's glory and faithfulness—the Holy One hears and answers our cries. The hope of God's glory allows us to patiently wait for salvation, even through the darkest hour.

SUGGESTION FOR MEDITATION: How has God revealed divine compassion to you? How will you respond?

When we consider this event from Moses' perspective, it must have taken courage and faith of heroic proportions to enter into God's presence. This was, after all, uncharted territory. We can only imagine how Moses felt being engulfed by God's glory for forty days and forty nights. A desire to remain in that holy place, surrounded by the loving presence of God forever seems likely.

But we sometimes lose sight of one of God's primary reasons for pulling us into divine presence. Yes, God wants us to experience love and grace; we leave the presence as changed people. Our faces may not glow as Moses' did, but those around us can tell we've spent time with God. (See Exod. 34:29-35.) Yet God doesn't draw us into presence for ourselves alone. When Moses leaves the Lord's presence he immediately goes to the people and tells them what God has to say. Hearing from the Lord brings responsibility. Spending time in God's presence dictated that Moses then go to others and share God with them as well.

The writer of the book of Hebrews tells us to "approach the throne of grace with boldness, so that we may receive mercy and find grace to help in time of need" (Heb. 4:16). We take this mercy and grace with us as we leave, offering them to those who haven't spent time at the throne of grace. We become God's hands, feet, and mouth to a world desperate for a fresh touch from God.

The children of Israel would have remained lost in the desert if Moses had hoarded God to himself. If our world seems lost and adrift, could the fault not lie with those of us who spend time basking in God's glory while failing to spread God's mercy and grace to others? The loving Lord isn't far away from anyone; God is as close as the nearest follower.

SUGGESTION FOR MEDITATION: **Who in your life needs a fresh touch of God's mercy and grace? How will you share it with them today?**

When they hear the voice, Peter, James, and John probably wish they were anywhere but on top of the mountain. Their minds can hardly grasp all they've already seen: Jesus' appearance shining like the sun, Moses and Elijah standing there next to him, and the cloud that envelops them all. Peter, James, and John know mere mortals are out of their league in this setting.

Then they hear the voice of God: "This is my Son, the Beloved; with him I am well pleased; listen to him!" The three mortals dive to the ground and cover their heads in fear. For the first time they understand the absolute terror that gripped the children of Israel at Mount Sinai when the voice of God called out the Ten Commandments in the hearing of the entire nation.

A hand touches the disciples' shoulders as they cower, hoping to survive the experience. The three look up. The cloud has lifted; Moses and Elijah are gone. Jesus alone stands before them. "Do not be afraid," he says. Yet, humanly speaking, how can they not be afraid? They've seen the real Jesus and his glory as the one true God in human flesh. Yet his touch and words of reassurance drive away their fear.

As we approach Transfiguration Sunday, we too hear the voice of God booming from the mountain. Coming face-to-face with a holy God, we know we've walked onto holy ground. We also feel the hand of Christ upon our shoulders. There before us is Jesus alone, the sole source of our hope and confidence. His touch and words of reassurance replace our fear with the confidence of God's love and acceptance.

SUGGESTION FOR MEDITATION: Place yourself next to Peter, James, and John. Allow their fear to sweep over you. Then feel the touch of Jesus, as well as the relief his love brings.

TRANSFIGURATION SUNDAY

As if the wonder of the Transfiguration wasn't enough for one day, the drama continues. I've always been struck by the contrast between the events on the mount of Transfiguration and what awaits Jesus and his disciples at the bottom. While Jesus' majestic splendor shines high on the peak, down below his other disciples battle the forces of evil.(See Matt. 17:14-18.) A man brings his demon-possessed son for healing, but they can't help. A crowd gathers, and the teachers of religious law start an argument.

We can only imagine the sigh of relief that rose from the disciples when they see Jesus coming down the mountain. *Finally*, they must be thinking, *Jesus is here. He'll take care of everything.* And he does. Jesus drives the demon out of the child and restores him to his father's care. The crowds walk away amazed; the religious leaders stew in their anger, and the disciples at the bottom wonder why they couldn't help the man and his son.

This sharp contrast between the stories of Transfiguration and the demon-possessed child reminds us that God doesn't call us to live on spiritual mountaintops. From time to time God invades our space and allows us to experience the splendor of divine presence. But God doesn't allow us to stay in that place. Instead the Holy One leads us down the mountain to a world of hurting people who need to feel the divine touch—through us. The distance between the two is quite short. We long to stay in God's presence on top of the mountain, but we can't. The crowd beckons, and there's work to be done.

PRAYER: Lord, I long to stay up on the mountain. I long to feel your touch and experience your glory. Yet you call me to go to a world filled with hurting people. Build up my faith that I may obey your call. Amen.

In the Garden

February 7–13, 2005 • *Nancy Mairs*‡

MONDAY, FEBRUARY 7 • **Read Genesis 2:15–17; 3:1–7**

All of us feel certain that we once dwelled in a garden of perfect innocence and that we would dwell there still if we hadn't fallen victim to temptation. But the story of the Fall deepens if we read it as a narrative in which disobedience, though its consequences may be dire, is necessary if we are to mature morally.

In this interpretation, God is less a forbidding father than an anxious parent who knows that once Adam and Eve (and all of us through them) become fully cognizant, they will recognize their own mortality. And so God admonishes them as we do our own children: "Don't do that, or else. . . ." Actions have consequences. However, like any loving parent, God doesn't lock Adam and Eve up but leaves them free to act on the advice—or not.

But from Eve and Adam's point of view, God is trying to keep them from growing up. The serpent suggests there will be no consequences. (Don't we always hope this when we do something we ought not?) Eve knows better. She replies, "God said, 'You shall not eat of the fruit of the tree that is in the middle of the garden, nor shall you touch it, or you shall die.'" But she eats anyway; and Adam, without protest, does too.

"Then the eyes of both were opened." Their innocence at an end, they embark on the journey toward moral development, one that each of us must take in turn, learning to choose, sometimes painfully, between good and evil.

SUGGESTION FOR MEDITATION: How have you responded to the freedom God has given you to choose between right action and sin? In what ways are you prepared to accept the consequences of your choices?

---

‡Poet and essayist who worships with Community of Christ of the Desert, a Catholic activist community dedicated to peace and justice; living in Tucson, Arizona.

The story of Eve and Adam recapitulates the exile of all of us from an undifferentiated and Edenic infancy and our entry into the moral world. The capacity to distinguish good from evil may render us, as the serpent hisses, "like God"; but if so, the resemblance (and a very limited one) comes at a steep price. We can now evaluate our own actions. In doing so, we often come up against a distressing reality: no matter how honorable our intentions, our thoughts and behaviors seem frequently to fall in the evil category. In short, we know ourselves to be sinners.

But sin is a subtler concept than it first appears, depending as it does on an understanding of God's law, which is not (though it may once have been) engraved in stone. Even the commandments that seem most universal may not apply to all people in the same way at all times. Certainly most of us agree that stealing is wrong yet would view the behavior of a drug-addicted burglar who breaks into a home and steals a family's Christmas presents as qualitatively unlike a father's theft of bread to feed his children. And both of these differ from a CEO's embezzlement that bankrupts a company and throws hundreds of people out of work.

Some people, troubled by ambiguity, reduce the world to just two categories, "good" and "evil" (which often means "everybody whose beliefs differ from my own"). They claim to know who or what belongs in each; but their certitude smacks of the sin of pride. Others repudiate the very idea that any law transcends self-interest, but their lives seem cramped and arid. Still others—and this includes not only Christians but practitioners of all faiths—pray for guidance in their decisions and actions and then for mercy for all the times their efforts fall short.

SUGGESTION FOR MEDITATION: How do you define sin? How do you recognize it in yourself? How do you acknowledge it to yourself and to God?

WEDNESDAY, FEBRUARY 9 • Read Joel 2:1-2, 12-17; Psalm 51:10-17

ASH WEDNESDAY

Often when I've attended an Ash Wednesday service, the priest has observed, looking out across the overflowing chapel, that more people come to church on this day than on any other. This day marks the beginning of the second great penitential season in the liturgical year, and such high attendance attests to a fundamental human characteristic: our preoccupation with wrongdoing. We know ourselves to be sinners, and we aren't satisfied simply to acknowledge our transgressions. We want to do something about them. People who envision God as a remote and fearsome judge may be motivated by the fear that they will be thrown into hell. Those of us for whom God is a beloved presence manifest in everyone we meet, believing that God grieves over our faults, seek to make amends to any we have injured. Regardless of impetus, we welcome Lent as a period for contrition.

Over the centuries, in accord with the Pauline condemnation of the flesh and encouragement of its mortification, some expiatory acts took on extreme forms. Some of these practices may persist to this day, but many would now question how anyone can have a healthy relationship with God while in a daze of pain and deprivation. What we need in order to please God, the psalmist sings, is not a holocaust but a willing spirit, a clean and contrite heart.

To achieve these does require discipline, of course. I elect to abstain from meat on Fridays during Lent, not as a means of self-castigation but as a reminder to reflect upon and rectify my shortcomings, but I wouldn't expect this practice to be meaningful for everyone. Our sins take many different forms; no doubt our penances will vary too.

SUGGESTION FOR MEDITATION: What elements in your life seem to push you away from God? How do you respond to God's call to return?

The thought of dying mystifies and appalls us more than any other. So death has long been imagined as a punishment, meted out, in biblical terms, to our first parents, Adam and Eve, and through them to the whole of humanity. All the same, death seems an awfully steep price to pay for a bite or two of a sweet, stolen fruit. Unless, in connecting the two, Paul means by *sin* something more than succumbing to the desire for forbidden fruit and by *death* something other than the exhalation that marks the flight of the spirit from its prison of flesh.

Most of us think of sin (insofar as we think of it at all) as a kind of glorified rule breaking. Like children, we want clear instructions and are made nervous by their absence. God, through Moses, laid down specific commandments; as long as we follow these, we figure we can't go far wrong. But mere obedience to the rules leads to a lockstep, lifeless conformity. Surely God wants more from and for us.

Through his life as well as his teachings, Jesus subsumes the Mosaic code and all its offshoots under a pair of directives: Love God and love your neighbor. God wants not a rote response to a set of rules but a lively and all-consuming love. If we can achieve this (and most of us can do so only sporadically and with great concentration), our innate perverse will to sin will dissolve, freeing us to do God's work in the world.

And will we then have achieved immortality? Of course not. The death that comes into the world through sin is not biological but spiritual. Whenever I separate myself from God through a failure to love, my spirit languishes until through the grace of God who never ceases to love me, even at my worst, I repent and return to my calling.

Suggestion for meditation: What causes you to fall out of love with God or others? What ways have you found to restore ruptured relationships?

Even after I've recognized my sin, confessed it to God, and achieved by one means or another an attitude of true contrition, I can't just congratulate myself and get on with my life. Something in my life urged or at least enabled me to transgress. Unless I plan to remain trapped in a squirrel cage of wrongdoing and regret, I will have to live differently from now on. I will inevitably sin again since I am human, but it had better be a different sin next time. Moral maturity requires that I learn from my errors in order to increase my reverence for and devotion to God.

Jesus names some of the disciplines that characterize a penitent life. Of these, fasting directs itself toward the individual sinner, using self-denial either as a punishment for misdeeds or, as in my case, a means toward mindfulness of and remorse for them. Prayer may focus either inward toward the self and its relationship to God or outward on behalf of others. Almsgiving is purely other-directed, an emptying of the self in service to the needs of both neighbors and strangers. In maturity, the sinner recognizes that just as the individual may stray from God, so may society at large. In order to be reconciled with God, each of us is called to make restitution for both personal and societal wrongdoing. Giving alms seems, I think, to imply more than merely writing out a check to a favorite charity. It means adopting a conscientious way of life that expresses a caring relationship with the whole of God's creation.

In all cases, Jesus warns us, we are to act "in secret" rather than parade our piety in public. Perhaps from personal experience, he understands that acting with one eye on the approval of others can lead to self-consciousness and self-congratulation, which distract from the sober purposes of prayer, abstinence, and good works: the return of the sinful soul to God.

SUGGESTION FOR MEDITATION: When do you feel most alienated from God? What practices draw you into closer communication?

The temptation of Jesus early in his ministry illustrates the fully mature moral response to which we all are called. Every detail in the account contrasts with Eve and Adam's trial. No longer are we shown a garden where every craving except one is satisfied, but rather a desert wilderness. Instead of a wily serpent, we have a featureless "devil." Eve succumbs to the serpent's blandishments and eats, even though she is not hungry; Jesus, though famished, resists. Most significantly, both quote the word of God to their tempters; but whereas Eve dithers and then permits the serpent to persuade her that God is wrong, Jesus relies firmly on scripture to counter each of the devil's offers.

Eve acts against God's orders and in her own interests: to please her palate and to gain wisdom. Jesus' resistance is entirely contrary to his interests. Not only could he allay the hunger gnawing at him after forty days without food, but he could find out for certain whether he is indeed the Son of God and, if so, he could possess untold worldly power. Many of us would settle for a great deal less. But Jesus has spent his time in the wilderness well. His vision is clear, focused not on his personal appetites but on right action.

Perhaps we cannot attain the moral perfection modeled by Jesus, but we are not morally helpless either. Time after time, we are given opportunities to choose, as he was. And like him, we can allow ourselves to be guided by principles we have developed by contemplating God's words. Each time we refuse to use others to advance our own ends and instead meet their needs, each time we forgive actions (including our own) that at first glance seem "unforgivable" and embrace the people (including ourselves) who seem "unlovable," we have drawn a step closer to him.

SUGGESTION FOR MEDITATION: When do you feel most like Eve? What do you do in response to temptation? When you fail to resist, what do you fear?

SUNDAY, FEBRUARY 13 • Read Romans 5:15-17;
                                2 Corinthians 5:20b–6:10

FIRST SUNDAY OF LENT

Good news! Your sins have been forgiven! This is the message Jesus came into the world to bring us: God loves us so dearly that, purely through grace and not through any merit we possess, God accepts us and cherishes us always. I began to grasp such love when I became a parent and learned that no matter how badly my children might act and how I might condemn their actions, I could not cease to love them. I could correct them. I could require them to make restitution for any harm they caused. I could encourage them to repent their actions and refrain from repeating them. But I could not withhold my love. And I'm only human!

The effect of sin is to create a chasm between the self and God so wide and deep that we forget that God waits for us, sorrowfully but with infinite patience, on the other side. God is not harmed by our sin—God cannot be harmed—but God grieves over the harm we do ourselves and one another. Through repentance and restoration, we can close the distance between us and be reconciled, literally brought together again. Oddly, through our sin we can thus be drawn closer to God, participating more fully in the mercy that flows from God through us into all creation.

All God asks of us—and this for our own sakes, not for God's—is that we accept the gift of grace that Jesus brings and put it to work in our lives. Like Paul, we become ambassadors for Christ, witnessing through our joyful demeanor to our experience of love and forgiveness. This is not a task to be put off for an instant. Now is the acceptable time! Now is the day of salvation!

SUGGESTION FOR MEDITATION: How has God's grace manifested itself in your life? How do you extend God's infinite love and forgiveness to others?

Heeding the Call

February 14–20, 2005 • Bonnie Hopper King[‡]

MONDAY, FEBRUARY 14 • Read John 3:13

Perhaps the only way for us to understand God's gift of grace is to stop pondering it and simply to start embracing the expression of God's love in Jesus Christ. The idea sounds easy enough, yet it is in actuality a difficult challenge, since we are usually thinking or talking rather than listening to or watching for God's presence in our daily lives. Even in prayer we are often scattered and anxious. Listening in deep silence for God to speak seems a daunting impossibility.

Yet the true and living God communicates to us in every moment of our lives the gift of the Son. Aware of the absence of "something," an absence that causes great pause and stillness, we feel a stirring in our souls and crave meaning in our experiences. We long to know the One, the only One, who has both "descended" and "ascended" on our behalf. In our effort to give ourselves over to God, we identify wounds in our soul and stumble as if in darkness. The strain of finding a purposeful direction is disconcerting and humbling. Yet we feel the purity of the heart of Jesus Christ drawing us to itself like a magnet.

If we are to heed God's call, we must first quiet the noise, still the activity, and clear the clutter in our lives. In the hushed stillness, we can feel the presence of God's promise. Unable to form words, we can yet know that God feels our emotions. Powerless to see the full arc of God's rainbow of love, we are given both insight and courage to honor the gift with all that we are.

PRAYER: Heavenly Father, forgive our distractions and anxious agendas. Help us to find that quiet, still room in our souls where we can open the gift of your love in Jesus Christ. Give us ears to heed the call of that gift. Amen.

[‡]Christian counselor, author, member of First Presbyterian Church; living in Nashville, Tennessee.

Abram (or Abraham as he came to be called) truly pioneered, serving as an important creative force in humankind's unfolding destiny. *Webster's Dictionary* defines the word *pioneer* as "one who goes before, as into the wilderness, into the unknown, preparing the way for others to follow." Whether exploring the physical or mental realm, the pioneer searches for life's uncharted experiences. The greatness of the adventuring pioneer resides in the fact that he or she pursues a mysterious goal despite frequent bouts with fear and failure.

Imagine Abram's consternation when God calls him to leave his country and kindred. It must have tested his faith to leave behind the familiar and dear and to travel by faith into the unknown. Abram responds to God's call and receives sufficient courage to travel to a foreign place with only a tent for shelter.

Following God's call can be a lonely journey. God's request to Abram did not reveal a plan. Obedience, especially with only a tiny corner of the picture visible, can be a daunting task. We do not want to risk letting go of the familiar. We wait for courage to bolster us before taking action. But living by faith means believing God will provide for our needs in every circumstance. When our hearts commit, courage will follow.

Abram could easily have denied God's voice, but his devotion to God kept him from falling into disobedience. True religious commitment requires not only a willing but a cheerful obedience, traits of the pioneer. If we evidence these pioneering traits, we can go where others have not been or lead the way for others to follow. If we bravely advance through the darkness, we will discover the blessing of divine illumination.

PRAYER: O God, as we heed your call, bolster us with the courage to obey your requests. Transform us from intenders to performers. Amen.

We become the beneficiaries of Abraham's pioneering faith. The promise to Abraham and his descendants comes through the "righteousness of faith," not through the law. How so? Laws control human conduct, which necessarily incurs outrage and judgment—the essence of sin. Yet God offers grace to all who have faith, not merely to those who justify their existence through works. Unification of believers, which creates a worldwide family, is the glorious outcome.

In our humanness we hunger for connection to others, and God understands this hunger. We find ourselves united both physically and spiritually with fellow believers in God's generous pool of grace. Yet, often we fail to rest on grace, since we have done nothing to merit God's merciful and everlasting love. Because of our sinful natures, we feel undeserving of God's grace. But if faith is sufficient, adherence to the law is not necessary to be part of God's new community. Hearts filled with the patience of grace speak the truth in love. Judgment loses its power and love flourishes. When our preoccupation with enforcing rigid laws becomes secondary, we are freed to claim the comfort of grace.

> Oh, the comfort—
> The inexpressible comfort of feeling safe with a person,
> Having neither to weigh thoughts,
> Nor measure words—but pouring them all right out—
> Just as they are—
> Chaff and grain together—
> Certain that a faithful hand will take and sift them—
> Keep what is worth keeping—
> And with the breath of kindness
> Blow the rest away.
>
> —Dinah Maria Craik, *A Life for a Life*

PRAYER: Gracious God, release us from the human burden of transgression. Give us your heart for the world, available to all who believe. Hold us in your faithful, loving hands. Amen.

Paul fervently claims that only grace can make a person righteous in God's eyes. Thus, grace rules out all human merit; God's grace provides not only salvation but safety and preservation for the one saved, regardless of imperfections. Therefore, grace removes any obligation to earn merits. The believer no longer lives under the law but comes to live under the grace bestowed by God.

"Abraham believed God, and it was reckoned to him as righteousness." The word *reckoned* carries a meaning from the world of accounting: indicating a column of figures to be added up or the sum total of that column. Yet, if we remove works from the calculations for justification, then a person has nothing about which to boast. Human pride impedes the vulnerability required to accept grace. Paul says that even the exceptional person cannot claim merit in God's presence.

The Christian faith requires more than humble vulnerability; it requires covenant. We can rest in the knowledge that God has made a covenant with us, through Abraham, that endures for all time. God has promised never to leave or forsake us. God's proclamation provides believers with the ultimate life insurance. And the policy arrives prepaid.

> I claim the fulfillment of God's promises,
> And rightly, but that is only the human side;
> The Divine side is that through the promises
> I recognize God's claim on me.
> —Oswald Chambers, *My Utmost for His Highest*

Abraham, our forefather, transmits the promise to those who follow. Justification by God's grace grants us hope and life eternal.

PRAYER: Dear God, we thank you for our heritage. We beg your encouragement to grow in grace, claiming the Christian heritage laid down by our forebears. Amen.

This psalm eloquently depicts the experience of pilgrims on the way to Jerusalem. Some scholars believe the verses represent a dialogue between those on the way and those staying behind; others understand these words as spoken between priest and people. As pilgrims approach the holy city, set high on a hill, their eyes will not only see the sentry but another guardian, the ultimate guardian—the Lord. The Lord never succumbs to fear or fatigue but watches over them by day and by night:

> [God] will silently plan for thee,
> Object thou of omniscient care;
> God . . . undertakes to be,
> Thy Pilot through each subtle snare.
>
> —E. Mary Grimes

Above all, the pilgrims rest in the knowledge that the Lord will protect them from danger during their journey. The psalmist claims the faith that neither those who go ahead or those who remain behind are ever left alone. Both our coming and our going are blessed by our vigilant Lord.

God may not keep us as we wish. We may feel the pangs of sorrow and hunger along our journey or stumble in pain as we seek to train our hearts. Yet the Lord will preserve our faith and protect us from the ultimate evil of being lost, alone or abandoned. This psalm calls us to live fully in the present life because God's promise sustains us. We will never be without God's love and care. We need only to lift our eyes to the hills to find divine help and protection.

PRAYER: Dear Lord, turn our hearts to your will. Guide us through the wilderness. Protect us as we seek shelter from the darkness of evil. Illumine our path. Amen.

We are made new through the devoted generosity of God's holy grace. This premise is the foundation of our faith, but the limitations of our humanity make it hard to grasp the concept of grace. Accepting grace requires the abandonment of old ways and a new responsiveness to God's touch. New life requires a new way of thinking.

Often we think of a pioneer as the person who goes forward without fear. But real pioneers, knowing what might lie ahead, have to muster the courage to take action. Nicodemus steps out into darkness toward an undetermined future. He surely feels great trepidation about approaching Jesus. Yet Nicodemus, a religious leader of the Jewish community, takes a bold step.

We may find our steps into the unknown halted by timidity. Fearing the unknown, we withhold our trust. We suspect the possibility of persecution. Nicodemus experiences these fears, but his courage and faith in God enable him to travel into the unknown. He realizes what he needs to do; he accepts the risk and steps into the unknown. God honors his courage by offering him the opportunity to be "born from above."

Nicodemus leaves Jesus a changed man. He may have desired to remain in the darkness, but his new birth contains the gift of courage; God empowers Nicodemus. Stepping into the light, he will assist in Jesus' burial, offering a mixture of myrrh and aloes to anoint the body. The once timid man will have the courage to stay with Jesus through the hardest of times.

God can empower a new nature in anyone who seeks it. Even with the availability of God's blissful grace, we may struggle to accept the gift. God sent the Son not to condemn but to save us. God's love can bear the weight of our humanness.

PRAYER: Gracious God, your perfect and eternal love is hard for us to comprehend. May we receive your promise and serve your will. Amen.

SECOND SUNDAY OF LENT

How can we be born again (born from above) when we are burdened by the oldness of our bodies? Limited by our humanness, we need concrete experiences that connect us with the Lord Jesus Christ as our personal savior. All spiritual history must have a personal knowledge as its bedrock.

We love imperfectly because we are human and often faithless. It has been said that we are as sick as our secrets. The shame of our hidden humilities erodes our courage to desire the truth. Yet we cannot let human insecurities diminish our desire to trust in God and to claim our new heart.

We began this week with the image of the One, the only One, who has descended from and ascended to heaven, an image too profound for the eye fully to grasp or the mind fully to appreciate. But like Abraham and Nicodemus, we know that we must move out of the shadows toward the light of new life. We can be "born from above" when we confide our guilty secrets to God, who already knows and forgives them, and accept the power of that forgiveness to ease our burden of shame. As the pain that once constricted our ability to love ourselves and others loses its grip on us, we can breathe in the fullness of God's love.

May we heed God's call to new life, born from above, praying not just with words but with our whole being. In our new life, may we love and forgive as we have been loved and forgiven.

PRAYER: Gracious God, encourage us to come to you in prayer, confiding our guilty secrets and painful disappointments. Open our hearts to receive and release your wondrous love. Amen.

Bearing Witness to Living Water

February 21–27, 2005 • *Cheryl Townsend Gilkes*[‡]

MONDAY, FEBRUARY 21 • Read Exodus 17:1-7

Painful survival issues make us ask troubling questions about God. On a bus tour of New Mexico's pueblos, art galleries, and Native American markets, the bus driver warned us about dehydration. I bought a big bottle of water and sipped it throughout the tour. Access to clean, healthy water for many in our world is a painful survival issue of the first order.

Facing a painful crisis of survival in the wilderness, the thirsty children of Israel confront Moses. Although God leads, it makes no human sense to these consummate herdspeople to pitch tents where there is no visible source of water! In their thirst, Egypt looks so much better. Their distress gives God an opportunity to act in a way that defies ordinary human perception. They ask, as we all do at times: "Is the LORD among us or not?" And God answers with a powerful revelation, calling Moses to use the same visible instrument of their liberation at the Red Sea, his rod, to smite the rock and to do it in front of the elders of Israel. One quick moment transforms the thirsty people and their leaders into witnesses of the living water that can only come from God.

In times of crisis and disappointment, we may wonder if God is with us. Moses and the people of Israel bear witness that God is with us and supplies our most fundamental needs. God, the Rock in the wilderness, becomes the living water we need.

PRAYER: Gracious God, help me remember that I face no wilderness moment without the miracle of your steadfast, living presence in my life. Amen.

[‡]Assistant pastor for special projects, Union Baptist Church, Cambridge, Massachusetts; professor and director of the African American Studies Program, Colby College, Waterville, Maine.

Make a joyful noise to remember

Sometimes we find it hard to remember that God is the source of all good things and of all that is necessary for life. Yet the importance of sacred memory means that we cannot leave it to chance. Songs aid our memory. I still sing the songs that taught me the order of the biblical books because it is faster than using the table of contents.

Oh, how quickly the children of Israel forgot about God's goodness in history! Oh, how quickly we today forget God's gracious presence in our everyday lives. Repeatedly the prophets remind God's people of their forgetfulness. Psalm 95 serves as a wonderful aid to sacred memory. The people of God must "make a joyful noise to the rock of our salvation." Through this psalm and others, the psalmist invites us to stand with raised hands, with voices, and with instruments of celebration—tambourines, violins, harps, and loud cymbals. And we are not to stand still! We are permitted to dance!

Whatever we do, we must give praise and glory to the rock of our salvation. The ancient Israelites must remember the waters at Massah and Meribah so that we may remember God our rock, our mighty fortress. We must remember the thirsty moments in our own wilderness wanderings and God's pouring forth water out of that desert rock. To remember we must sing about the ways God pours forth goodness in the midst of our need. If we open our hearts through the transformation that comes with the joyful noise of praise, then we will see God's action in the midst of our troubling circumstances.

PRAYER: Precious Lord, I thank you that you are a great God. Help me to remember that you are my maker and my shepherd. Keep your hand upon me this day and every day. Amen.

The Gift of Living Water

All of Jesus' actions and encounters in the Gospel of John foreshadow and anticipate his passion—an anticipation upon which we reflect and meditate in this season of Lent. In his journey to the cross, Jesus purposefully goes to the places the righteous avoid. Jesus goes to Samaria; he encounters a people of limited vision and fractured lives. They suffer under the same yoke of Roman oppression as their distant kin in Judea but without the grandeur of an established priesthood and the comfort of Roman accommodation. The Assyrian conquest of the Samaritans in 722 BCE stigmatized them. The Judeans have no dealings with the Samaritans.

Jesus, however, chooses to interact with the despised, the stigmatized, the rejected, and the lost. He confronts this Samaritan woman with his humanity by asking her for water. She expresses her surprise, "How is it that you, a Jew, ask a drink of me, a woman of Samaria?"

When we, in God's presence, recognize our shortcomings, limits, faults, and failures, God surprises us with the gift of God's self. This woman came to the well at a time, about the sixth hour, that indicated her shame and her community's exclusion. Jesus meets her at the well at the moment she wants to meet no one. Jesus informs her that the gift of God is available and that he is ready to provide living water. And we can anticipate the moment, about the sixth hour, when Jesus endures incomparable and almost unimaginable humiliation on the cross. Perhaps this Samaritan woman reminds Jesus' disciples and bears witness to us all that it was not only the cleansing blood that poured forth from Jesus' wounded side but also the gift of living water.

PRAYER: Loving God, help me to hunger and thirst after your righteousness. I thank you for your gift of living water. Continue to fill my cup, and let it overflow. Amen.

Water for Spirit

It is hard to imagine the Spirit of God, referred to in my faith tradition as "the Holy Ghost." As a child I often referenced the cartoon character, Casper, the friendly ghost. As I grew in the faith, I quickly recognized the limits of such thinking. But even as an adult, as a Christian, as a member of the clergy, the concept of the Spirit of God is not an easy one to convey. That Spirit is what came upon the prophets of old when they spoke forth a word from the Lord. The Spirit is fire, speaking out of a burning bush, descending on Elijah's sacrifice on Mount Carmel, or sitting on the heads of disciples in Jerusalem. The Spirit is oil, anointing those whom God would use in sacred service. The Spirit is a mighty windstorm that defeats armies and speaks to sufferers like Job. Apprehending the Spirit of God creates such difficulty for our imaginations that theologians avoid it and denominations engage in serious controversies about its "operation."

Jesus understands and anticipates our difficulties. He tells the Samaritan woman that he has living water, and then he also tells her that there is a revelation of God that transcends the marginal imagination of the Samaritans and the established order of Jerusalem: God is spirit. We worship God by bearing truthful witness to God's work in our particular lives. God is bread when we hunger, water when we thirst. God is oil when we need light, light when we sit in darkness. Jesus reminds the woman then and us today that the Holy Spirit is also our living water. It bathes us for membership in the people of God and provides for our eternal survival despite the difficulties of our wilderness journeys, despite our distance from the established order of things.

PRAYER: Comforting God, empower me to seek your will in my life. Enable me to bear witness to the presence, love, and truth of your Spirit in my life. Amen.

From waterpot to witness

When I was a little girl, opera singer Eileen Farrell (1920–2002) recorded an album titled *I've Gotta Right to Sing the Blues.* My aunt took me to the record store to see the album and to explain that this world-class opera star was making an important statement about African American blues music. Even though the judges of high culture might snub her record, Miss Farrell was declaring her freedom to sing whatever she felt was great music—including the blues! That object lesson encouraged me to transcend the boundaries and limits that others would impose.

Jesus meets the woman at the well and tells her everything she has ever done. The woman looks beyond the antipathies between Samaritans and Judeans and sees a prophet, an anointed man of God, someone who could converse about the hope of the world: "Messiah is coming. . . . [who] will proclaim all things to us." When she raises this subject with Jesus, he reveals himself as the one: "I am he, the one who is speaking to you."

People experience a change in their lives when Jesus says "I am" to them. At the well in Sychar, this woman's life turns upside down. His encounter with this woman transforms her from a furtive water seeker who makes her trip to the well at noonday to avoid a hostile community into an evangelist, a witness, a bearer of good news who runs from her waterpot back to the community that rejected her. Her encounter with Jesus gives her the right to bear witness to the Messiah's presence in their midst. "Come and see a man!" Some believe her; some come to see and hear for themselves. What a joyful revelation: "We believe, for we have heard for ourselves, and we know that this is truly the Savior of the world." Meeting Jesus in spirit and in truth gives us the right to bear witness to the gospel!

PRAYER: Liberating God, meet me in the places where no one else will go. Touch me and transform my life; make my soul a witness for you. Amen.

Death for our life

I feel sure that when the Samaritan woman went to the well, she could have easily sung the Negro spiritual: "Nobody knows the trouble I've seen. Nobody knows my sorrow." She meets a man at the well who is a supposed enemy, yet Jesus brings peace to her heart and salvation to her and her community. I am sure that when she left, she could have shouted the refrain, "Jesus knows all about our struggles!" Radically transformed, she no longer perceives herself as the enemy. Instead she runs from the well rejoicing in hope as a child of God.

Salvation is like water for the thirst-crazed pilgrim in a dry desert who is close to the point of death. Paul understands the extremity of the human condition and wants the people in the early church to understand the depth of the glorious gift of God's salvation: "While we were still weak, at the right time Christ died for the ungodly." When we found ourselves at the point of death, pushed to the extreme margins of existence, and in our sinfulness considered to be "enemies" of God, we were given a gift of eternal life that is almost unthinkable. Right when we needed it, Christ died for us, the enemies of God. "Christ died for the ungodly."

Christ's death brings us back from the brink of death; we have new life. Jesus' resurrected life reconciles us to God, giving us peace and grace. Instead of beating us down, experiences of tribulation build us up, developing our capacity for patience, hope, and joy. Having received the atonement, we have a new life as a child of God.

PRAYER: All-knowing God, thank you for giving yourself for me. Increase my faith. Help me to stand fast in your grace. Amen.

SUNDAY, FEBRUARY 27 • Read Psalm 95

THIRD SUNDAY OF LENT

The listening witness

Who'll be a witness for my Lord?" The proper response is, "My soul is a witness for my Lord." The people who stand in God's presence, lifting their heads, hearts, and hands in joyful praise, bear witness to God's work and power in their lives. In the clandestine worship services of American slave communities, worshipers found the presence of God in their lives so miraculous that they had to temper the noise of their praise so it didn't invite punishment. Yet God's presence in their lives often overcame their fear of punishment, so they sang, "I said I wasn't going to tell nobody, but I just couldn't keep it to myself, what the Lord has done for me!" The Spirit of God helped them bear witness.

Those who fail to bear witness do not see the truth of God as the source of salvation, as the source of living water. They not only harden their hearts and provoke God, but their spirit of error can destroy their community. It took the Israelites forty years to reach the Promised Land. All of the people heard God's voice and witnessed the signs and wonders in the wilderness. Yet only two men survived to bear witness.

If we will hear God's voice, we must choose an opposite course of action than those who hardened their hearts in the wilderness. We must rejoice in God's presence, remembering that the deep places of the earth and the strength of the hills are in God's hands. We must make the kind of noise that bears witness and brings others to seek the living water poured out from the one American slaves called "a Rock in a weary land."

I came to Jesus, and I drank
Of that life-giving stream;
My thirst was quenched, my soul revived,
And now I live in Him.

PRAYER: Healing God, I praise you for your creative and transforming power in my heart and life. Amen.

Anoint Us to Your Service

February 28–March 6, 2005 • *Yeo Khiok-khng (K. K.)*‡

MONDAY, FEBRUARY 28 • Read 1 Samuel 16:1-5

The term "anointed one" comes from the Hebrew word *messiah* or the Greek word *Christ*. It carries the tenor of being sent by one in authority to do an important task. In biblical times prophets, priests, kings, and apostles were often anointed to be God's transformative agents. Some say that Confucius had a messianic mission in life. The teaching of this "crownless emperor" has ruled China for the last two thousand years. Clearly Mother Teresa, an anointed one of God, brought divine love and mercy to the poor in Calcutta.

Today's scripture tells of God's decision to anoint David as king. At God's initiative, Samuel goes to Bethlehem to anoint a new king over Israel, while the current king still sits on the throne. Samuel fears King Saul's anger. But trust and obedience are also required of those who seek the anointed of God.

The elders of Bethlehem also express fear, and they approach Samuel trembling. Yet Samuel finds himself sent by one in authority to do an important task—Samuel, the "anointed," will anoint. Those God calls and sends find themselves anointed to a life of sacrifice and sanctification. They become instruments of God's salvation in the world.

The life of Jesus offers the clearest pattern of service for anointed ones in God's kingdom. When we, like Jesus, choose to serve God, we inherit God's superabundant life. In living a sanctified life, we belong to God and are called as God's beloved.

PRAYER: Lord, grant us simplicity to behold the passion of Christ on the cross, that we may know the joy of serving you and live a holy life to your glory. Amen.

---

‡Malaysian Chinese Christian; New Testament professor at Garrett-Evangelical Theological Seminary; ordained preacher of Chinese churches in Chicago; lecturer of Bible in China and the Far East; living in Skokie, Illinois.

People look on outward appearance, but the Lord looks on the heart. God will not allow physical stature to be the deciding characteristic in the selection of Israel's next king. The Lord does not choose David's brothers. While the Lord may use the beautiful, the rich, the knowledgeable, the Lord looks upon the heart and determines a person's will and character. Anointed ones of God have hearts oriented Godward.

Mencius, an early Chinese philosopher, believed that the heart differentiates human beings from other animals. The heart, as the core of our being, serves as a metaphor to describe the centrality of our attitudes, emotions, and wills. Therefore, if we serve God with an "attitude problem," even our diligence will not make our heart right with God. If we do not know peace with God, then our service will lack peace and joy. If we let our way and will overwrite the kingdom rules of God, then our ministry will end in bankruptcy.

In a world packed with advertising gimmicks, how has the Christian church focused on the outward appearance of ministry: the size of the building, the number in attendance? How many of our churches have been aligning themselves with popular culture? In what ways have we unintentionally let the spirit of commercialization anoint us? Through what means have we turned the place of worship into a trading institution of loss and profit? Christian life cannot be contained in a balance sheet of "if I do such and such for God, then God will reward me with this and that." We cannot calculate the mercy of God, because divine grace is priceless.

The Spirit of the Lord is upon David. The same Spirit is upon us today, calling us to look beyond the externals and granting us truth, grace, and strength.

PRAYER: Lord, teach us how to empathize with the needs of the world. May your Spirit anoint us to be prophets and priests in the world. Amen.

This well-known psalm speaks of God as the great Shepherd and the Host of Life who cares for, supplies, guides, and protects us through all the ups and downs of our lives. God finally brings us home in God's presence.

I came to love this biblical God through the realization that God, creator of the universe, becomes part of creation. I used to know God as the cosmic principle, the righteous judge of all. In studying the scriptures, I began to appreciate a more personal God, one who cares about the details of my life. I begin to imitate the character and personality of God, especially the God-in-Christ. The Lenten Jesus makes me aware that he is the good shepherd (John 10:11) who lays down his life for me. Jesus is the great shepherd of the sheep (Heb. 13:20) who intercedes for me and is merciful to me. God in Christ is the chief shepherd (1 Pet. 5:4) who protects and saves the sheep.

The psalm describes life in its pastoral setting. To me, that means life, while full of change, has moments of divine intervention in which God showers blessings on us. I left Malaysia, my birthplace, more than twenty years ago. The pilgrimage of studying, teaching, and serving God in the United States has been a life of joy and surprises all the way. God the Shepherd is the central metaphor of my remembering God's goodness. God supplies my needs and carries all my burdens. God leads me all the way. "Surely goodness and mercy shall follow me all the days of my life" (RSV).

The season of Lent can be dry and dull but also refreshing and exhilarating. Oases exist in the desert; springs may gush from hard rock. The cross speaks of the pain and agony of God's anointed one. It also portrays the wound of divine love of God's beloved one. How near is God to us? As near as our acknowledgment of the Great Shepherd who gave his all on the cross.

PRAYER: Lord, open our eyes to behold the miracle of the cross, that we may find life amidst death, hope in despair, joy despite sadness. Amen.

Thursday, March 3 • Read Ephesians 5:8-10

Now in the Lord you are light. Live as children of light" (RSV), The epistle writer admonishes the Ephesian Christians. They struggle with a cosmopolitan culture of fragmentation, political correctness (in pluralism), and narcissism (in relativism of various philosophies). The unity theme in Ephesians grants the readers the vision of the whole: Christ, the unifier of all things (1:10). There is a grand narrative that, according to God's eternal and loving plan, God creates, saves, directs, and sustains our lives. Therefore, we do not live in vain. Christians ought to know God's plan for the universe and live a dynamic life in the world as children of light.

To live as children of light requires countercultural thinking and the ability to transform cultural assumptions. For many years I have taught New Testament in major universities in China. I tend to begin by identifying with the Chinese cultural material, such as Confucian ethics, Taoist cosmology, Buddhist spirituality, or even the Marxist critical theory. While I hesitate to present the biblical worldview or may present the biblical perspective as one of many, I am often invited by the audience to be more apologetic and bold. Chinese students and professors attending my classes want me to present the uniqueness of Christ so that Christ will shed new light on the economic, political, and social struggles of the present Chinese societies.

The writer of Ephesians understands that we cannot live outside our culture. As children of God, we learn to engage our wider social reality in theological critique. Thus, we see in the writings and lives of Moses, David, Augustine, Luther, Bonhoeffer, and King the long tradition of holding firm God's light in their places and times so that God's light continues to redeem the world. We can be candles for God today.

PRAYER: Light of all lights, shine on and through us, that we may be candles of hope, life, and joy to a despairing, dying, and crying world. Amen.

The text contrasts the fruits of light with the works of darkness. The fruits of light are good, right, and true; the works of darkness are empty, sterile, and futile. This passage reminds me of a dark period of Chinese history—the Cultural Revolution (1967–77).

Political, economic, and family systems were in chaos because secrecy and mutual condemnation were the rules of the game. Family members and close friends would secretly report their own relatives and friends to the authorities without having to substantiate the truthfulness of their reports. What was done in secrecy then bred distortion, exaggeration, and even lies. Some did it out of self-gain, some out of jealousy. What was done in the dark produced conflict, broken relationships, the dismantling of a system of justice. Those secret reports brought about humiliation and finally violence and death to millions. It was a period of turmoil within and alienation from the outside world.

The transformation of darkness comes by exposing it to the light. The Chinese government began to introduce rules of law as a justice system and accountability for personal and social relationships. What is done in the light breeds trust, goodness, and truthfulness. This principle works in government, as well as in church institutions and interpersonal relationships. We become transformative agents in the world as we work in the light.

The quotation "Sleeper, awake! Rise from the dead, and Christ will shine on you" is a baptismal liturgy. It reminds readers, both ancient and modern, of their baptismal vow to be bearers of Christ's glory and light. We have to be bold and prophetic, merciful and priestly; above all, we have to walk in the light of God's word and seek to bear fruits of that light.

PRAYER: Lord, help us to know your goodness and your truth that we may be your faithful witnesses, bearers of the holy in a world that desperately yearns for your light, love, and faithfulness. Amen!

SATURDAY, MARCH 5 • Read John 9:1–23

The Gospel of John is a book of signs, miracles, and works of Jesus that reflect the glory of God. In this passage Jesus, "the light of the world," heals the man born blind to reveal God's redemption in the world. Only the Gospel of John refers to Jesus as "the Lamb of God" (1:29, 36); that is, Jesus' words and works redeem God's whole creation. In John's Gospel Jesus is the Lamb of God sacrificed at Passover (see 13:1; 18:39; 19:14). With Christ as the Lamb of God, an insignificant blind man becomes a crucial character within the scheme of God's salvation.

Do not underestimate God's care for the seemingly insignificant details of our lives. If only we have eyes of faith, nothing in our lives lies outside the reach of God's hands of salvation. Medical, philosophical, and scientific explanations of our problems and sufferings often fall short of redemption. "Who sinned, this man or his parents, that he was born blind?" That issue is less important than that "God's works might be revealed in him." The Light of the world comes to give sight to people, so that they may see God's salvation and recognize God's being—full of grace and truth.

Notice how the writer plays on the words *anointed*, *go*, *Siloam*, and *Sent*. Jesus' healing of this man has a messianic meaning. The sacrificed one is the redeemer of the world. The redeemer anoints the blind to fulfill his life purpose of manifesting God's glory. Indeed, at the end of the healing process, Jesus charges the recipient of divine salvation to be God's sent, to bear witness to God's glory. The healing occurs at the Pool of Siloam, meaning the Pool of the Sent.

God's anointed ones need not be royal, great persons; God often chooses and anoints ordinary people to be Light bearers.

PRAYER: Lord, thank you for opening our eyes and healing us. Thank you for entrusting us with the task of bringing hope and light to the world. Amen.

FOURTH SUNDAY OF LENT

John's Gospel often uses irony to reveal truth and reality. Kenneth Burke, a scholar of religious language, concludes that if language is metaphorical, then irony is the master, because reality is ironic. If God is the ultimate reality, then the most meaningful of all realities is God.

In the Gospel of John, fragmented events are whole, contradictory phenomena are meaningful, and goodness eventually triumphs over all negatives. Seeming not to choose the miracle of life for God's beloved son on the cross, God nevertheless transforms sin and death into life, a divine irony. Jesus' decision to drink the cup of judgment and to bear death on the cross becomes the greatest miracle of all. In another divine irony, the hour of his death is the hour of glorification.

Ironically, those who have eyes cannot see Jesus Christ as the Son of God, yet those who are blind see it clearly. The faith response of the man born blind contrasts starkly with that of the Pharisees. His recovery of sight brings him to worship Jesus, for he now understands that he has eternal life through faith.

It will be tragic if we allow our knowledge, technology, and culture to blind us to the divine identity of Jesus. The influence of postmodern culture has led many believers away from faith. Yet God still heals and performs in this scientific age. God still intervenes, not just in human history but in our daily life.

PRAYER: God of irony, teach us to submit ourselves to you, knowing that you are the God who gave us your beloved and who raised Jesus from death. Amen.

The Time in Between

March 7–13, 2005 • Susan Henry-Crowe[‡]

MONDAY, MARCH 7 • Read Psalm 130

Holy Saturday, the day between Good Friday and Easter Sunday, is a lost day in the Christian year, the brief season after the excruciating experience and before the breaking forth of new life. After a traumatic event, survivors find themselves in this kind of space: between life and death. Not dead. Not living either. Locked in an indefinable middle where they wait "more than those who watch for the morning."

Our texts this week call us to examine the meaning of this time in between, so painful and unbearable that "out of the depths" we cry to God. We begin this journey in the valley of death, of dry bones in a period framed by the anointing of David and the revival of Israel. Between those two events, the Israelites learn the futility of the Exile and and the hope of freedom. In Romans 8 we hear Paul address the tension inherent in living a truly committed Christian life during the period between Christ's ascension and his return. In John's Gospel story of Lazarus, we see Jesus breathe life into a man newly dead but not yet released to death by the grieving hearts who loved him.

Today's psalm expresses the depth of human anguish when disaster befalls humankind and the longing of the distraught soul for redemption. The "in between" is a space of despair but also of witness and the possibility of life emerging out of death. Here in the fifth week of Lent we find ourselves to some extent in a time in between. With the psalmist we anxiously "wait for the Lord" and in God's word we find hope.

PRAYER: O God of the in between, do not let us go. O God, whose spirit breathes life into death, breathe the hope of new life into our despair. Amen.

[‡]Dean of the Chapel and Religious Life, Emory University, Atlanta, Georgia; lecturer, preacher, teacher, workshop leader.

It is the time in between destruction and death and the season of hope and resurrection. Today's scripture follows a tragedy of great proportion. The Exile was a national disaster. The Judeans have lost the land promised to their ancestors. The last of the Davidic kings has been taken captive. The Temple lies in ruins. It seems like the end. The people must have felt like the citizens of Hiroshima, Dresden, Baghdad, or Pearl Harbor as the bombs dropped on their cities. It must have felt like the end of an age, the end of life as it had been known.

The spirit of the Lord takes Ezekiel and sets him in a great plain covered with dry bones—like a city bombed. Yahweh poses this question to Ezekiel: "Can these bones live?" Can these brittle, destroyed bones live? The prophet responds, "O Lord GOD, you know." The Lord commands Ezekiel to prophesy to the bones. Ezekiel does and the bones come together, covered with sinews, flesh, and skin. But they do not come to life.

It is the time of death and destruction. How does the community live before new life comes? The world as previously experienced is now gone forever. Known life is destroyed. How does a community live through Holy Saturday? The horror of Good Friday is over and Easter has not yet come. How does the community live in between the time of terror before the mystery of resurrection?

As Christians in this in-between time, we live silently. Not silently alone but silently in community. Discovering Holy Saturday helps us find new ways through life. We must be present to it. We are called to live in new ways in the times in between. Only when Yahweh calls for the breath of the four winds do the bones come to life. This Breath of life will come in due season but until it does, we must wait. In silence.

PRAYER: **O God of dry bones, be with us.**
O God of the silence, be with us.
When there are no words, be with us.
When we know no way, be with us.
When there is only the time in between, be with us. Amen.

WEDNESDAY, MARCH 9 • Read Ezekiel 37:11-14

These verses interpret Ezekiel's vision. This vision promises life—not a general resurrection but the revival of the people beyond Exile. The vision stresses that this revival is corporate: the restoration of the people of God. It is accomplished by word and spirit, the word of God through the prophet and the life-giving spirit as a divine gift.

Ezekiel's vision belongs not to him but to the people—wonderful news to those who consider themselves dead. The vision promises release to the exiles, good news to those who have been beaten down by sin. It is good news for those who suffer under the weight of the sins of their ancestors, the vision of life where death appeared all around.

As the dean of the chapel and religious life, often I have the joy and the responsibility of being present to people as they struggle with their own identities, their hurts, their wounds, and the sins of life. The struggles are painful and difficult. They come for spiritual guidance, sometimes bringing parents with them. As family members learn of their child's struggles, they often cannot hear the message that all will be well. So we sit in the midst of uncertainty, confusion, and sadness in the time in between when dreams and hopes are dead, lost, and gone with no certainty that life will come.

Into these brittle bones, Yahweh breathes. And early in the morning when tears still flow, the solar plexus aches, nausea is barely repressed, and terror abounds there comes the faint fluttering of life. A question, a thought, an inkling of hope. The vision promises the restoration of all of God's children: the children, the parents, the grandparents, the friends, the loved ones, the fearful ones, the ancestors, all those in exile—all of these will be restored to life.

PRAYER: O God of Holy Saturday, be with us. Hold us when the tears will not stop. Enfold us when we are shocked by fear and terror. Sustain us until we are aware of the fluttering of life. Keep us in your care until life is restored. Amen.

We all have obsessions, distractions, and behaviors that prevent us from being the kind of person we hope to be. Our walls of protection and security, comfort and safety often become "tombs" in which our hope, our need to love and be loved, our dreams of forgiveness and reconciliation disintegrate and die. We long to hear the words of Jesus, "Lazarus, come out!" The dead man comes out, tied hand and foot with burial bands, and his face wrapped in a cloth. "Untie him and let him go."

The final scene in the film *The Truman Show* finds Truman's friend going to the tomblike basement to find Truman. He is not there! He is in a boat out on the water. We see the drowning scene when Truman lies on the boat with arms spread out and left for dead. But . . . he gasps for air. Possibly this signals his new life, his resurrection. When Truman reaches the end of the set and notices the sky is only a painted canvas, he ascends the stairs to hear the voice of the Creator. He then goes forth into the unknown to live in the world!

The Christ who calls Lazarus from his tomb calls us from our tombs to live life to the fullest, to bring the love of God into our hurting and entombed world. As Jesus called Lazarus to life, may we hear that same call to life—to free ourselves from the tombs, the expectations, the obsessions, the distractions, the competition, and cravings that bind us, that prevent us from knowing God in the love of others and the love we offer.

PRAYER: O God who frees us from death, give us courage to live life fully and unashamedly.
When we are entombed, free us.
When we are distracted, help us to focus on life.
When we are obsessed, liberate us.
May we find joy in service to your people.
May we find light in darkness.
May we find life in death. Amen.

FRIDAY, MARCH 11 • Read Psalm 130

As Holy Week approaches, particularly Good Friday, I attempt to imagine what Mary, the mother of Jesus, must have felt. How does a parent live with such deep grief? As a mother, I cannot let myself imagine seeing my child executed. I have tried over the years, and I cannot. It is too painful, too horrific, too terrifying, and too grievous.

We are all more acquainted with grief than we would like. Some of it is our own; some we share with others. Some depths we cannot plummet, yet we find ourselves immersed in deep grief. How do we live? In what do we hope?

This psalm speaks to the depths, the watery deep, of death and deep distress. It speaks to inconsolable grief, to terror in the night, to unspeakable and unbearable pain caused by sin. Good Friday is the result of sin, pain, and fear, unfaced but put on another—Jesus. Good Friday represents radical love misunderstood and not tolerated by the world, a radical love put to death.

Sin and death do not have the last word. The psalmist reminds us that God's nature is to forgive, even the attempts to kill love. God's forgiving love is the heart of faith. We hear the words of comfort, "But there is forgiveness with you, so that you may be revered."

In these times we wait. We wait for hope. "I wait for the LORD, my soul waits, and in his word I hope." In the face of despair, anguish, in unspeakable pain, we wait. We wait in our vulnerability. We wait for God's redemption, for God will redeem Israel from all its iniquities (sins).

PRAYER: **In the terror of the night, hear our prayer.**
In the despair of loss, God, hold us.
In the waiting, come to us.
In the end, redeem us. Amen.

In *Mere Christianity*, C. S. Lewis, like Paul in Romans 8, addresses the tension inherent in living a truly committed Christian life in the time in between:

> The real problem of the Christian life comes where people do not usually look for it. It comes the very moment you wake up each morning. All your wishes and hopes for the day rush at you like wild animals. And the first job each morning consists simply in shoving them all back; in listening to that other voice . . . letting that larger, stronger, quieter life come flowing in. . . . Standing back from all your natural fussings and frettings; coming in out of the wind.

Often we think that Paul uses the terms *flesh* and *spirit* to differentiate between body and soul or between the material world and the spiritual world. This is not the case. Paul understands flesh (*sarx*) to characterize the path chosen by the self-sufficient person who chooses not to turn toward the divine help of the Spirit. Living in the spirit (*pneuma*) means accepting the gift of the indwelling Spirit. It means being open to communion with God so that God can lead us toward life and peace.

Let us return to the idea that the time in between death and life is not only the space of despair but also can be "the space of witness, of the possibility of life emerging out of death." What makes the movement possible? Love makes the transition possible. Not only is it love but divine love. Living in the Spirit means accepting the gift of the indwelling Spirit, being open to communion with God so that God can lead us away from death into life.

PRAYER: **O Spirit, who dwells with us before**
the morning comes, stay with us.
O Spirit who flutters in the time in between,
sustain us.
O Spirit, who breathes life into death, be with us.
Amen.

SUNDAY, MARCH 13 • Read John 11:38–44

FIFTH SUNDAY OF LENT

The freeing of Lazarus from death and restoration to life sets in motion the events that lead to Jesus' death, a death full of anguish and hopelessness. It is the end: the end of life, the end of hope for freedom from the bonds of fear and oppression, the end of a new community of love and freedom.

But Jesus' death brings Mary to the tomb in the time after death. And in the darkness of the morning there are flutterings, utterances. At the tomb, Jesus utters Lazarus's name. At the tomb, Jesus utters Mary's name. At the tomb, Mary utters Jesus' name. It is the utterance of love, the encounter between human and divine love. The utterance of love—the breath of life. Names of loved ones are spoken. Love stands in the way between the darkness and the dawn, between death and life. Love is in the silence. Love is in the waiting.

This is the way and the work of Love.

PRAYER: O God of silence . . .
       O God of the night, we wander.
       O God of the time in between, we wait.
       O God of utterances, our hearts flutter.
       O God of Love, we hear our name.
       Fragile and vulnerable we know you in love. Amen.

Preparation

March 14–20, 2005 • Debra K. Farrington[‡]

MONDAY, MARCH 14 • Read Matthew 21:1-11

Lent can bring out the best and the worst in me. It gives me the opportunity to think more clearly about my spiritual life. Sometimes I like what I see; sometimes I don't. As I approach Holy Week I prepare for even more challenge. Holy Week takes me through the lands of praise and fear, of celebration and betrayal. This week's readings reflect the confusion of the time ahead.

Every year members of my church reenact this confusion. We gather outside the church on Palm Sunday and receive palm branches to wave about. Our live donkey sometimes cooperates in the march to the church and sometimes doesn't. Children run about because it looks like a parade to them. The liturgy begins, and we all join in while walking to the sanctuary with palm fronds waving and donkey braying.

Though I like this annual ritual, I also know what's coming later in worship. We'll hear readings about betrayal, about darkness. In the space of one hour, we'll go from waving palms and shouting "Hosanna!" to saying "Surely it is not I who betrayed you, Rabbi, is it?" And we'll remember that we are betrayers of Christ, our king, just as Judas was. Perhaps if we didn't know the story so well, we could march more triumphantly into the sanctuary, but we know what is going to happen during Holy Week. This week I begin my preparation for what lies ahead.

PRAYER: God of the journey, help me listen for your word to me in the midst of the confusion. Amen.

[‡]Publisher for a religious publishing house; author of books on Christian spirituality; member, St. Andrew's Episcopal Church; retreat leader; Harrisburg, Pennsylvania.

Do you know how movies sometimes lull you into a sense that things are going along just fine, and then this quiet but ominous music begins to play? You're not even aware of it at first, but your stomach begins to knot a little; your back muscles tense. Something is coming, something that will startle or scare you.

Well, that's how today's reading strikes me. This psalm begins with such confidence. God's steadfast love endures forever. God has answered us and become our salvation. The stone that the builders rejected has become, instead of refuse, the chief cornerstone. God is marvelous, and we rejoice. And then—hear that music playing quietly in the background yet?—there is verse 25: "Save us, we beseech you, O LORD! O LORD, we beseech you, give us success!"

The psalmist moves quickly back to praise, light, and thanks for God whose steadfast love endures forever. Sometimes I wish Lent passed as quickly as verse 25 in this psalm. A quick "save me, O Lord," and then on to Easter, without having to pass through the events that I know are coming, without having to hear again the stories about betrayal and pain. But every year the season of Lent reminds me that I am one of the builders that rejected the stone that became the chief cornerstone, and that, more often than I'd like, I do things that deny God's steadfast love. Save me, I beseech you, O Lord! O Lord, I beseech you, give me success.

PRAYER: God of forgiveness, we give you thanks for your steadfast love that endures forever. Amen.

As I write this meditation it has been exactly six months since I was diagnosed with multiple sclerosis. I've had a few dark and difficult days, and I'm sure to have a few more before my life on earth is over. But oddly enough, the last six months have been some of the richest time I can remember.

I know that sounds weird. My feelings have surprised my friends as much as they've surprised me. But I've discovered something immensely liberating about a disease that forces you to recognize that you're not really in control of everything that happens. After recognizing that fact, giving the reins back to God, and being grateful for God's help and guidance, acceptance of human limitation is easier than it used to be.

The prophet who writes to us from his exile says much the same thing. God opens his ears, and he is no longer rebellious. The Lord helps him, and he is not disgraced. God helps him, so who can declare him guilty? This praise and confidence comes from a person who knows God as partner. God has liberated the writer from the need to be in control and have all the answers.

I wonder if Jesus thought of these words as he faced the events at the close of his earthly life? This passage resonates with so many of the stories of Jesus' life. Jesus had the tongue of teacher; his words sustained the weary. He was not rebellious, did not turn back from his difficult journey. Jesus turned the other cheek. Did he think about Isaiah 50:9 as he heard his sentence of death? Did this passage comfort him, providing the confidence he needed to do what he must, as it does for me?

SUGGESTION FOR MEDITATION: Imagine yourself reading this passage in difficult circumstances in your own life. How do its promises help you?

I have become like a broken vessel," laments the psalmist. Immediately I think of Humpty Dumpty. Humpty Dumpty sat on a wall / Humpty Dumpty had a great fall / All the king's horses and all the king's men / couldn't put Humpty together again.

The world is full of people who feel like Humpty, sometimes once in a while and occasionally for long stretches. War, famine, illness, poverty, and violence are part of daily existence in the lives of many in our world. People from whom all others flee (verse 11) are an all-too-familiar sight in the streets of our cities. Our own troubles and the pain of those we see on the streets, and the nightly news or in the newspapers can leave us feeling like the psalmist's broken vessel. How could we feel otherwise? All the king's horses and all the king's men/ couldn't put Humpty together again. And if the king can't help, how can we?

But the King we know can and does help. Our times truly reside in the hands of the King, our God, whose face shines upon us, every one of us, and saves us. And knowing that God delivers us from persecutors and enemies brings courage—maybe even the courage to make small changes that matter to someone in need. Maybe the courage to walk alongside Jesus as he journeys toward the cross. Maybe even the courage to admit that we are broken and to let the King repair what is broken in us and put us back together again. So be it.

PRAYER: Gracious God, help me see not only the brokenness of others but my own brokenness. Let me be open to your healing touch so that I too can help heal the world rather than leave the broken pieces shattered on the ground. Amen.

FRIDAY, MARCH 18 • Read Philippians 2:5-11

On Fridays my colleagues and I order Chinese food for lunch, eat together, and shoot the breeze. At the end of lunch we crack open our fortune cookies and read our fortunes aloud. My cookies often tell me the same thing: You are honest and straightforward. When I read today's famous passage, my honest and straightforward reaction is this: This humility stuff is hard.

Saint Benedict quoted this famous passage in his Rule, his guidelines for monastic life. Submit to your superior in all obedience, he wrote, and imitate Jesus who submitted to God's will, even to the point of death. Ascend the ladder of humility, Benedict says, and you will reach heaven. Exalt yourself instead of God and you'll never get there.

Imitating Jesus seems impossibly difficult to me. So I look around me for others who are doing a better job of it than I am. I think of a colleague, well known for his preaching and pastoral skills, who is so sought after that he has speaking engagements almost every week. And still, he's a deeply humble person. He thanks me repeatedly for any small thing I do for him. Though he has every right to be arrogant, I've never seen any pridefulness in him. Everyone who talks with him feels like the center of his undivided attention while he listens. So, perhaps I will set my sights on imitating my colleague, at least as an interim step—not in an idolatrous way. I know he's not Jesus. But he knows and loves Jesus, and he's climbed higher on the ladder of humility than I have. If I can learn to be as obedient and humble as he is, maybe I can climb another rung toward the humble Jesus.

PRAYER: God of humility, help me in my struggle to learn humility. Help me take one small step farther up the ladder toward you this Lent. Amen.

If these verses were part of a movie, we'd all be hissing. Judas, speaking to the chief priests, quietly says, "What will you give me if I betray him to you?" And I think, *I'd never do that. I'd never be that cold and calculating.* It's easy for me to criticize Judas, to think I'm better than him, but I'm not. More often than I'd like, I betray Jesus too.

Recently I bought a pocket computer, one of those tiny handheld jobs that keeps track of your life. It reminds me of upcoming meetings with a little alarm and then a screen that gives me two choices: dismiss or snooze. I tap "dismiss" if I want the alarm to cease and "snooze" if I want another reminder. I never hit "snooze." Reminding me once is enough but doesn't always guarantee right action on my part. I think my pocket computer needs a key to press that indicates not only my awareness of the action needed but impetus toward that action.

See that homeless man? Dismiss or snooze? Look at my calendar that leaves little time for others. Dismiss or snooze? Full recycle bin, so paper goes in the trash. Dismiss or snooze? Violence on TV, on our streets, in our homes, and around the world. What can I do about it anyway? Dismiss or snooze?

In these and so many other ways, I betray Jesus—not all the time but pretty often. And yet, the miracle is that Jesus doesn't hit the "dismiss" button on me. He comes with a cup, gives thanks, and offers it to me. "Drink from it, all of you," he says to each of us. So we drink and begin again and keep working on pressing the "right action" button.

PRAYER: God of the cup, forgive my everyday betrayals of you. Give me the courage to take the right action today and all my days. Amen.

PASSION/PALM SUNDAY

And here we are on Palm Sunday. Having made it this far through Lent and knowing the stories of betrayal and pain that will be told again this year, as they are this week every year, I'd rather skip ahead to Easter. I don't want to live through the trial, the crowd chanting "Crucify!" yet again, and the horrible walk to the cross and Jesus' death. This week is too hard. Maybe we could just skip Holy Week this year and go straight to Easter.

But it doesn't work that way. A naturalist in Alaska once told me about the barren rock that is left after ice and snow recede from glaciers. Birds, wind, and water throw seeds and nutrients onto the rock. If the rock is even a little porous, it holds on to what's tossed there and begins to create new life. Small life comes first, then medium-sized life, and finally trees begin to grow. If trees come too early, they lack what is needed for survival and die.

Maybe experiencing Holy Week resembles the rock's experience. Maybe we have to be porous to absorb what Holy Week has to teach us. Then we let those small beginnings grow into deeper understandings as the events of the week unfold. If we go straight from Palm Sunday to Easter, maybe we won't develop the strength and stamina for survival. I wish there were a shortcut to Easter, but there's not. So let the stories be told again this year. They are the nourishment we need for new life.

PRAYER: God of the journey, help me listen to these difficult stories yet again. Help me absorb the nourishment they offer, so I may continue to grow into the person you call me to be. Amen.

The Deliverance of the Lord

March 21–27, 2005 • *Victor Michael Singletary*[‡]

MONDAY, MARCH 21 • **Read Hebrews 9:11-15**

Why does Jesus go to Jerusalem? Given his foreknowledge of his pending persecution, unjust trials, and crucifixion, Jesus appears insane in his determination to go to Jerusalem and confront the religious and political powers. What drove him to follow such an inexplicable and deadly course? The author of today's scripture reading provides an enduring answer.

Quite simply, Jesus enters Jerusalem to fulfill his destiny as the atoning sacrifice for humankind. I favor Saint Anselm's position about the theory of atonement: The devil had to be given his due. Because of Satan's success in causing the fall of humankind in the garden of Eden, he took humankind, God's highest creation, captive. Accordingly, Satan demanded a ransom in exchange for the liberty of humankind and the restoration of fellowship with the Lord: he requires priceless blood.

The author of Hebrews posits that Jesus goes to Jerusalem to fulfill his role as the great high priest of humankind who enters the Holy of Holies. However, Jesus does not enter an earthly tabernacle, nor does he offer the cheap blood of animals. Jesus offers his own precious blood, invaluable and sufficient for eternal redemption.

Lastly, Saint Anselm suggests that not only does Christ's sacrifice pay the ransom; it completely conquers the work of the devil. In Christ, the ransom is paid, automatically liberating all captives, past, present, and future. Jesus goes to the holy city to enter the Temple and cleanse it of the moneychangers. In condemning their actions, he precipitates the actions that lead to his crucifixion in which he ironically fulfills his destiny as the ransom for humankind.

SUGGESTION FOR MEDITATION: Why did Jesus go to Jerusalem?

[‡]Senior pastor, First Baptist Church Capitol Hill, Nashville, Tennessee.

God chooses the venue of servanthood in which to reveal the divine character, which is love. Søren Kierkegaard, the great Danish theologian and religious existentialist, referred to this historical surprise as the "great paradox." The divine takes on human form in the person of a lowly servant to educate all persons about the love of God.

According to Isaiah, the servant of the Lord was called and named by God before birth, "formed in the womb to be [God's] servant." God "hid" the servant, "polished" him, and prepared him to be the one "in whom I will be glorified." Finding the servant's mission to restore Israel "too light a thing," God gives the servant to all people, "that my salvation may reach to the end of the earth."

We can end the age-old theological debates about whether God set up Adam and Eve for the Fall. Isaiah posits that before the Fall God had already provided a mysterious and majestic resolution to this dilemma—a servant, "a light to the nations," who would redeem humankind. Though "deeply despised, abhorred by the nations, the slave of rulers," God in Christ the Servant extended salvation to all people in all times.

Many faith traditions offer moral and ethical insights on God's character, but only Christ, the superlative disclosure of God's essence, offers a direct relationship with a loving God who willingly pays the ultimate price in order to give life to those who believe. As theologian Paul Tillich concluded, Christ is the clearest revelation of God in human history.

SUGGESTION FOR MEDITATION: How may I become like the Lord Jesus Christ, a servant who clearly demonstrates the love, faithfulness, grace, truth, mercy, and peace of Almighty God?

No good deed goes unpunished." Those of us who humbly presume that we live in right relationship with Almighty God and endeavor to live to God's honor and glory must accept that we will be misinterpreted and grossly misunderstood. Today's psalm, a lament reminiscent of a contemporary blues song, speaks the agony of the righteous.

Interestingly, we are most prone to misunderstandings by fellow religious folk who characterize us as spiritually arrogant and unbearably sanctimonious. Yet we strive to do God's will as we understand God's revelation in our lives.

Jesus Christ encounters this phenomenon in his dealings with the religious authorities of his time. His insight into God's love freely extended that love to everyone, regardless of social status or economic background. Jesus heals freely, preaches to anyone who listens, and teaches everyone who receives. Yet, he journeys to Jerusalem to observe the dictates of his faith and discovers that the Temple has been made a "den of thieves" rather than God's "house of prayer." Not surprisingly, he forcefully speaks out against such dastardly deeds. In so doing, he earns the murderous condemnation of the religious establishment. They determine that this illiterate, poor, and self-righteous carpenter must give his life in exchange for his spiritual arrogance.

The psalmist captures the plight of the righteous in today's reading. In the face of imminent assassination, the protagonist pleads for divine help. He summons God's assistance in thwarting the schemes of the religious rulers. He begs God to come quickly to his rescue. Essentially, he asks that the bloodthirsty people who seek his life fall prey to their own shenanigans. Similarly, we who strive to fulfill the will of God as we humbly understand it, must ask God to handle those brothers and sisters whose misreading of our intentions lead them to plan to harm us.

PRAYER: O God, come quickly and save. Amen.

Thursday, March 24 • Read John 13:1-17, 31*b*-35

Maundy Thursday

A few years ago, I delivered a sermon titled "Sweet Smelly Feet." Needless to say, it remains memorable in the nostrils more so than the minds of the congregation. Yet that sermon illustrates the purposes of the evangelist in recounting the story of John 13. In that passage, the Lord Jesus washes the dirt-encrusted, callused, and smelly feet of the disciples. More significantly, he does so in the midst of dinner.

In this one act of extreme humility and love, Jesus teaches the disciples everything that he has previously endeavored to show during the three years of his public ministry among them and exclusive tutorial with them. He demonstrates that his perspective of God rests significantly upon an understanding of God's love, which empowers us to love everyone regardless of the cost. Pride and power are not components of this definition of God's love.

Whereas the law can be summarized in the two greatest commandments, which Jesus teaches elsewhere in the Gospel, they must be lived practically each day. As we obediently follow the leading of the Holy Spirit in the multifaceted ways in which God leads us to serve others, we manifest our understanding of the definition of agape, God's supreme type of love. The spiritual life is not a theory but the daily willingness to live with integrity according to the principles and values of one's faith.

Jesus, in this immortal ceremony of foot washing, annihilates the ulterior motives of power, prestige, and self-aggrandizement that linger within the crevices of the disciples' mind. On this Holy Thursday, I pray that his example forces us to evaluate our personal desires and that we will humbly yield our self-centered objectives to the will of God. Thereby, we can live as divine servants, instruments of God's peace, and vessels of God's love.

PRAYER: O Lord, make me a servant in the image of Jesus. Amen.

FRIDAY, MARCH 25 • Read John 18:1–19, 42

GOOD FRIDAY

Arguably, Good Friday is the holiest day of the year. You may insist that Easter is the holiest. However, the events of Good Friday were necessary to bring the dawn of Easter. Moreover, unless we can see the salvation of humankind in the tragedy of Good Friday, we cannot access the power and resurrection of Easter.

The Johannine evangelist straightforwardly and briefly records Peter's first denial of Christ in today's Gospel passage. We find Peter warming by a charcoal fire, along with the servants and officials of the religious authorities, because it was cold. That simple act symbolizes Peter's denial of Christ and the monumental events of his earthly ministry. The next day, Good Friday, Peter looks upon the crucifixion with horror and disgust. Rather than comprehending the atonement and sacrifice of "the Lamb of God who takes away the sin of the world," Peter seemingly determines that Jesus has failed, leaving him disappointed that the revolution against Rome will not commence.

Like Peter, we fall prey to dismissing the necessity of Good Friday. We relegate the events to legend. Sometimes, we spiritualize them to the point of meaninglessness. In addition, we warm ourselves by the secular and humanistic fires of skepticism, philosophy, science, and technology. We conclude that the crucifixion of one carpenter with a common name in Jerusalem two thousand years ago has no personal significance: We are Peter as he warms by the world's fire.

The author of Hebrews encourages us to see Christ's broken body as the rending of the curtain that separated the Holy of Holies from the rest of the Temple. Humankind now has direct access to the Lord and Creator of the universe. The tragedy of Good Friday provides this restoration between God and humankind. Yet each of us must resist our tendency toward denial and see the Lord's salvation in the brutality of the cross.

PRAYER: Lord Jesus, help me to believe steadfastly in your atoning work. Amen.

EASTER VIGIL

Secluded in their attempt to avoid arrest and crucifixion, the disciples must have felt like the world's biggest fools. Drawn by divine sanction and miraculous power, they had left everything to follow Jesus with the expectation that he would restore Israel to former glory. In their utter disappointment following Jesus' crucifixion, they surely thought the three exciting and dramatic years of his public ministry were all for naught.

On the Saturday that we call Easter Vigil, the discouragement of the grieving disciples gives us some insight into the disenchantment of the Hebrews with Moses' leadership. Like the disciples, they have "looked back," and to their great surprise and horror, Pharaoh and his mighty army are about to overtake them. In their self-centered fear, they ask Moses, "Was it because there were no graves in Egypt that you brought us to the desert to die?" (NIV) Perhaps feeling very foolish, they must wonder how they could have fallen for Moses' elaborate scheme to escape enslavement in Egypt. Serving the Egyptians now seems to them "better . . . than to die in the wilderness."

Like the distraught disciples in the time following Jesus' crucifixion, the children of Israel wonder, *What will become of us? How will we rejoin life?* But Moses assures them, "Do not be afraid. Stand firm and you will see the deliverance the Lord will bring you today" (NIV). And as we know, both the desperate Israelites and the grieving disciples lived to experience the miraculous power of a loving God, who "will fight for you."

In the midst of the hopelessness and despair of Easter Vigil, we must remain steadfast in our faith in the Lord and in our expectation of resurrection. We "need only to be still."

PRAYER: Lord Jesus, give me the strength to be still and to remain unwavering in my faith in you. Amen.

SUNDAY, MARCH 27 • Read Psalm 118:1-2, 14-24

EASTER SUNDAY

The celebratory nature of Psalm 118 warrants its characterization as a "Psalm of New Life and Victory." For Christians, Easter Sunday most clearly demonstrates the faithfulness of almighty God, who "did not give [us] over to death."

In raising Jesus from the dead, God permanently cancels the effects of death and bridges the chasm that had previously existed between the divine and humankind. "This is the gate of the LORD," the psalmist tells us. "I thank you that you . . . have become my salvation." Today Christians everywhere will join the chorus as "shouts of joy and victory resound in the tents of the righteous" because "the LORD's right hand has done mighty things!" (NIV).

The psalmist acknowledges in the midst of his jubilant song the times that God allowed life's circumstances to chasten him. Yet God never permitted any situation to conquer him. Just as Jesus, rejected by the religious authorities of his day, became the "chief cornerstone" of salvation, so God uses our trials to transform darkness into light. Because God will equally and ultimately transform every defeat into victory, the psalmist can exult, "I shall not die, but I shall live, and recount the deeds of the LORD."

Every day is Easter for disciples of the risen Lord and Savior. We rejoice with a song of new life and victory. With every dawn we rise and say with the psalmist, "This is the day that the LORD has made; let us rejoice and be glad in it."

PRAYER: O Lord, fill me with your resurrection power, that I may give thanks to you, whose steadfast love endures forever. Amen.

The Resurrection Difference

March 28–April 3, 2005 • Jim Somerville[‡]

The note on Psalm 16:10 in my Bible says, "The psalmist expresses confidence in God's power to deliver from terrible death." A good verse to know when facing the prospect of a terrible death, isn't it? The battlefield, bone cancer, crucifixion. Jesus knew the Psalms and often quoted them. From the cross he cried out the heartbroken words of Psalm 22:1: "My God, my God, why have you forsaken me?" Did Psalm 16 come to his mind? Did he quote it on the night of his betrayal as he anguished in the garden, as he stood before Pilate? Did he say aloud or whisper to himself, "You do not give me up to Sheol, or let your faithful one see the Pit"? Was it wishful thinking on his part or on the psalmist's to voice these words at all?

I don't think so. The psalmist has reason to trust in God. In verse 6 he says, "The boundary lines have fallen for me in pleasant places; I have a goodly heritage." Knowing that God has been trustworthy in the past gives him confidence for the future. Even if he should face "terrible death," he counts on the God who has always been with him to be with him at that time. For this reason he says, "I keep the LORD always before me; because he is at my right hand, I shall not be moved."

Jesus had reason to trust in God and in the hour of his death, I could hope that he called these words to mind and whispered to himself: "You do not give me up to Sheol, or let your faithful one see the Pit."

PRAYER: O Lord, you who were faithful to your son Jesus, who did not let your Holy One see corruption, be faithful to us now and in the hour of our death. Amen.

[‡]Pastor, First Baptist Church, Washington, D.C.

In what was certainly one of the most effective, if not one of the best, sermons ever preached, Peter makes some interesting sermonic "moves." He begins by claiming boldly that God has raised Jesus from the dead! Then he backs up that claim with Old Testament scripture. Peter also uses his knowledge of his audience. He is speaking to "men of Judea" and all those who live in Jerusalem, people who loved both the Old Testament scriptures and the king who had written so many of their favorite psalms— King David. Peter appeals to both.

"Do you remember what David said?" he asks, quoting from the words of Psalm 16: "I saw the LORD always before me, for he is at my right hand so that I will not be shaken; therefore my heart was glad, and my tongue rejoiced; moreover my flesh will live in hope. For you will not abandon my soul to Hades, or let your Holy One experience corruption." And then Peter explains, David did "experience corruption." He died and was buried and his tomb still remained in Jerusalem. David was not referring to himself when he said this; he was talking about the Messiah who would be one of his descendants (and therefore, by extension, his "flesh"). It was he whose flesh would not "experience corruption." Then Peter puts together this interesting syllogism: (1) The Messiah will not experience corruption; (2) Jesus did not experience corruption; (3) therefore, Jesus is the Messiah!

It works. Peter's hearers make the move with him from propositional truth to experiential truth, and at the end of that sermon, three thousand people are baptized. Peter helped them accept David's words as a foretelling of the death, burial, and resurrection of the Messiah.

PRAYER: Dear God, help us trust the truth of scripture even when it is hard for us and to live our lives in faithful obedience to your word. Amen.

It is all well and good to preach powerful sermons on the foretelling of the death, burial, and resurrection of the Messiah, but usually we understand God's will best in hindsight. Not too long before Peter's famous Pentecost sermon, he hadn't been at all sure about God's plan.

Let's go back several weeks before Pentecost when, as Peter himself puts it, "Jesus of Nazareth . . . [was] crucified and killed" (Acts 2:22-23). On that awful Friday Peter watched as the one sent from God was delivered into the hands of "those outside the law." Peter himself played a role in that delivery. Although he had promised to stick with Jesus to the bitter end, he hadn't—by most accounts—been able to stay awake with him for even one hour of prayer. He hadn't succeeded in preventing Jesus' arrest, although we can hardly fault him for giving it a foolhardy try. He hadn't had the nerve to acknowledge his relationship to Jesus even when asked about it point-blank. In fact, he denied it three times. In Luke's account Jesus turned and looked at Peter after his third denial, and Peter "went out and wept bitterly" (22:61-62).

On the night of Pentecost, a different Peter stands confidently before the crowd in Jerusalem. The Peter of denial had been a broken, cowardly person, filled with remorse. This one seems ready to take on the world. What has happened? Resurrection; that's what has happened. After recalling the finality of Jesus' death Peter says, "But God raised him up"—a divine conjunction, that little word. *But* hope was shattered. *But* Peter was a ruined, broken failure. *But* in this Pentecost sermon Peter bears witness to God's power to raise the dead.

And Peter—of all people—should know.

PRAYER: God, help us remember that things often look hopeless, that we often feel helpless, and that often we can see no way out. But with you all things are possible. Amen.

The disciples huddle together behind locked doors "for fear of the Jews," John says. Remember that "the Jews" is John's usual designation for the enemies of Jesus and not a reference to Jews in general. The disciples feared the people who had arrested Jesus, "tried" him, and then took him to Pilate to have him condemned, flogged, and crucified.

Why shouldn't the disciples be afraid? They might be next!

But then an incredible thing happens: Jesus walks into the room. The one who had suffered and died now stands before them alive. He says, "Peace be with you," and shows them his hands and side as proof of his identity. And then, "the disciples rejoiced when they saw the Lord."

The first sermon I ever preached was on this passage. In those days I used the Revised Standard Version, which reads: "the disciples were glad when they saw the Lord." I remember thinking of it as an enormous understatement. "Glad?" I preached. "They were glad?" And then, with a little help from *Roget's Thesaurus* I said, "What about ecstatic? What about euphoric? What about blissful, mirthful, joyful, gleeful, beaming, leaping, capering, cheering, 'hopped up,' 'high as a kite,' and 'happy as a clam at high water?'"

Glad couldn't begin to describe the disciples' feelings.

I recently reminded a despondent friend of this story and said, "You know, those disciples moved in a single moment from the depths of despair to the heights of rapture. Jesus did it for them. I'm praying he'll do it for you. There is no despair so deep, no door so locked that the risen Christ can't walk in and resurrect hope."

PRAYER: Lord Jesus, enter the locked rooms of our lives, those places where we tremble with fear, with rage, with depression. Enter in and say "Shalom" and bring us the joy we thought we would never feel again. Amen.

John's version of Pentecost differs from the story in Acts 2 and is far less dramatic. No rush of a mighty wind here, only the warm breath of the risen Christ; no tongues of fire dancing on the heads of the disciples, only a solemn commission. But something happens here all the same.

"As the Father has sent me, so I send you," Jesus says, and in that moment the disciples become apostles, "sent ones." But sent to do what? What was Jesus sent to do? In the beginning of John's Gospel we learn he was sent to give those who believed the power to become children of God (1:12b). Is that what the apostles are sent to do? To help others believe and become God's children? At the end of that initial section the writer states that no one has ever seen God, "the only Son, who is close to the Father's heart, who has made him known" (1:18). Is that what they are sent to do? To make God known to the world?

The options exhaust us. Following Jesus through this Gospel leaves us gasping for breath. And, as the author says, if everything he did and said were recorded "the world itself could not contain the books that would be written" (21:25). If the disciples are going to be sent as he was sent, they will need some help; Jesus anticipates that need.

In this story Christ breathes on his disciples and tells them to receive the Holy Spirit. The Greek word for spirit is *pneuma*, from which we get *pneumatic*—the power that raises a bulldozer's scoop full of earth and rock. He gives them the power to forgive or retain sins. The Greek word for power is *dunamis*, from which we get the word *dynamite*—the power to bring down sheer granite cliffs. Something happens in this story, all right, something earthshaking. The risen Christ comes to his disciples with gifts of Spirit and power . . . and sends apostles on their way.

PRAYER: "Breathe on me, Breath of God, fill me with life anew, that I may love what thou dost love, and do what thou wouldst do" (Edwin Hatch, 1878).

I've always wondered where Thomas was while all the other disciples rejoiced with the risen Christ. Was he out buying groceries at the time? picking up his dry cleaning? Or was he so grief-stricken by Jesus' death that he simply wanted to be alone?

We sometimes saddle Thomas with that scornful nickname, "Doubting Thomas." It might help to remember that this Gospel mentions Thomas in two other places: he is ready to die with Jesus (11:16) and eager to follow Jesus (14:5). He doesn't sound like the quitter we sometimes imagine him to be. The doubt we accuse him of might not be the opposite of faith but its necessary companion: the refining fire that burns away everything but wholehearted belief. When the other disciples say they have "seen the Lord," he insists that he will not believe it until he has put his finger in the mark of the nails and put his hand in Jesus' side. Thomas desires a faith as tangible as that.

And to the amazement of everyone (including ourselves) Jesus grants his request. He appears a week later and offers Thomas precisely what he has asked for: "Put your finger here and see my hands. Reach out your hand and put it in my side. Do not doubt but believe." Thomas, however, finds that he doesn't have to touch Jesus after all. Seeing is enough. "My Lord and my God!" he exclaims.

But Jesus seizes the teachable moment. If Thomas can believe without touching, by sight alone, then surely there are those who can believe without seeing, by faith alone, and how lucky are they! "Blessed are those who have not seen and yet have come to believe," Jesus responds. And, of course, he's talking about us.

PRAYER: My Lord and my God, when I can't touch you or see you, let me reach for you with the hands of faith, look for you through the eyes of faith, and find you present through the miracle of faith. Amen.

When I taught religion to college freshmen I would bear down on those last two verses of John 20: "Now Jesus did many other signs in the presence of his disciples, which are not written in this book. But these are written so that you may come to believe that Jesus is the Messiah, the Son of God, and that through believing you may have life in his name."

"Do you hear that?" I would ask. "This whole Gospel was written so that you might become believers. If you're not a believer by this point…the Gospel has failed." And then I would lean over the lectern and say with a smile, "You wouldn't want that to happen, would you?"

No. You wouldn't want that to happen. Because John tells us that those who believe "have life in his name." And the writer of First Peter tells us that through the resurrection of Jesus those who believe are given "a new birth into a living hope…and into an inheritance that is imperishable, undefiled, and unfading, kept in heaven." We celebrate this living hope in church every Sunday, and not only on Easter: the resurrection of Jesus gives us life here and now and the promise of life eternal. One of these days, says the writer of this epistle, Jesus will come again, and the faith you have kept will result in "praise and honor and glory." But even before that time comes—because you love him and believe in him—you can rejoice with an "indescribable and glorious joy," because already, right now, "you are receiving the outcome of your faith, the salvation of your souls."

For the writers of First Peter and the Gospel of John, faith is not only pie in the sky by and by but something sound, on the ground, while we're still around. Eternal life begins the moment Christ lives in us.

PRAYER: Lord, you know that life is what we most desire. Give it to us, by faith, not only there and then but here and now. And on this Lord's Day, as we celebrate the risen Christ, may we be moved to "rejoice with an indescribable and glorious joy." Amen.

The Body of Christ Risen

April 4–10, 2005 • Sister Mary Michael[‡]

MONDAY, APRIL 4 • Read Luke 24:13–27

The two disciples on the way to Emmaus reveal to Jesus their disgruntled and disheartened natures, sharing dreams of Jesus as the long-awaited messiah who would redeem Israel. They express mistaken ideas that may have caused Jesus sorrow. They are not the only ones who misunderstand Jesus. Two other disciples had mistaken ideas of his reign, evidenced by their mother's asking for special places of honor for them. Another disciple tried through betrayal to force Jesus into his understanding of a messiah.

"Then beginning with Moses and all the prophets, he interpreted to them the things about himself in all the scriptures." When we recall Jesus' explanation of God's plan for the world's salvation, we are tempted to think how dense the disciples were in clinging to mistaken ideas. Yet we sometimes cling to our own set of mistaken ideas, holding out hope that Jesus "was the one to redeem" our nation, our marriage, our unfair work setting. Then we experience our own version of the disappointment of the disciples on the way to Emmaus and feel disheartened. We seek the grace that came in the breaking of bread and in the revelation of the risen Christ among us.

Thomas à Kempis offers needed wisdom: "Drink of the chalice of thy Lord lovingly, if thou desirest to be His friend, and to have part with Him. . . . If indeed there had been anything better, and more beneficial to [our] salvation than suffering, Christ certainly would have showed it by word and example." The breaking of bread remains Christ's most common example of revelation in our ordinary lives.

PRAYER: Redeemer of the world, strengthen our love for you so that we become open to your revelation. Amen.

[‡]Member of the Episcopal Society of St. Margaret, having served in Montreal, Utica, Port-au-Prince, Philadelphia, and New York; now living in the Mother House in Boston, Massachusetts.

You and I are the body of Christ risen—Christ alive on earth here and now today. People will believe and give themselves wholeheartedly to Christ because of what we say and do, or they will believe less than ever before.

During the seven-mile journey from Jerusalem, Jesus prepares the two disciples for their first Eucharist. Their experiences of Passover and perhaps of the meal in the Upper Room differ greatly from their experience in Emmaus. As Jesus sits at table with them, he takes, blesses, breaks, and gives bread to them. Their eyes are opened, and they know him. Then they make confession: "Were not our hearts burning within us while he was talking to us on the road, while he was opening the scriptures to us?" Notice their amazement and gratitude! We tend to think of confession as a time to speak of sin. Here confession offers a note of grace. The disciples confess wonder and awe, amazement and praise. The risen Christ has elevated the lowly and lifted the burdens of those who are oppressed!

We may connect the thanksgiving meal at Emmaus with other words in Luke: "This is my body, which is given for you. Do this in remembrance of me" (Luke 22:19). In remembrance and thanksgiving, we receive the broken bread even as we go on our own journeys of faith.

Dom Gregory Dix, writing about the Eucharist in *The Shape of the Liturgy,* said about Christ's command to do this in remembrance of him: "Was ever another command so obeyed? For century after century, spreading slowly to every continent and country and among every race on earth, this action has been done, in every conceivable human circumstance, for every conceivable need from infancy and before it to extreme old age and after it, from the pinnacles of earthly greatness to the refuge of fugitives in the caves and dens of the earth." We all hunger for this bread, and we still implore our Lord Christ for this living bread.

PRAYER: Christ, make yourself known to us as we break bread on the journey. Amen.

WEDNESDAY, APRIL 6 • Read 1 Peter 1:17-23

We are the holy people of a holy God who requires our obedience. When we remember God's use of frail, weak human beings to do great things, we sinners can take courage. Our holiness does not come from relationship to God alone or to our devotional life. Indeed, consider the people addressed in First Peter: The salutation addresses "the exiles of the Dispersion . . . who have been chosen by God"(v. 1).

Sometimes exile seems a natural condition of our times. We struggle alone and feel cast off. We hope that someone will help us, but we do not ask for fear that our asking might show weakness or dependence. Because of such a sense of exile, division seems to rule many lives. Even though we may experience exile, First Peter reminds us that we are a people in community, a community of love and support based on life in the risen Christ.

The epistle writer urges us to "live in reverent fear during the time of your exile." I invite you to meditate upon this condition of reverent fear. For the epistle writer, "reverent fear" comes from a deep sense of atonement, of Christ's death and resurrection. Such reverent fear is less the feelings of panic or terror and far more a sense of awe.

Thomas Merton, Trappist monk, once said that learning to love one another is the most creative and difficult work to which any Christian is called. I suspect that one difficulty of loving remains rooted in our sense of exile. "Love one another." We hear those words and think that this command is simple and basic, but love in the midst of exile calls for vulnerability and transparency, qualities that seem rare in exile. The risen Christ invites us to set aside the bondage of exile and to take on the freedom of love.

PRAYER: **Christ, open our ears and hearts to hear your living and enduring words to us. Grant us the grace to obey them so that we may become all that you would have us be. Amen.**

Because of our baptism we have been born anew and Christ lives within us. How do you understand the experience of being born anew? Do you understand this spiritual birth as a process or as a mountaintop spiritual experience? Is this spiritual rebirth renewed each day?

Because of our baptism we have been born anew, and Christ lives within us. Despite the universal proclamation of Christianity, even something as unifying as the transformation we experience in Christ can become divisive as we split into our different theological understandings of conversion. We have been born anew, and our lives will never be what they once were because we know now that Jesus Christ loves us.

Despite our theological divisions, I think that the author of First Peter would invite us—perhaps in strong language—to consider a basic truth: Whether we can name a conversion moment or claim a gradual unfolding of God's love in our lives, what matters is that our lives reflect what we claim. The risen Christ invites each one of us to live in the loving reign of God.

Alan Jones wrote in *Living in the Spirit*: "At our worst and darkest moments, we can affirm that we are God's handiwork, that [God's] image has marked us forever, that the most real thing about us is the Holy Spirit who dwells in every human heart." We have been born anew, and the mark of Christ is on us!

PRAYER: "Trust in the LORD forever, for in the LORD you have an everlasting rock" (Isa. 26:4). Amen.

The first four verses of Psalm 116 speak powerfully to me as the perfect example of the living and enduring word of God. Six years ago I had a massive heart attack. My doctor told me afterward that I had actually died—the cords of death entangled me; the grip of the grave took hold of me. But the doctors' skill got my heart functioning again; they did by-pass surgery and later added a pacemaker. Our compassionate God has granted me six more blessed years at our Mother House in Boston where I continue to serve in ministry.

As one who has lived in a convent for fifty years, I believe that most of the people who visit our center for retreats or conferences come because they really wish to know—not just know *about* but know—our Lord better than ever before. How can we help people know God more deeply? If persons expressed such a desire aloud to me, I would first take them to a window and tell them to look at the beauty and glory of God's creation.

I would invite them to our community prayer service. Four times a day we gather to sing our praise and gratitude to and express our love for our Lord Christ. I would urge them to attend our daily Eucharist to be nourished and empowered by our Savior's words and his meal.

I would suggest that they spend time alone in our Oratory in the presence of the sacrament, being still and listening for the living word of God. I would advise them to begin reading God's love letter to humanity—the scriptures. I would urge them to search for the face of Christ in every human being they encounter, beginning with the faces of those they love the most.

I would urge them because, like the psalmist, I love the Lord. The snares of death encompassed me; I suffered distress and anguish. In my time of dying, like the psalmist, I also called on the Lord to save my life. I do so every day.

Prayer: Grant, O Christ, that we may see you more clearly, love you more dearly, and follow you more nearly. Amen.

Our psalmist asks how he can repay the Lord for all the blessings God has given him. Remember that he wrote about a sickness unto death in the beginning of this psalm; the snares of death, the pangs of Sheol encompassed the psalmist. In the midst of deathlike despair, healing happened and new life was given!

We can no more repay God for the gifts we have received than we can repay the apostles for their faithfulness or our families for their provision. Having received these gifts, we let our lives express gratitude. Near the end of our week of thinking about the gifts of God, we raise the question asked by the psalmist: How can I ever repay the Lord for all the good things God has done for me? The psalmist charges us to lift up the cup of salvation and call upon the name of the Lord. We hear also that we shall fulfill the vows we made to the Lord in the presence of all God's people.

I wonder about the nature of the vows made by the psalmist. Were they especially significant or were they like the vows you and I may have made? Most of us made vows during a profession of faith. We take vows or make promises at marriages. Some of us made vows at ordination. All of us took special vows (or our sponsors did for us) at our baptism. That was the most important day of our life, the day that we became a member of the body of Christ alive on earth today. We vowed to renounce evil, to follow the teachings of Jesus Christ, to do everything in our power to bring God's reign of love on earth in the here and now.

I can only speculate about the psalmist, but I like to think that he also vowed to renounce evil and to do everything for God's sake, so that others would know of his commitment to the reign of God. How indeed can we mortals ever repay our Lord for the gifts that flow so abundantly?

SUGGESTION FOR MEDITATION: Reflect on the vows you have made. What purpose do those vows serve?

We began this week with the two disciples on the way to Emmaus and the revelation of the risen Christ in the breaking and blessing of bread. Today we read about another revelation of the risen Christ in the act of proclamation. Both breaking bread and uttering speech are common activities. They happen every day, and often we expect little from these acts. But even now—thanks be to God!—our ordinary, everyday actions may reveal anew the risen Christ.

Acts 2 offers us glimpses of the first century and reflects our own hope. After the Pentecostal outpouring of languages and communication beyond national and ethnic borders or barriers, Peter addresses the crowd. Is Peter preaching or teaching? Does it matter? Peter does for the crowd what Jesus did for the two on the way to Emmaus: Peter explained the history of God's salvation. Far more important for us is the response of the crowd. "they were cut to the heart and said to Peter and to the other apostles, 'Brothers, what should we do?'"

We may have asked that question of someone we loved and trusted, someone whose life radiated God's love. We repented and were baptized. We sensed forgiveness. Ever since that moment, we have come each day to realize again the newness of God's love for us and for the world.

Peter adds more to the equation: "Save yourselves from this corrupt generation." The text does not invite us to run from corruption. I do not believe that the apostles or even Jesus expected the community of faith to live in isolation from those who did not follow the teachings of Christ. Peter expects the new believers to receive the power of the Holy Spirit and be empowered to reach out to others for the sake of the risen Christ. Our readings this week encourage us to speak to others about God's reign, particularly the risen Christ revealed in the breaking of bread and the opening of scripture.

PRAYER: O God, be known to us in daily practices of word and table. Reveal your radiant love through us to others. Amen.

Abundant Life

April 11–17, 2005 • *Sue Joiner*[‡]

MONDAY, APRIL 11 • Read Psalm 23:1-3

Restoring

Psalm 23 is one of the best-known and loved scriptures. Many people, including those who have long abandoned the church, can recite this psalm from memory. Often quoted at memorial services to comfort the grieving, this psalm has a strong message for those who are living. The first line summarizes the psalm's message: "The LORD is my shepherd, I shall not want." Trusting God to provide frees us from anxious striving. Psalm 34:10 says, "Those who seek the LORD lack no good thing."

Psalm 23 speaks of peace and tranquility. It promises that God will care for our basic needs, a reminder that God holds the big picture. While the small stuff distracts me, God tunes in to the greater needs of all creation. Occasionally I need to recall that my very life depends on God and that the same God who cared for Israel during the Exodus and the long years of exile is the God who cares for me today. I rouse myself, step out of my habits and routine, and acknowledge the one who feeds me.

On a recent trip to Europe, I found myself most aware of this God who "restores my soul" while sitting in the Swiss Alps near a lake in Austria. The beauty of the mountains and the serenity of the lake filled me with peace. Somehow, away from all that normally clamors for my attention, I found myself resting in God in profound ways and in those moments did not "want." My soul was restored. Psalm 23 affirms God's soul-restoring promise for all.

PRAYER: God of all life and breath, we thank you for this living word, for this reminder that our lives depend on you. Restore our souls as we seek you each day. Amen.

[‡]Associate minister, First United Methodist Church, Corvallis, Oregon.

Comforting

This verse has been called the theological center of Psalm 23. No matter how threatening or dangerous the situation, God's provision is enough—not that the threat is unreal—but God is ultimate. The psalmist no longer refers to a God "out there" but shifts to a particular intimacy with God. Even though we find ourselves in valleys of pain and despair, God is with us. God is with us throughout our lives, every step of the way.

So often God's presence becomes clear to us after the fact. We stumble along through times of grief and loss—barely coping. But as we later reflect on this time, we see God's comfort and care for us.

God's comfort and care come in many forms: through the love of a family member or friend, in our own prayer, or in the colors of a rainbow. Sometimes in the loneliest of moments, we experience a sudden awareness that we are not alone. God's tender compassion surrounds us in all times and places.

Each morning, my dog and I walk through a wooded path in our neighborhood. Often we are the only ones out and the only sounds are those of nature waking—birds calling to one another, leaves blowing in the breeze, and the nearby stream continuing the journey begun the day before. Some days it is still dark when we walk; the path is not clear. Somehow in those early moments, I know that God is with me. Those moments strengthen me throughout the day. After several years of walking this path and feeling God's comforting presence, I am shaped by God's loving embrace and know that it will sustain me in all circumstances. I am grateful for God's presence in the darkness and in the light.

PRAYER: Comforting God, thank you for your presence with us in the darkest valleys. Thank you for your loving compassion that sustains us each day of our lives. Amen.

Feeding

With the image of God as host at the table, we encounter a God who gives life to the world. It is important that our table be open to all God's people. St. Gregory of Nyssa Episcopal Church in San Francisco believes that the Communion table is also the table where we, as the body of Christ, host the world. The Communion table at St. Gregory is the one from which the church serves the hungry from their food pantry. This same table is used to serve refreshments for fellowship time following worship.

When I discovered the centrality of the Communion table at St. Gregory, I realized that the Communion table in many congregations sits empty most of the time. Yet we worship a God who feeds our deepest hungers—not just in worship. This same God longs for us to feed the world. Occasionally we see pictures of hungry children on television. Do we connect those pictures with the table from which we are fed? We know that Jesus' body was broken and his blood was shed for the world. Do we remember our role in sharing that holy food with all who hunger?

God prepares a table for us without waiting for us to be worthy. But that is not the last word. The psalm assures us that God's goodness and mercy will pursue us throughout our lives. We dwell with God no matter where we are.

Affirming our faith in Psalm 23 can transform our lives. When we are fed at God's table, we are changed. We commit ourselves to feeding the world with the same generosity.

PRAYER: Generous God, you feed all of our hungers, and you call us to feed one another. May we learn to feed one another as you have fed us. Amen.

THURSDAY, APRIL 14 • Read 1 Peter 2:19-25

Returning

This text closes with those who have gone astray returning to the one who guards our souls. How easily we stray from the source of our lives. I once read a cartoon with two sheep talking. One says to the other, "All we like people have gone astray." We may be lost, but God is not. Returning, we find ourselves welcomed by the one who cares for us in profound ways. This passage shows us that the one who suffered for us is the one who awaits our return.

Some of our favorite stories involve the element of returning. As children, we learn about Hansel and Gretel who have lost their way and finally find their way home. In *The Wizard of Oz*, we journey with Dorothy who, in the midst of her adventures, longs to be home in Kansas. Eventually she finds her way home, and we are relieved. One of the best-loved Gospel stories in Luke 15 relates the story of a young man who leaves home with his inheritance, squanders it, and finds himself in misery. He returns home to beg for a slave's place in the household, only to find a father waiting for him, ready to celebrate. Rather than suffering further "consequences" for his actions, the son is received into a gracious father's loving arms.

Wherever we find ourselves in this story, often called the parable of the prodigal son, the good news is always staggering. Like the father in this story, God eagerly welcomes us when we return and throws a party in our honor. Such outrageous news is too good to be true! God's gracious welcome refuses to be limited by human understanding. When we return to God, we experience graciousness that is beyond our imagination.

PRAYER: Welcoming God, thank you for receiving us with open arms. We are grateful that you do not wait for us to understand your welcoming embrace before offering it to us. Amen.

Hearing

I grew up in the city and have to confess that sheep are a mystery to me. I pastored a rural church where some of the members owned sheep. One thing I learned from them is that sheep utterly depend on the shepherd. In both Psalm 23 and John 10 humans and sheep have much in common. We resist a comparison to sheep because we have difficulty acknowledging our complete dependency on the Shepherd. We want to live life on our own terms. When our own terms fail us, we struggle to admit our great need for God.

The relationship between sheep and shepherd is characterized by the shepherd who calls the sheep by name and the sheep that recognize the shepherd's voice. Sheep follow the shepherd, trusting the one who knows them by name.

The Igniting Ministries commercials for The United Methodist Church include a series of commercials called Love Letters. In one of those commercials, God says, "I miss being asked for my advice and loving you enough to always tell you the truth." In another, God says, "I miss our late-night conversations. I've tried to call, but there's no answer."

Can you hear God's voice calling you? God calls in the midst of busy schedules, in the early morning quiet, in the music we sing, in the people we encounter, in walks through our neighborhood, in much-needed vacations, in the ordinary moments of our lives. When we listen, we find that God knows our name and shows us the way. Trusting God, we step out in faith.

PRAYER: Loving God, thank you for calling to us. Open our ears to hear you and our hearts to trust you. Amen.

Receiving

Once again we hear the promise of pasture and an assurance that we will find food and water with the shepherd. The great promise in this text is that of abundant life. Our attempts to make our lives secure show that we have forgotten this promise. God intends that our lives be rich and full. The catch is that God intends that *everyone's* life be rich and full. We work hard to secure life for ourselves, often at the expense of another. Trusting this promise means trusting that God's abundance is for all.

A former colleague, Isaiah Jones, wrote a song about this text that claimed "abundant life is yours." This song never failed to get people on their feet clapping and dancing as they sang of God's abundance. Somehow in that time of dancing and singing, we knew without overtly stating it, that God's abundance is for all, an end to hungering and thirsting for *all* people.

We may picture abundance in many ways: a table overflowing with food, a field of wildflowers, a rainfall after a drought, a family welcoming a newborn, a congregation singing with enthusiasm, water dripping from a newly baptized person, a couple professing marriage vows to each other, the celebration of a life lived well, surprise visits from a loved one, the colors of a sunset. There is no limit to the abundance God promises and offers us each day. Jesus gave us a deeper understanding of the abundant life. The accounts of his life among us tell the story of his encounters with people. Jesus made the most of every moment. He stopped to touch and heal people. He opened himself to every opportunity that God offered. Abundant life involves making the most of each day and seeing God's potential in every person.

PRAYER: Life-giving God, open us to receive the abundance you have to offer. Remind us that you desire abundant life for all. Amen.

Growing

This week's readings have painted a picture of the abundant life that comes from God. This abundance is always found in the life of community. This picture in Acts of the early Christian community provides a glimpse into what is possible. The people's enthusiasm and openness evidence God's transforming power. They willingly share possessions, prayers, food, and love for God and one another. The staggering result is explosive growth.

In a time when many mainline denominations are losing members, what effect might it have on the church to live out the truth of this text? It is tempting to dismiss this text as ideal, but this story shows us our purpose. Christian community requires more than halfhearted, occasional participation. Instead, it calls forth our best efforts, our most generous selves, our highest praise, and lives that reflect sincere gratitude. This community calls us to deeper unity, but such unity is only possible when all are included around the table. This scripture teaches us how to be the church. When we are truly the church, no one hungers.

John Wesley understood that truth when he created class meetings and called people into mutual love and accountability. These early groups followed the principles of Acts 2. Today, many churches are rediscovering the power of small groups. The groups that thrive are the ones that most resemble Acts 2. Such groups not only sustain their members but reach beyond the bounds of the group to feed those who hunger.

PRAYER: God of us all, you created us to live in unity. Help us to trust you and one another and be generous with what we have that all may know the power of your transforming love. Amen.

Preparation for Inspired Living

April 18–24, 2005 • *Hank Blunk*[‡]

MONDAY, APRIL 18 • **Read Acts 7:55-60**

I don't know that this is exactly the way it happened," said the old Native American storyteller of his tale, "but I know the truth of the story." Today's story in Acts raises our suspicion. It seems mysterious, mystical, not real. We can't see, touch, hear, smell, or taste it. We can't prove it empirically or scientifically.

And seeing is not believing. We don't always know what we are seeing, touching, hearing, smelling, or tasting. Our senses are easily misled. We must train and condition them to perceive. Someone in my remote recollection said, "Inspiration favors the well-prepared mind." Stephen, a person of "good standing, full of the Spirit and of wisdom" (Acts 6:3) was prepared to see.

Stephen "gazed," while we glance, glimpse, even gawk. We sneak a peek. Gazing is a lost art, perhaps protecting us against the cultural overload of sights, sounds, and images. But fixing our attention in a steady, intense gaze is an important skill. Stephen's "gaze into heaven" indicates focused concentration that comes from practiced knowing of what and for whom he looked. What he saw strengthened him and gave him courage.

We can never know whether this description of Stephen's experience accurately reflects what happened, but we can know the truth of it. Witnessing God's mystery comes with preparation, wisdom, and the Spirit.

SUGGESTION FOR MEDITATION: What in my life impairs my ability to see the mystery of God's glory?

PRAYER: God of glorious mystery, remove my inability to see. Give me courage to be of good standing, filled with your Spirit and wisdom. Amen.

[‡]Retired Presbyterian clergy; a watcher for God through prayer, study, and the life of the church; husband, father, grandfather; companion of Benedicta, a yellow Labrador retriever; living in Elkhart, Indiana.

My times are in your hand...
  save me in your steadfast love.

A primary element of biblical faith asserts that God is always present but not at our disposal. God, the context in which we live, is not a convenience when a situation eludes our cleverness and control. Faithful living implies a trust in the God whose "steadfast love is *better* than life" (Ps. 63:3, emphasis mine)

As I write these words, some of those into whose hands we entrust ourselves are wobbling. The stock market has lost nearly forty percent of its value from just months ago. We still feel a sense of dis-ease from the 9/11 attack on the World Trade Center, Pentagon, and U.S. way of life. Children have been kidnapped; several of the largest corporations in the world have declared bankruptcy, the investments of thousands cannibalized by exploitative executives and "cooked books." The credibility of both religious leaders and the church wanes as a result of abuse of authority and cover-up. I could go on and on.

"My times are in your hand . . . save me in your steadfast love." Such inspired faith in times of turmoil comes from the preparation of knowing God's steadfast love and recognizing that God is not a giant vacuum cleaner to suck up the messes we make; a local convenience store where we pick up a few items we need, any time, day or night; or a broadband cable service offering whatever we choose with the flick of our remote control.

SUGGESTION FOR MEDITATION: What are the "everyday gods" to which I entrust myself and my security? In what place in my life do I trust God's steadfast love?

PRAYER: My times are in your hand, O God. Save me in your steadfast love in Jesus Christ, who entrusted himself to you, even on the cross. Amen.

Like newborn infants, long for the pure, spiritual milk. . . .

Casey, eight years old, wanted to "read all of the Bible." I suggested that he start with Mark rather than go from Genesis straight through. A week later, he had read Mark's Gospel. "What is it about?" I asked. He replied, "There are no birth stories and no stories about the resurrection. It is about Jesus' adult life and ministry, from his baptism to his crucifixion." And Casey was right. In seminary I studied the Gospel of Mark for a semester and knew little more than this eager third grader in one week!

If "inspiration favors the well-prepared mind," the likes of Casey will be prepared. The ancient discipline of *lectio divina* consists of reading a brief text slowly, four times:

- First, to hear the passage and get the sense of the story or the words of counsel.
- The second time, to listen for a word or phrase that beckons, a "word to me" that speaks of comfort or challenge.
- The third time, I listen for that word or phrase and my feelings—the resistance, the hope, the encouragement we have not heard before.
- And for the fourth reading, I listen again—this time opening and emptying myself so that God can work that promise or transformation in me!

"I have read through the Torah," said the student to the rabbi.

"It is not how much you have gone through the Torah," replied the rabbi, "but how much the Torah has gone through you!"

SUGGESTION FOR MEDITATION: How do you get the "pure, spiritual milk" you need?

PRAYER: Wondrous God, who by your word and spirit nourishes and nurtures, feed us with pure, spiritual milk that we may grow into salvation. Amen.

Come to him, a living stone . . . and like living stones, let yourselves be built into a spiritual house, to be a holy priesthood.

Some of the preparation for inspiration comes when we involve ourselves in activities and causes beyond ourselves. American culture's emphasis on individualism, personal fulfillment, and competitiveness makes this a hard lesson for us to grasp.

Three of my grandsons spent several months in Togo, a small country on the west coast of Africa. Almost immediately, the neighborhood boys invited them to play soccer, or "football" as it is commonly known through most of the world beyond the United States. My grandsons noted two aspects of play that differed from their previous experience: The Togoan boys set up smaller goalposts than did boys in the United States, and they exhibited more interest in passing the ball around until someone had a good shot than in rushing down the field to kick a goal.

Phil Jackson, sometimes called the "zen master" of professional basketball, has won record-setting championships with the Chicago Bulls and Los Angeles Laker teams by emphasizing passing, team play, and increasing the number of assists rather than individual points and star performances.

First Peter says that our baptism becomes our invitation to community and fellowship, to become a part of something larger than our individual interests and accomplishments. We are invited to a great mystery—to be part of the living Christ in whom God lives, to become a holy priesthood, to become part of a mystery greater than ourselves!

SUGGESTION FOR MEDITATION: What attitudes, hopes, or fears keep you from giving yourself to the mystery of being a living stone? What steps would make you more available?

PRAYER: God, make me a living stone in Christ, the spiritual house; make me part of your royal priesthood. Amen.

FRIDAY, APRIL 22 • Read John 14:1-6

"I am the way, and the truth, and the life."

People often read this familiar passage for comfort and solace at at the time of a death: "Do not let your hearts be troubled....In my Father's house there are many dwelling places....I go to prepare a place for you." We sometimes refer to this passage as "spirituality of consolation."

Thomas the questioner, always wanting to know more, asks, "How can we know the way?" Jesus responds, "I am the way, and the truth, and the life. No one comes to the Father except through me." Some people interpret these words as a "spirituality of exclusivity," insisting that salvation comes only through Christ and emphasizing the way, the truth, and the life.

Since Jesus directs his words in response to Thomas's question, it seems more likely that they reflect a "spirituality of awareness." Jesus says that if we want to understand what this life's journey is about to look to him. He is the way of God, what God intends us to be. He is the truth of God, how God is. He is the life God wants for each of us: a life of close relationship, healthy and life-giving intimacy, goodwill, and good deeds.

SUGGESTION FOR MEDITATION: What way of Jesus do I need to travel on this journey? What truth of Jesus do I need to take with me on my journey? What aspects of Jesus' life would make my life with God fuller and richer?

PRAYER: Eternal God, in whom we live and move and have our being, you always give us what we need and more. Give me the grace to welcome the way, the truth, and the life of Jesus into this life you have given me to live for you. Amen.

"Whoever has seen me has seen the Father."

Historically, in creeds and confessions, the church has used philosophical language to explain how the Father can be seen in the Son: "being of one substance with the Father" or "having the same being with the Father. . . ."

At this point the analogy of osmosis may help: "the tendency of fluids to pass through a membrane and so equalize concentration on both sides." It is a matter of relationship and the influence of close relationship. At the beginning of his Gospel account, the Gospel writer states: "No one has ever seen God. It is God the only Son, who is close to the Father's heart, who has made him known." Close to the Father's heart. That is the mystery of relationship—and influence.

When my son Joel was about twelve years old, someone observed that he walks the way I do. When my friend mentioned that characteristic, I felt I partially knew the truth of that fact. Shortly thereafter, on a sunny day, as I approached the large glass entryway of St. Luke Hospital, I saw the familiar walk of my father reflected to me: his gait, a little shuffle; his posture, a little slouched. Of course I was seeing myself, but it looked like my father. Now I see the same walk in my grandsons! How can we explain such matters?

Osmosis. Being close to the Father's heart is part of the preparation for inspired living. The influence of relationship, sometimes intentional copying but more often subtle, unconscious, and unintentional—but real just the same.

SUGGESTION FOR MEDITATION: **What of God do I see in me? What of God do others see in me? How can I live closer to the Father's heart?**

PRAYER: **Compassionate and loving God, help us live close to your loving heart, which we know in Jesus Christ, that you may be seen in us and experienced through what we say and do, both in our lives and in the lives of others. Amen.**

"Very truly, I tell you, the one who believes in me will also do the works that I do and, in fact, will do greater works than these."

Are you prepared for this? Do you hear what Jesus says? First, the mystical: "I am in the Father, and you in me, and me in you!" (Other texts also speak of this interrelationship, for example, John 14:10-11; 15:4). We usually think of God, Christ, you, and me as separate, individual entities. But no! Christ in God. You and me in Christ. Christ in you and me.

The second item that catches my attention is the part where Jesus states that those who believe in him "will do greater works." Because of our interrelationships with God in Christ and Christ in us, we will do what he has done and more. Inspiration favors the well-prepared mind!

Florence, a wife, mother, nurse, teacher, friend, grandmother, and great-grandmother is an interesting person in her own right and especially a saint of God. She knew God's grace, justice, and compassion in Jesus Christ; she respected creation and things of the earth. She was hospitable, committed to peace, and had a deep sense of God's presence.

For years before her death, Florence worried that her life had not amounted to much. But four generations of her family now spreads from coast to coast in the United States, interracial and serving people through teaching, medicine, music, nutrition, social work, immigrant law, nursing, military, ministry, housing— and in a spirit that is Florence in them and Christ in her! Florence's life in Christ continues to produce "greater works."

SUGGESTION FOR REFLECTION: What keeps me from knowing Christ is in God, Christ is in me, and I am in Christ? What greater works is God inviting me to?

PRAYER: O God of great and little things, do your work through me that I may be a partner with you in creation and re-creation, through Jesus Christ. Amen.

Definitions of Difficult

April 25–May 1, 2005 • *Jennifer E. Copeland*[‡]

MONDAY, APRIL 25 • **Read 1 Peter 3:13-18a**

Better to suffer for doing something good than to suffer for doing something evil. Better not to suffer, I'd say, but that does not seem to be an option. Indeed, suffering is not an option and to admit this is not resignation to fatalism, for suffering is part of created existence. The more literal among us fancy the story of Satan's presence in the garden of Eden working his wily ways on Adam and Eve. The theological pundits look to the original sin explanation that humanity is predisposed toward sin and only capable of good when aided by God's grace. The fact remains that the world is not perfect. Now, what will we do about it?

Actually—nothing. Christians believe that God will finally consummate a new way of being in God's world, the way described by and embodied by Jesus. God is working God's way of goodness in the world; our role is to live hopefully into that future, trusting in the future in spite of the present.

Hope based on God must necessarily find expression through particular historical activities even though the hope itself cannot derive from these activities. Our confidence in God's hope-filled future reveals itself in tangible acts of faith carried out in the concrete world of living and dying. Hope does not resolve evil or conquer death. Hope changes our perspective so that suffering is no longer an irreducible entity wreaking havoc in our lives. Rather, like all of history, suffering is subject to God's hope-filled future, a future full of grace and beauty.

SUGGESTION FOR MEDITATION: Do all the good you can, by all the means you can, in all the ways you can, in all the places you can, at all the times you can, to all the people you can, as long as ever you can. (paraphrased from John Wesley)

[‡]United Methodist campus minister, Duke University, Durham, North Carolina; member of the South Carolina Annual Conference.

TUESDAY, APRIL 26 • Read Psalm 66:8-20

Come and hear, all you who fear God, and I will tell what he has done for me.

As a psalm of thanksgiving these verses present an interesting perspective. They come from a place of survival rather than celebration, from a time of trial rather than triumph. The psalm recounts some difficult times in Israel's history and also lays claim to some desperate personal situations. Obviously, the days of difficulty and desperation are past, perhaps reason enough to celebrate, but the memory of them haunts the writer with a type of post-traumatic presence. Many of us fail to thank God when life goes smoothly; imagine pausing to give thanks in the midst of tribulation. Yet this writer remembers to do both. When in trouble he promised God his praise, and now he has come to deliver.

Remembering difficult circumstances can serve to heighten our sense of thanksgiving. The psalmist knows that he has much to be thankful for on this day even if getting here has been a rough road. Witness his extravagant liturgical exhibition of burnt offerings from several categories, all as a reminder to himself that God is good. His faith in God's goodness has brought him to this place, and his witness offers sustenance to those still treading the difficult way. What begins as a rehearsal of God's mighty acts in the exodus of Israel soon becomes internalized by the one who has experienced firsthand the saving grace of God.

The great deeds of God throughout history are magnificent to recall. Greater still is the reassurance of God's presence in our own lives, the knowledge that "God has not rejected my prayer or removed his steadfast love from me." Thanks be to God for the chance to sing that song.

PRAYER: God of love, we thank you for all with which you have blessed us even to this day. Amen. (*United Methodist Book of Worship*, Service of Death and Resurrection, Prayer of Thanksgiving)

Yet you have brought us out to a spacious place.

Our society is built on a system of setting goals and achieving them. Businesses set up strategic plans and then allocate resources on the basis of effectiveness; churches devise long-range plans and then establish committees to report on their accomplishments; individuals lay out a course for career, family, and retirement and watch their portfolios to mark milestones. Life is tied up in a tidy little package replete with maps and checkpoints from which we set about the task of controlling events around us so that they will fit into the box. Some of my greatest disappointments in life have come when I didn't get the next treasure for my chest.

Interestingly enough, though, when things haven't gone my way, the way they have gone becomes my way. Always I expected a way out, a way through, or a way around; and always the way appeared, though seldom, if ever, in the form I anticipated or even desired. With credit to Quaker wisdom, I can attest that "way will open." Hindsight illuminates that it is a way that would not have been possible had I been designing the course.

This doesn't mean we live as programmed automatons plodding along a preestablished course. The great tension of free will comes in acknowledging how our own choices weave within the design of our lives. Goals help up to a point, but really the journey is the greatest testimony of our faith. When our self-designed goals conflict with the journey, we still continue the journey, trusting in God not only to meet us at the end but also to greet us at crucial stops along the way.

PRAYER: Lord, make me what you will. I put myself fully into your hands: put me to doing, put me to suffering, let me be employed for you, or laid aside for you, let me be full, let me be empty, let me have all things, let me have nothing. I freely and with a willing heart give it all to your pleasure and disposal. Amen. (John Wesley's Covenant Service)

What are you looking for? That is the question posed to Mary Magdalene when she showed up to anoint the body of Jesus for burial and found the tomb empty. "I am looking for Jesus," she replies, speaking, unbeknownst to her, to Jesus himself. Sometimes knowing what we are looking for doesn't help us find it. A few days before the encounter with Mary, Jesus had told his disciples before he left them in the upper room that they would find what they were looking for. They had only to follow one simple guideline: to love him and keep his commandments. Heeding this counsel sets off a chain reaction that culminates in our finding what we are looking for. Loving and keeping Christ's commandments implies love for Christ; love for Christ results in being loved by God; being loved by God ensures the presence of the Holy Spirit through which Christ is revealed. The revelation, however, isn't always what we expect. Just ask Mary.

What were you expecting? Another newborn? A teacher, healer, miracle worker? The Incarnation? No one expected any of that the first time around, but that's what we got. Jesus is quite clear about the coming reality—I am leaving, he says, but you will not be alone.

What should we expect this time? Maybe this: a group of college students who spend one night each week preparing and serving the evening meal at the local soup kitchen. After only a few weeks, folks actually start to remember names and stories. Imagine the biomedical engineering major getting a high-five from the bipolar, legally blind, recovering alcoholic washing dishes beside her. He knows she had an important test this week; he cares that she passed. She knows he's been on the wagon for three months; she cares that he made it another week. When we love the commandments, we will find the revelation of Christ we're looking for. Good luck recognizing it.

PRAYER: By your spirit make us one with Christ, one with each other, and one in ministry to all the world. Amen. (*United Methodist Book of Worship,* "The Great Thanksgiving")

When Jesus told the disciples they would find what they needed by looking to him, he spoke to an intimate, well-known group of supporters. Paul, however, faces a tougher crowd—a crowd of Athenians steeped in scholarship, philosophy, and polytheism. Where the disciples always seemed to need a bit more information, these Athenians suffer from information overload.

Paul considers them "extremely religious . . . in every way," offering the requisite compliment that always helps to get someone's attention when we have something we want them to hear. No doubt, the folks at the front of the crowd stood just a little straighter, and the folks at the back nodded their heads in approval: "Yes, we are extremely religious, aren't we?" As are we: we can recite The Apostles' Creed without thinking about it or rattle off the page number of our favorite hymn. As Paul carefully illustrates to the Athenians, however, knowledge is not enough if we don't know the right things. What good is the page number of a favorite hymn if we never attend worship to sing it? Even knowing The Apostles' Creed loses its usefulness if the words tumble without thought or meaning from our lips.

In this instant-gratification, techno-driven, information-saturated world in which we live, perhaps it's time to take stock of exactly what we need to know. Paul offers some precise information: God made the world and everything in it, so even our very lives are a gift from this creator God. God is Lord over the heavens and the earth, so our every action is accepted by this redeemer God. God stands at the end of all our journeys, so we live and move and have our being in this sustainer God.

PRAYER: Almighty God, because you made us for yourself, our hearts are restless until they find rest in you. Amen. (Saint Augustine, *Confessions*, Book 1, Chapter 1)

"If you love me, you will keep my commandments."

A command implies something we do, as opposed to a feeling that ebbs and flows according to its own whims. Though we often confuse love with a feeling, feelings are not commanded. Love, Jesus tells us, can be commanded; and Jesus commands us to do it.

I always take the opportunity to remind the couples I meet with to plan their weddings that on the day of their wedding they must answer the question, "*Will* you love this person?" Contrary to Hollywood, I won't ask them, "Do you love this person?" Of course they do or things wouldn't have gotten this far! But marriage is not about the past or even about specific emotions at a particular moment; it's about the command to love. *Will* you love this person acknowledges that love is an act of the will. An astonishing one hundred percent respond on the day of their weddings, "I will love this person." Too bad nearly fifty percent of them forget those vows during the ensuing years before death does them part.

The myths of our society feed the insatiable quest for personal happiness at the expense of our commitments. If it feels better to love a different person, we go with the feeling and forsake the command. Jesus would have us live a different way—a way that acknowledges ardor can wane but love must not, passion may diminish but love must not, health will deteriorate but love must not. Love is an act, not a sensation, though appropriately channeled love can create some extraordinary sensations. The sensation follows the act, however, and it is the act that defines our faithfulness to the call of Christ. The command to love looms large throughout the Gospels, but we carry it out in the everyday activity of living faithfully.

PRAYER: Send therefore your blessings upon us, gracious Lord, that we may surely grow in love and godliness together. Amen.
(*United Methodist Book of Worship*, Service of Christian Marriage)

We can't read these verses without considering baptism. The water analogy to Noah is enough to conjure up visions of total immersion, and First Peter's overt reference to baptism elicits scenes of squirming infants clad in white-laced gowns. The context, however, reminds us that baptism is not a quaint, private affair. Baptism is initiation into the way of Christ, a way that could include the suffering described in the preceding verses of this letter. Clearly, we don't suffer because we are Christians in the way that we train because we are athletes or practice because we are musicians. Christians will, however, face adversity because their way of being in the world often runs contrary to the flow of the world's current. Oftentimes this adversity achieves the status of suffering. The baptized don't opt out of suffering any more than Jesus opted out while sweating drops of blood in the Garden of Gethsemane.

Baptism doesn't call us to a life of pain; it calls us to a life of commitment. Baptism doesn't call us to a life of suffering; it calls us to a life of self-giving. Baptism doesn't call us to a life of individuality; it calls us to a life of community. Funny how commitment, self-giving, and community can be such burdens in our life when we're still held hostage to the myth of personal satisfaction. When we're able to relinquish this fantasy of individuality, however, concepts like commitment and self-giving and community take on connotations of joy and thanksgiving.

Of course, there's no end in sight. The baptized life is never complete; it proceeds daily towards perfection in love, "an appeal to God for a good conscience." It is the only life worth living.

PRAYER: Initiate us into Christ's holy Church, incorporate us into God's mighty acts of salvation, and give us new birth through water and the Spirit. Amen. (*United Methodist Book of Worship*, Baptismal Covenant)

Why Are You Standing There?

May 2–8, 2005 • Robert King[‡]

MONDAY, MAY 2 • Read Acts 1:6-14

Imagine what it must have been like for the apostles during the forty days after Jesus' resurrection. It boggles the mind to try to understand what they saw, heard, and might have felt. Now, to top off everything, Jesus ascends before their very eyes! Adding to the shock, two men suddenly appear and ask them why they are standing there! What possibly could happen next!

What an incredible experience to have known Jesus in his physical form, to have felt his tangible presence and love, and to have personally witnessed his miracles. But, while we may think that it would have been easier to believe had we seen Jesus, the accounts in the New Testament seem to show otherwise.

The disciples didn't have the two-thousand-year history of the church, sometimes good and sometimes bad, that we have to rely upon. So many evidences of God's love and transforming power have occurred between their time and ours. Under the circumstances, Jesus' ascension must have left them feeling abandoned. The small community of believers, destined to be Jesus' witnesses to the ends of the earth, responded to their fear and confusion by withdrawing to a secluded room. There, the scripture tells us, they devoted themselves to constant prayer. Persecuted, uncertain, faithful, the disciples turned to prayer for strength as they awaited empowerment by the Holy Spirit.

We may wonder at their inability to comprehend what was happening, yet we can't help but be amazed at what they were able to accomplish when empowered by the Holy Spirit.

PRAYER: Come, Holy Spirit, and fill the hearts of your faithful. Kindle in us the fire of your love, and help us to spread that word to a hurting world. We are your hands. Amen.

---

‡Layperson and member, First United Methodist Church, Larned, Kansas; active in Emmaus and Kairos movements.

As I write this, there are the usual problems and conflicts throughout the world. Humans continue to argue, fight, and kill one another. Hunger continues to occur too often. Divorces still happen. Crime is still rampant. Addictions abound.

Yet this psalm promises help to those who need it. It promises that God knows who the fatherless are and protects them, that he will defend the widows (and presumably the widowers), that he leads the prisoners to prosperity. Finally, it promises homes for the desolate and punishment for the rebellious, which bears witness to the work of God. So why aren't things getting better? After all, God has promised all this will happen.

There is an old story about a statue of Christ found in Germany after World War II with the hands blown off. The sign underneath reads, "Christ has no hands but ours."

Maybe the reason things aren't getting better is because God is waiting for us to be the hands that bring about the solution to our social problems. We are called to be Christ's witnesses. It is our responsibility to reconcile with our enemies, to feed the hungry where and when we can, to make our marriages work, to look at our own addictions, to care for orphans, to comfort the bereaved, and to remember the prisoners.

Just as the psalmist witnessed to God's action through the ages in today's reading, we too can be joyful witnesses in the present.

PRAYER: Christ, I acknowledge that you are counting on me, and I am counting on you. Help me to be reconciled to my enemies, to do what I can to help feed and clothe the needy, to care for the orphans and comfort the bereaved, to visit those in jails and prisons, to be your hands in this hurting world. Amen.

Jesus is glorified by his disciples? How could he possibly make such a triumphant claim about his disciples when he surely knows what is coming! Judas will betray him; Peter will deny him. He will be unfairly tried, beaten, mocked, and crucified. This is glory?

Obviously, the glory of Jesus differs from our concept of glory. Like the disciples, we in this modern age don't glorify sacrifice and service in the way Jesus taught us. Yet that is exactly what most of the Bible is about. Throughout the Old and New Testaments, we are called to humble ourselves and serve God.

The glory Jesus talks about transcends his immediate situation, and, on faith, we can believe it transcends our immediate situation now. Jesus has promised that those who follow his commandments will be glorified before God the Father. Sounds so simple, doesn't it? Humble ourselves and serve the Lord with gladness. Great stuff! Simple yes, but so hard for us humans with our big egos and paralyzing fears to do. Yet the power and protection of God are greater than the biggest ego or worst fear.

"Holy Father, protect them in your name that you have given me, so that they may be one, as we are one." The promise Jesus gives us is the power of the Holy Spirit to help us transcend ourselves when we call on the Spirit to help us. I know that I cannot possibly be the person I ought to be without God's power. But now I know that I can call on the Holy Spirit to help me glorify Jesus and to be his witness in the world.

PRAYER: Christ, I want so badly to share in your glory, but I'm often reluctant to pay the price of servanthood and sacrifice. Come, Holy Spirit, and help me overcome my ego and truly walk with Jesus. Amen.

ASCENSION DAY

Every once in a while we experience a great Aha, when we finally get an important idea and internalize what it means. Witnessing Jesus' ascension may have finally been just such an Aha moment for many of the disciples. Up to this point, the disciples have been unable truly to understand what Jesus is all about. One last time Jesus explains the mission fulfilled in him and the mission ahead—the proclamation of repentance and forgiveness "in his name to all nations." Having promised his disciples the gift of the Holy Spirit, Jesus ascends. And the disciples, who return to their homes with "great joy," are thereafter "continually in the temple blessing God." They finally get it.

But wait! Jesus' charge to spread the gospel of repentance and forgiveness is not only for those present at the time of his ascension. All believers who follow those first disciples are expected to carry on that task. Through the power of the Holy Spirit and the word given us in the scriptures, we are to preach the gospel at all times and wherever necessary. Whether in the local county jail, a prison, a nursing home, a soup kitchen, a hospital, or our place of work, we are to share the good news that begins in our hearts and spreads outward. Let us accept Jesus' charge with "Aha" understanding and joy, continually blessing God as we live the love given us in Jesus.

PRAYER: Lord God, thy kingdom come within my heart. Help me to practice and preach your gospel of repentance and forgiveness with joy. Amen.

FRIDAY, MAY 6 • Read 1 Peter 4:12-14

Kairos is a ministry designed to help prison residents create a Christian community within their environment. Trust me, the prison environment is not a place where Christians are in the majority. The Kairos experience takes place over three days in much the same way as Emmaus or Cursillo weekends. When the Kairos team members complete their time with a group of prisoners, we send them out into the environment of the prison yard to live the Christian life. Sometimes I'm overjoyed at the reports we receive.

After the first Kairos weekend held in the Hutchinson Correctional Facility in Kansas, the participants began meeting at the beginning of their "yard time" to hold hands and pray. Imagine that sight—African American, Caucasian, and Hispanic murderers, rapists, and child molesters getting together in that hostile environment to hold hands and pray—a direct violation of the culture and mores of the yard. That's what I call a "fiery ordeal." Yet those prisoners are "blessed, because the spirit of glory" rests on them.

What the early Christians went through to form the church obviously was much worse than what guys face in the yard, since they were literally crucified for witnessing to their belief. Yet prisons are tough places in which to hold unpopular beliefs, and often any Christian group is looked down upon as an organization for "losers."

I wonder what would happen if a group of men in my town got together every day at noon, stood in a circle on the courthouse lawn, held hands, and prayed! How would others in my town view such a practice? Would I be inspired? embarrassed? outraged? Would I "shout for joy when [Christ's] glory is revealed"?

PRAYER: Christ, I want to share in your glory, but I'm often unwilling to face the embarrassment of public witness. When I am "reviled for the name of Christ," help me to remember I am blessed. Amen.

Bringing his glorious song of praise and thanksgiving to a close, the psalmist presents three ideas for our consideration. First we are to sing praises to the "rider in the heavens, whose power is in the skies."

This morning I had a sense of the terrible nature of some of God's creation as I watched television radar warn of a hurricane bearing down on the Caribbean and possibly the Atlantic coast of the United States. Certainly we in the Midwest who face tornadoes in spring also know the awe-inspiring power of God's created order. Sooner or later we all come to understand the psalmist's observation: "Awesome is God in his sanctuary."

Yet the psalmist asks us to consider a second idea, that, in spite of God's awesome power, the God of Israel will bestow power and strength on God's people. Hinting at a promise of the Holy Spirit to come, the psalmist assures us that God will ride out every storm with us, not only comforting us but helping us glorify God in our suffering.

Finally, although the versions in my Parallel Bible vary on other specifics, all the translations of the psalm's ending are identical: "Blessed be God!"

We may acknowledge we don't understand the many-faceted nature of God or the terrifying aspects of God's creation. But like the generations of disciples who have accepted the charge first given by Jesus to his inner circle of disciples, we understand that we are meant to bless God with our every thought and act.

PRAYER: Majestic God, we are inspired by the terrible beauty, complexity, and completeness of your creation. We lift our voices in praise. Blessed art thou, O God of the universe. Amen.

SUNDAY, MAY 8 • Read 1 Peter 5:6-11

The book of First Peter provides hope for communities and persons facing persecution. I often suggest that our Kairos participants (see Friday's meditation) read it for encouragement.

This closing passage, in particular, offers counsel on glorifying God in our suffering: We are urged to humble ourselves, let God take our worries and cares, maintain order in our lives, resist evil, trust the Lord, and remember others who suffer in his name. In due time, we are told, God will "restore, support, strengthen, and establish" us.

While we may know the power of the Holy Spirit to transform us, many of us have learned that such a transformation may be far from a "burning bush" experience. Rather, we have found ourselves only slowly learning to humble ourselves, give up the concerns of our lives, and trust "the God of all grace."

As a recovering alcoholic of many years, I have turned often to the "Big Book" of Alcoholics Anonymous. One great phrase at the end of Part I always catches me: "You will surely meet some of us as you *trudge* the road of Happy Destiny"* (emphasis mine). The last thirty-six years have indeed been for me a matter of *trudging* as I have dealt with my character defects, sins, and growing faith in God. I pray your trudging is taking you farther down the road of Happy Destiny.

If you are trudging down the road of Happy Destiny too, perhaps you are learning as I am, how to answer the question that began our week together: the answer is also our call. When we go to church, treasure our spouse and children, and love our enemies, we glorify God, "who has called [us] to [God's] eternal glory in Christ."

PRAYER: **Loving God, thy kingdom come, thy will be done on earth. Amen.**

---

*Alcoholics Anonymous (New York: Alcoholics Anonymous World Services, Inc., 1955), 164.

The Spirit with Us, among Us, in Us

May 9–15, 2005 • *Ada María Isasi-Díaz*[‡]

MONDAY, MAY 9 • Read Acts 2:1-4

A sound, a mighty wind, tongues as of fire! How wonderfully generous and exuberant of the Spirit to be among us in such a rich way! How considerate of the Spirit to be present in ways we can feel, hear, see, smell! The Spirit delights in our humanness, in our need for apprehending with our senses, in our desire to have what we believe confirmed by signs.

The Spirit continues to be among us in ways that we can touch, see, feel, smell, hear. The Spirit came that first Pentecost in unexpected ways. The same is true today. The Spirit comes to us in the beggar we ignore, in those imprisoned for whom we want nothing but punishment. The Spirit comes in those we love so very much. The Spirit came rushing to strengthen, embolden, sustain, and ensure the confirmation of Jesus' disciples in the commandment of Jesus to love and serve one another.

By the time the Spirit came, the group of disciples had a new member: Matthias. He replaced the despondent Judas who failed to believe that Jesus would forgive even his betrayal. By then the men who had fled at the time of the crucifixion had returned and joined Jesus' mother and Mary Magdalene—the first witness to the Resurrection—and the other women who stood watch at the foot of the cross. The Spirit came to confirm what they were creating: a community of believers.

SUGGESTION FOR MEDITATION: Today as you go about your daily activities, try to envision the Spirit's presence in everyone you meet. Remember the Spirit did not simply come in the past but continues to be present here and now.

[‡]Professor of Christian Ethics and Theology, Drew University, Madison, New Jersey.

The touch of the Spirit changes everything. At that first Pentecost the newly born community of believers was transformed from a cozy group whose members knew one another very well into a broad community of people who came from everywhere. Imagine! Mary the mother of Jesus and John to whom Jesus entrusted her, Peter, and Mary Magdalene—all leaders from the beginning, as well as the other women and men who had known Jesus now have to face a different sort of people. All the Jews who have gathered in Jerusalem, be they from Parthia, Elam, Mesopotamia, Cappadocia, Pontus, Asia, Phrygia, or Egypt, are the first to hear in their native languages the word of God preached by Jesus' followers. It's as though the coming of the Spirit has reversed the story of the tower of Babel (Gen. 11:1–9). The community of those who believe swells to thousands! (Acts 2:41).

The community of Jesus' followers centered on inviting and including, not rejecting and excluding. Would there be any doubt that today that community would welcome those who speak Spanish? Is there any doubt that, filled with the Holy Spirit, we are to open our hearts to African Americans, Native Americans, Asian Americans, Hispanics, and Euro-Americans? We may exclude no one. As followers of Jesus we welcome unruly teenagers, fragile elderly persons, those with mental or physical challenges, those in love with persons of their own sex or the opposite sex. We may exclude no one.

This is what Peter preached: The Spirit has been poured out upon all flesh. Yes, not on some of us only but upon *all* flesh. The Spirit allows us to envision all-inclusive communities and supports us in our commitment to make them a reality in our church and society.

PRAYER: Come, Spirit of God! Set us afire with the gift of tongues, the gift of inclusiveness. Bless us with the gift of effective love. Amen.

Now there are varieties of gifts, but the same Spirit." All gifts are welcome no matter who brings them. Gifts that are for the good of all are manifestations of the Spirit. How do we judge this? If they help us to imitate Jesus' welcoming spirit, the gifts are good. Jesus did not exclude even the Pharisees. They excluded themselves by putting conditions for their participation: others were to be excluded.

We need all the gifts. We need the wisdom of our elderly who want to teach us what they have learned throughout their lives. We need the knowledge of those willing to think differently because they learn from nature and from the struggle to survive. We need the faith of those who know that to believe is to be called to a life of justice. We need the gift of healing divisions that set us one against the other because of our differences. We need the gift of miracles that are ours to perform by working hard to build a society that includes all.

We need the gift of prophecy so we can gather the hopes and expectations of the poor and the oppressed about a world in which they and all others can flourish. We need the gift of distinguishing between spirits to be able to judge what benefits the whole community, not just the rich and powerful. We need the gift of various tongues—the Spanish of the Hispanics, the Creole of the Haitians, the mother-tongue of all who come to our shores so our perspective can become more inclusive. We need the gift of interpreting tongues so those who do not speak our language may contribute their own unique gifts.

SUGGESTION FOR MEDITATION: "For in the one Spirit we were all baptized into one body." What does all being part of one same body require of me?

THURSDAY, MAY 12 • Read John 7:37-39

The Jews are looking for Jesus. Instead of hiding, Jesus is "standing there" and calling out to the crowds without hesitation, "Let anyone who is thirsty come to me, and let the one who believes in me drink." For what do we thirst? For money, prestige, privileges? Do we label such persons as power hungry? What of those who dare to say that they thirst for simplicity? Do we speak of such persons as lacking ambition and drive? Do we label them as losers? Yet, it may be the losers who will approach Jesus to drink from what he offers: faith. Jesus invites us to believe in him, to believe in the one who sent him and who sends each of us, to believe in the goodness of others, to believe in ourselves.

The opening years of the twenty-first century have been devastating: war among nations and terrorism from groups that have no other method of political discourse to call attention to their struggles. Violence is a slap in the face of God, an unequivocal way of saying that some of us are bad.

Yes, evil exists in our world, for sin has marred God's creation. Yes, we are cruel and selfish. However, as Christians, we believe that God continues to be with us and among us. We believe, to quote Anne Frank, that "in spite of everything I still believe that people are really good at heart." That is why Jesus can stand there and invite all to come to him for a drink of fresh water, for comfort, and for encouragement. Once we have drunk from Jesus, we become the source of refreshment for others. Then from us will "flow rivers of living water."

SUGGESTION FOR MEDITATION: I must take Jesus' words seriously. If I drink from Jesus, then others will be able to drink from me. How am I a source of comfort, encouragement, and refreshment for others?

What do these "rivers of living water" flowing from Jesus carry? For what do we thirst more than anything else? Perhaps we thirst for vision, the vision of a world where justice and love have kissed and brought forth peace. We thirst for a future that is more than a repetition of the past; a future that, respecting the ever-creating presence of the Spirit in our world, moves us beyond the limitations established by the few privileged ones in our society. Prophecy is precisely that: proclaiming everywhere the vision of what we need to do to make possible the unfolding of God's reign in our world.

In the Hispanic community we challenge one another to be people of vision by singing this song, which I offer here in free translation:

> Prophesy, my people, prophesy once again.
> May your voice echo the cries of the oppressed.
> Prophesy, Hispanics, prophesy once again,
> announcing a new society to the poor.

I consecrate you as prophet [says Yahweh]. Have no fear, have no doubts. As you walk through history, be faithful to your mission. Announce to the people that God will renew the covenant of justice, and love will flourish once again. Denounce those who oppress so they will be converted, turning their faces once again to God.

May this be your hope and your mission: to construct the reign of God, the society of love. Be a sign of God's covenant, be light from a rising sun, be rivers of living water.

SUGGESTION FOR MEDITATION: To be about vision and prophecy we have to stand with the most fragile and vulnerable, with our most oppressed brothers and sisters. Quenching our thirst from Jesus' living water invites us to this task, demands it of us, and gives us the grace to do it. Do I dare?

SATURDAY, MAY 14 • Read Psalm 104:24-34, 35*b*

This beautiful psalm of praise thankfully acknowledges how marvelous God is. Verses 24-25 praise God for creation. The text is reminiscent of the breath of God sweeping over the waters as the initial act of creation. But creation is not a long-ago event but an ongoing project. By sustaining creation, God continues to create. Verses 27-29 speak about divine feeding of creation, filling creation with good things. This food is given "in due season," not routinely. Our sustenance is God's constant preoccupation, not a task taken care of in a general way or once and for all. God is the loving mother who prepares our breakfast, who walks us to school, who worries about how others treat us, who puts us to bed at night. If God fails to sustain us, we "are dismayed"; we die.

Sustaining creation is not a repetitious act guided by a same-as-always attitude. God's sustained creation is forever new. Verse 30 refers to God's spirit coming to renew the face of the ground. Often we think of renewing as a going back to what was. Yet the word *renew* means to move ahead, taking into consideration what creation is now and learning from what creation has been. God renews by moving this creation ahead toward the fullness of divine reign. In sending the Spirit, God becomes involved with creation in a new way, for creation is always in the process of becoming something new.

SUGGESTION FOR MEDITATION: **In creating us with a high degree of self-consciousness, God marks us as cocreators; God involves us in sustaining creation, in helping to bring creation to its fullness. How do we affirm that involvement?**

PENTECOST

In our busy world Sundays are days to do the laundry and take care of matters we did not get to during the week. If we take time to relax and rest, we do so to feel refreshed for the duties of the coming week, not because we want to reenergize ourselves to praise the Lord in the coming week.

The psalmist invites us to "sing to the LORD as long as [we] live." Not only on Sunday but all the days of our lives we should praise God, marvel at God's goodness, and bless God time and again. Such self-abandon requires a total centeredness. We must understand what lies deep within us in order to release it and turn toward the one we praise.

True praise emerges from our depths. We can concentrate wholly on God when we are completely at peace with ourselves, which is the true spirit of the sabbath. Without an honest sense of ourselves and an appreciation for the importance of rest for our souls, we cannot have that sabbath spirit.

This wonderful God has taught us through Jesus that the way to "sing to the LORD" is in loving one another. With a sabbath spirit—rested, centered, and "pleasing to [God]"—we can concentrate on the hurts and needs of one another, praising and rejoicing in the Lord with every tender touch for as long as we "have being."

SUGGESTION FOR MEDITATION: Imagine God, the nurturing mother, coming home from work and soaking in the bathtub. Later she sits on the porch, a shawl over her shoulders to protect her from the evening air. Rocking gently, she smiles as she watches us loving one another. Her smile broadens as she hears our song to her: the music of the glass of water we offer the thirsty, the prisoner we visit, the old woman we bathe, the baby we nurse, the love we share.

Stewards of God's Graces

May 16–22, 2005 • *Johanna N. Green*[‡]

MONDAY, MAY 16 • **Read Genesis 1:1-26**

In the beginning . . . God created the heavens and the earth." What a profound statement of the essence of the beginning! These words were the favorite of one of my childhood teachers. He enjoyed telling us children that no matter what we heard about anything else, we could be sure of this one truth: God was in the beginning and created the heavens and the earth.

Much has transpired since the recording of the Bible's first words. Science and revolutionary hypotheses have caused some of us to rethink what once we never questioned. Others of us have become so distracted by the busyness of our lives that we take God's creation for granted and overlook the beginning, the how and why of it all.

Yet God's creation and the method by which God brought it into being establish a basis and a manner for our daily living. There was order in God's production of this terrestrial planet, and the end product "was good." The orderliness of creation testifies to God's wisdom.

We live in a much more complicated space than in the beginning. We eagerly move in many directions without rhyme or reason. However, let us not neglect the orderliness and purpose by which we were made and by which we should live. In the words of a gospel song, "Order my steps in your Word, dear Lord; guide me every day. Lead me, guide me, teach me your will. I want to live worthy according to your will." In what ways have I embraced order as a course of action for my activities and endeavors?

PRAYER: We thank you, God, for the grace of your creation and the ordered pattern you have set for our lives. Amen.

Assistant minister, pastoral care, Metropolitan African Methodist Episcopal Church, Washington, D.C.

148

God's order and purpose culminate on the sixth day in the creation of humankind, to whom God assigns "dominion" over "every living thing that moves." To all creatures that breathe, God gives "every green plant for food," but humans alone receive God's blessing and the charge to "be fruitful and multiply, and fill the earth and subdue it."

The grace of God in the creation of humankind is sweeping. God provides our every physical requirement for survival and offers us unearned status as rulers of the earth. But because we have been made "in the image of God," we are expected to be responsible stewards of God's infinite graces. As caregivers of God's creation, we receive specific instructions: we are to nourish our bodies, to multiply, and to fill the earth. Have we listened carefully to that charge? Its implicit responsibilities can prove a difficult task.

We are to fuel our bodies with good food and properly attend to their care. We also nourish our minds with positive learning. When blessed with offspring, we see to their welfare. And as we fill the earth, we tend to those in need of the same life-giving resources and nourishment we seek for ourselves.

Our concern for and care of our environment—the land, the sea, vegetation, animals—is also required by God's grace. We must watch for commercial greed and unreasonable actions by entities that may foster destruction in areas of God's creation. We direct our efforts toward life-giving environmental efforts.

Through attentiveness and openness to the Spirit's guidance, we can learn to be responsible stewards—in partnership with God—of God's creation. If the rhythm and dance of our lives are to the glory of God, perhaps we will hear an echo of God's word in the beginning: "It is very good."

PRAYER: Thank you, God, for the blessing of physical and spiritual nourishment. May I be a steward worthy of your grace. Amen.

WEDNESDAY, MAY 18 • Read Genesis 1:26–2:4a

Once again, God gives us a pattern for living. "Rest," in this context, is a spiritual discipline that could become part of the regimen of our lives. Though individuals may address this discipline differently, rest falls under the category of proper care of our bodies, an essential to living as God would have us live.

In our fast-paced age, events and involvements, as well as our zest for production and outstanding performance, exhaust our physical, mental, and emotional strength. In words penned for a hymn, Charles Tindley aptly described our circumstances: "We are often tossed and driven on the restless sea of time." Yet at the creation God patterned a design for our well-being: proper rest as necessary for productive lives.

In scheduling our lives, we might strive to set aside one day a week for intentional worship, meditation, and rest. Worship and meditation can build and enhance our faith in God. Rest of both body and mind from labor can invigorate and renew us for further work in the vineyard. Remember, we are partners with God in the care of God's creation. We cannot address issues and needs that come before us when drained of physical and mental energy.

As if to emphasize the importance of rest to a healthful pattern of living, God "blessed the seventh day and hallowed it." The day of rest is not simply a day of relaxation but a time set aside to acknowledge and glorify the goodness of God's creation.

PRAYER: Lord, bless me to be a more disciplined person, not only scheduling but taking respites from the demands of my life. Guide me, as a steward of your creation, to seek a balance of work and rest that glorifies your handiwork. Amen.

From the treasure of biblical resources provided for worship, we can follow the direction and sing with the choirmaster, "O Lord, our Sovereign, how majestic is your name in all the earth!" We cannot help but reflect on God's goodness through the gifts of life and community on earth, through the gifts of knowledge and wisdom freely given God's people, and through the gifts of empowerment along with the resources to manage God's creation.

We can sing praises to God as the choirmaster directs, but the requirement goes deeper. With knowledge and wisdom comes responsibility. Our dominion, through God's empowerment, extends our care, builds and replenishes. We tend the sheep *and* the grounds on which they graze, as well as the waters through which the fish swim. Our charge includes significant responsibilities.

Often we have not taken these responsibilities seriously. We see and enjoy those things within our immediate purview. However, we often forget the many poor decisions and actions we take that widely impact other people and the environment.

Nonetheless, God has appointed us stewards, managers of creation. We approach this work with thought, order, and sincerity. Then, alone or with a choir, we can seriously and sincerely sing praises to the Lord, our sovereign God, for God is a good God; God is a great God.

Suggestion for meditation: Think on God's goodness in your life. Ask the question: In what ways do I take my blessings and responsibilities for granted? Can I sing comfortably, "How majestic is your name in all the earth"?

FRIDAY, MAY 20 • Read 2 Corinthians 13:11

Paul, a convert to faith through the call of Jesus, the son of God, grasped the pattern of responsible living. Because he saw his role as one of furthering the faith, he became a courier of the message, meeting with young Christian communities and, when absent, communicating with them by letter. At the close of this second letter to the Corinthian community, Paul urges openness to the Spirit and to the teachings of God through Jesus. Order and care for one another, he instructs, are vital parts of the Christian community's agenda. Attitudes of the community's individual members should promote goodness and peace among them.

We understand some of the Corinthian community's experience: Living in community, particularly when like-minded communities are physically distant from one another, is not always easy. Individuals have different thoughts and perceptions. Understandings of the message may register differently not only among distant communities but also among the individuals within those communities. Often households have differing opinions on issues.

Paul tells us, however, that if we "put things in order," we will have peace. If we travel attentively the path of learning opened to us at the beginning of study and follow its guidelines, we ultimately will embrace, with our companions, the study goal. This does not mean we will not slip. But if we persevere in putting things in order, watching for guidance, and supporting one another—we will rise and stay on the journey together.

Order, love, and concern for one another are always the end goal. Paul promises that if, as stewards of God's graces, we attend to that goal, "the God of love and peace" will be our constant companion.

PRAYER: Lord, help me live a disciplined life as I strive to be an honest steward of your order, love, and peace in the world. Let your light shine through me. Amen.

We are God's stewards and disciples in Christ's flock. We are called to shout the good news of Jesus Christ, not in words only but in the way we live; to share life, love, and faith with others in order to widen the community of believers; and to be life givers, bringing love and peace to all with whom we come in contact.

This understanding of the earliest Christian generations is what Paul continues to share in his travels and through his letters to communities with whom he has established relationships. Recognizing that the wealth of eternity, the power of the kingdom, the precious cargo of human lives, and the very oracles of God found in the scriptures have been entrusted to these young communities of Christian believers, Paul encourages them to "greet one another with a holy kiss."

Paul understands the stewardship of God's graces as a sacred mission. God's stewards are to regard each other with reverential respect. When they are with each other, they stand in the company of saints.

Paul further understands that life in any millennium poses many challenges, but particularly so for Christians. In our own age, accelerated technology and shifting interests compete for our attention. Yet Paul assures us that if we nurture and hold onto our faith, we will receive the gifts of the Trinity: "the grace of the Lord Jesus Christ, the love of God, and the communion of the Holy Spirit."

Paul's instruction to the Christian church at Corinth remains for Christian churches all over the world today. We are to live in harmony and community with one another, to study and practice our faith together, and always to be mindful of the holiness of our charge.

PRAYER: We thank you, God, for ordering life and trusting us with the care of one another. Enable our faith with your love, the grace of Christ, and the communion of your Spirit. Amen.

SUNDAY, MAY 22 • Read Matthew 28:16–20

TRINITY SUNDAY

In Matthew's descriptive closing, Jesus delivers a message to his disciples in a post-Resurrection appearance, reminding them of his authority in heaven and on earth, commissioning them to fulfill their responsibility of discipleship, and assuring them with the promise of his never-ending presence through the Holy Spirit. Our belief and trust in this edict truly are the framework for our faith and our inherited commission.

As stewards of God's graces, we have been given a tremendous responsibility. Realizing our weaknesses, we know well that we must prepare ourselves through study of and reflection on the lessons found in scripture, thus becoming more able to teach others. But of utmost concern must be our desire to pray constantly for openness to the divine presence of the living God. Many of us know through experience that it is an enabling energy. The mere realization that God has promised to be with us to the close of the age is remarkable. The experience of that presence goes beyond description.

Girded with this blessed assurance, we can accept the awesome responsibility of Jesus' commission with confidence and love. Jesus has charged us to widen our community on the grandest of scales—to "make disciples of all nations." With the authority given to him "in heaven and on earth," he has deputized us to baptize "in the name of the Father and of the Son and of the Holy Spirit." And he has challenged us to teach obedience to all his commandments.

Let us embrace our mission as stewards of all God's creation, empowered by "the grace of the Lord Jesus Christ, the love of God, and the communion of the Holy Spirit" (2 Cor. 13:13).

PRAYER: Lord, help me to empty myself so that I can be filled with your holy presence and feel your touch on my life. Guide me as I strive to fulfill my responsibility of discipleship. Amen.

Faith and Obedience

May 23–29, 2005 • Jenny Impey[‡]

MONDAY, MAY 23 • Read Psalm 46

I have on my desk a calendar based on *The Worst-Case Scenario Survival Handbook*. Each morning a fresh page offers useful advice about fending off alligators, jumping from roof to roof, and surviving parachute failure. No alligators live in my area. I limit my flying strictly to large planes, but still I read the advice each day. It brings a smile to my face and, you never know, one day I may just need the advice. It certainly puts my day into perspective!

In today's reading the psalmist paints a worst-case scenario. He invites us to picture the worst possible thing that could happen and reminds us that even in that situation, we can find peace. God is a refuge and our strength, present with us and supporting us. The creation might be in chaos, its very foundations shaken by earthquake, hurricane, or global warming; human beings might do their worst in acts of terror or war, but God's dwelling place will remain secure. However terrible the situation, the waters of chaos can become a life-giving stream that will nourish God's people.

What a thought to take into a Monday. Whether the chaos resides on our desks, in our relationships, or in the world around, God is with us. God, our refuge and strength, is a very present help in trouble. The psalmist encourages us to take time today to be still and to remember who God is.

SUGGESTION FOR MEDITATION: Think of the worst thing that might happen or has happened today. Repeat the words *Be still* slowly until you *are* still. Add the words *and know that I am God* and remember who this God is. Whenever you feel up against it today, stop for a moment and repeat the words.

[‡]Minister, High Street Methodist Church, Maidenhead, England.

TUESDAY, MAY 24 • Read Romans 1:16-17; 3:22b-28

John Wesley struggled to be right with God. He prayed, studied the scriptures, performed good works, and preached the gospel. However, all his efforts seemed to be for nothing. When faced with the possibility of shipwreck on the voyage to Georgia, he found his trust in God severely lacking in contrast to the Moravians, who showed no fear. The storms of life help us discover what lies at the core of our being.

Today's passages get to the heart of the gospel and set out the theme of Paul's letter. In Christ, God has acted powerfully to save all people without distinction. All can be saved, and all must be saved. All of us, from the greatest to the least, from saintly person to obvious sinner, need restoration to a right relationship with God. We can do nothing to earn or deserve this grace and cannot achieve it ourselves. It comes as a gift of God, to be received in faith.

Wesley continued his struggle until May 24, 1738, when he went very unwillingly to a society meeting in Aldersgate Street. There someone was reading Luther's preface to the Epistle to the Romans, when, "about a quarter before nine, while he was describing the change which God works in the heart through faith in Christ, I felt my heart strangely warmed. I felt I did trust in Christ, Christ alone for salvation: And an assurance was given me, that he had taken away *my* sins, even *mine*, and saved *me* from the law of sin and death."

Wesley's confidence and ours comes when we cease our striving and simply accept the fact that we are accepted. In Jesus, God has reconciled us to God's self.

SUGGESTION FOR MEDITATION: Peter Bohler advised Wesley to "preach faith till you have it; and then because you have it, you will preach faith." In what ways will you live out these words today?

Salvation is by faith and not by works, but real salvation is lived out in faithful obedience. Jesus reserves his harshest words for "insiders," those who consider themselves to be people of faith but who are in danger of becoming hypocrites.

Wesley realized that his good works would not bring about his salvation, but even after his heartwarming experience he never ceased to do them. His continued faithfulness in acts of worship and devotion, in acts of justice and of compassion were the outworking of his salvation.

People in today's reading affirm the basic creeds of the church; they refer to Jesus as Lord. They do their work in the name of Jesus and seem to be effective in their ministry. But therein lies the problem—it is *their* ministry, not God's. They deceive themselves. They say the right words and do the right actions but still place self rather than Christ at the center.

God wills the salvation of the whole world. Therefore, any privatized faith that seeks to create God in human image rather than allowing ourselves to be shaped into God's, is not a faith that leads to salvation. It merely seeks to use God for our purposes, for good or for ill; using God rather than allowing God to use us.

True disciples attempt to discern God's will in every situation and to allow themselves to be shaped in the divine image. Only those who act on what they hear will find life. Jesus aims his words at those who want acceptance without change, forgiveness without repentance. Rather than presuming on divine generosity, we need day by day to reorient our lives Godward.

SUGGESTION FOR MEDITATION: Reflect on the day ahead or the one just past and offer that day to God, praying at each stage, "Your will, not mine, O Lord."

The nearest I've been to a hurricane is on the other end of a telephone. I'd heard reports of a hurricane about to hit Bermuda and so found myself telephoning friends on the island to assure them of my love and prayers. They spoke of their preparations for the storm. In the background I could hear and almost feel the storm raging as the gusts of wind blew around the harbor. I could also hear the laughter of friends enjoying a game, knowing they could do nothing except wait. The next morning I phoned again and could hear the stillness and calm. There the sun was shining and birds singing. The island, however, was devastated with boats thrown halfway up the hill; trees stripped bare and uprooted; buildings and coastline crumbled.

The whole experience seemed surreal. No one could have known beforehand which buildings would be hit. All looked alike from the outside, but some had better foundations and others did not fall in the path of the eye of the storm.

So it is with faith. What holds us firm when the storms come is not our outward faith but our inner foundation. The two men in today's story probably read the same scriptures and went to the same synagogue, but the storm exposed their foundations. We lay our foundations of faith by living the way of Jesus: a way of forgiving, of turning the other cheek, of prayer, of fasting, of giving, of trusting. The life of faith we see in the Sermon on the Mount (Matt. 5–7) is not static but a dynamic conversation with a God who daily invites us to a life of faithfulness and obedience.

SUGGESTION FOR MEDITATION: The crowds were astonished because Jesus taught as one with authority; his words and deeds were one. Reflect on the Sermon on the Mount, and ask yourself, What words must I live out today?

I was driving along High Street the first time I heard it—a silent, insistent voice telling me to visit a particular person. While tempted to continue on my way, I turned the car around and knocked on her door. A shocked relative answered and said, "How did you know? Mum's just died."

Since that time I've learned to act on that silent, insistent voice. Sometimes I come away from a mission fulfilled, having recognized the voice of God and understood God's command and acted on it. Other times I wonder why I was sent and feel a bit of a fool.

Noah, "a righteous man, blameless in his generation," naturally recognized the voice of God and understood that he must act without hesitation on what God had commanded him. Yet in the eyes of the world at the time, he must have looked foolish building his boat and assembling a collection of animals. Perhaps he felt as foolish as he looked. But Noah "walked with God." Quite simply, what God said, Noah did.

What God had declared good in the beginning had been utterly ruined through the corruption of human beings. Then God said, Noah did, and the ruined earth received a new beginning. Because Noah listened to the voice of God and responded in trust and obedience, "every living thing" was preserved to "abound on the earth" and to "be fruitful and multiply."

SUGGESTION FOR MEDITATION: Listen for the silent, insistent voice of the Holy Spirit today. Consider that your response, or lack of it, can be a means of grace or ruin. Allow yourself to be caught up in God's plan of salvation for the world.

SATURDAY, MAY 28 • Read Romans 3:22b-31

For seven years I had the privilege of serving a church whose members came from at least twenty-three different countries. As each of us made assumptions about the "right" way of doing things, tensions often arose. Did we dance our offering up the aisle African style or secretly place it into the collection bag? Was worship to last exactly an hour or would we pay less attention to time? Should we use the worship book or be more spontaneous? Rarely was everyone happy as we struggled to be a sign of God's reign in the midst of a sometimes-divided community. However, at the major festivals of the Incarnation and Resurrection, worship seemed to take off as we valued each and every tradition and blended different styles into one glorious whole. Barriers came down as we focused not on ourselves but on Jesus. Such times offered no room for boasting, no room for cultural pride. Our divisions paled into insignificance when faced with the overwhelming grace of God.

"There is no distinction...." We are one human race. The same fate awaits all, and the same means of salvation is offered to all. We share both in plight and solution. Why do we find this understanding so hard to accept? Paul clearly states that faith excludes boasting. Salvation does not result from our being chosen above others or from our good works—but from our self-emptying to be filled with God's grace. That grace both justifies and redeems. To be saved is to be caught up in God's plan and purpose to reconcile the whole creation to God's self.

SUGGESTION FOR MEDITATION: Reflect on whether you look down on people or judge them as inferior. Remind yourself that Christ died for them. Ask God to help you see them anew.

In the Hebrew, the beginning to this psalm reads, "God is *for us* a refuge and strength." God, worthy of our trust, has the power to help. God is profoundly for us.

God may be for us, but that doesn't mean that God is always on our side. To the forces of evil and to those who would wage war, the words *be still* are less a gracious invitation than a divine imperative and command: "Stop fighting" (GNT). "Know that I am God." Don't depend on your own strength. Trust in God alone. Look to God to see what makes for peace and security, for God rules all nations and judges both nations and people. God constantly works to bring an end to war and shut down the weapons of destruction.

Sometimes the way we act and speak gives the impression that our security, be it national or personal, depends on ourselves and our own strength, on our technology or weapons. We attempt to justify the curtailment of others' rights in the name of security. In such times, God says, "Let be then; learn that I am God" (REB). Stop what you are doing, pause a while, and remember that I, not you, rule the world. Look and see what I am doing, and get on board.

The God in whom we trust will protect and provide for us but will not shape the divine self in our image. As we shape our lives around the Holy, God becomes our refuge and strength.

SUGGESTION FOR MEDITATION: Reflect on the areas of conflict in your life. Where do you need to hear the words *stop fighting*? How might God become your refuge and strength in these situations?

Amazing Promises

May 30–June 5, 2005 • Paula J. Gravelle[‡]

MONDAY, MAY 30 • Read Genesis 12:1-3

Water dripped down the forehead of five-year-old Taylor on the day of his baptism. The sign of the cross was made. Just as a final prayer was to be offered, Taylor tugged on my hand and said, "I can't feel it. Can I have more water?"

How often that is our cry, "Please may I have more—more faith, more hope, more strength, more forgiveness, more . . . because I don't feel it right now." It is as though the water of God's promise in our lives has dried up. We are parched and wonder if we will ever be refreshed.

Perhaps Abram feels dried up when God's call invites him to journey to a new place. Abram hears the promise of his being a blessing to others. He may not understand it, but at that moment he trusts that God's word of blessing will not dry up. Abram receives the promise and the blessing and begins a life-changing journey. It wasn't easy, but even during the dry spells Abram persevered and held on to the promise.

It the midst of our dry spells we can remember God's promise to Abram and its fulfillment; we can recall God's promise to the prophet: "My word . . . shall not return to me empty, but it shall accomplish that which I purpose, and succeed in the thing for which I sent it" (Isa. 55:11). We can cling to God's promise made flesh in Jesus the Christ and rejoice that the promise of baptism is new each day. The water drips down our foreheads; we don't need more, because the promises of God that sustain us are more than enough.

PRAYER: God, open me to the reality of your promise and presence in my life. When my spirit feels dried up, pour your life-giving water over me so that I delight in your blessings. Amen.

[‡]Director of Pastoral Care, Ellis Hospital, Schenectady, New York; ordained Lutheran minister.

God said to Abram, "To your offspring I will give this land." What an incredible claim! Abram is an old man. His wife Sarai is well past childbearing years. Yet here is God making promises about children that are no longer hoped for but have instead become a painful reminder in the hearts of both Abram and Sarai of dreams unfulfilled. Rather than railing at God for a promise that seems impossible, Abram builds an altar in the place where these words of hope are shared so that God can be worshiped there. Abram trusts God even when he cannot comprehend God's promises to him.

That particular promise became reality in the lives of Abram and Sarai with the birth of Isaac. According to the chronology of Genesis, Isaac was born approximately twenty-five years after the promise was given. That is a long time to wait. Despite times of questioning, doubt, and anger as Abram and Sarai journeyed to a new land, they trusted the surety of God's word.

The fulfillment of God's promises did not cease with the birth of Isaac. God's promises reached into the hearts of the prophets who spoke boldly of Yahweh's commitment to the people. Mary opened herself to the seeming impossibility of God's promise, and Joseph chose to continue his journey with Mary. And when God's promise was born into the world, countless people through the ages not only believed the promise but lived it. Even in the midst of heartache, failure, grief, and betrayal, the promise of God's mercy, justice, and salvation made visible in Jesus has given and continues to give sustenance for the journey.

PRAYER: Help me to believe, gracious God, that your promise to me is as real as your promise to Abram and Sarai. Clinging to your promise, may I fully live my life's journey as your beloved child. Amen.

The writer of Psalm 33 celebrates the magnitude of God's word. Loud shouts of joy, along with the music of lute, harp, and strings, blend together into a melody of praise. The psalmist rejoices that through God's word creation came to be. He offers praise because God's intent for creation is righteousness and justice.

In our time, words of hate, cries of violence, and shouts of division too often drown out the melody of praise for righteousness and justice. Discordant sounds pound in our ears and blare more loudly in our hearts as we question God's care of creation. How do we praise when injustice seems to reign supreme, when righteousness is a distant vision, when divisiveness is predominant, and when God's own children turn away from hope? How do we sing a new song when burdened by the weight of unfulfilled promises and broken dreams?

The *Comadres* in El Salvador, women whose men have been "disappeared" by the government, live in an unsettled darkness as they search for the men and boys they love. In the midst of that darkness, they praise God daily for God's presence, guidance, and gift of hope in their lives. They praise—not because all is well in their world—but because God's word is sure, God's *hesed* (steadfast love) fills the earth; God's promise is at work even if not yet realized. The melody of their praise gives rise to a spirit of trust that strengthens these women in their mission. They know the earth is full of the steadfast love of the Lord, and so they sing.

PRAYER: God of all creation, may songs of praise fill my heart and spill from my lips so that the discordant sounds of my life become melodies of rejoicing in your steadfast love. Amen.

There is little doubt that the apostle Paul followed the letter of the law. He believed that adherence to the law brought people into a right relationship with God. The law left no room for nuance—it was to be obeyed, no further discussion needed.

By the time Paul writes his letter to the Romans, however, he has opened himself to the promise of God in Jesus the Christ. Paul has two acknowledgments: First, if following the law circumvented relationship with Jesus, then the law was to be discarded. Second, God welcomed people into divine embrace because of God's gift of faith, not because they followed the letter of the law.

Paul's story of conversion from entrenchment in the law to living by faith bears witness to our struggle to be faithful in a world that often views rules as unbendable, law as ultimate authority, and change as suspect. Living as people of faith, we focus on our relationship with Christ despite the situation in which we find ourselves; that relationship gives us worth. When we live by faith we know that mistakes can be forgiven and brokenness can be healed. When we live by faith we know that rules and laws are necessary for living together in community, but nothing surpasses the importance of God's promise to us and presence with us.

Following Jesus' example, Paul wants the Romans to understand that their relationship to God takes priority over strict adherence to the law. We can apply the message of Romans to our own lives—we follow the law not to find a right relationship with God but as a way of living out the fact that God has already called us into that relationship. The gift has been given.

PRAYER: God of all mercy, thank you for the gift of faith. Guide me so that living out of that faith I bear witness to your love each day. Amen.

Paul lifted up Abraham's faith as an example to the Romans, pointing out that Abraham believed that God was able to do what God had promised. They needed an example that God's word was sure; that God could bring wholeness out of chaos; and that despite their weakness, clinging to God's promise would strengthen them.

Emma, only fifty-eight years old, resided in a nursing home, her body crippled with the effects of rheumatoid arthritis. Although she could no longer hold a spoon to feed herself or move into a sitting position, Emma rarely complained. Her mind and spirit were alert and bright. She had kind words for any who entered her room and exemplified unwavering faith in God's promise of wholeness.

One Sunday morning a nurse entered Emma's room and found her with tears running down her face. When questioned Emma responded that the tears were tears of joy. She had just listened to a hymn on the radio and felt wrapped in God's embrace. She said to the nurse, "I used to think my life had no worth because this disease destroyed my body. Then one day I realized that I had the opportunity to enter into a ministry of prayer for others in a special way. My body doesn't move, but my heart does. And I trust that one day I will be dancing with God."

Emma, like Abraham, believed that God could do what God had promised. Even though she lived in pain, she chose to cling to what gave her strength—her faith in God. Her life is a witness to each of us when we find ourselves struggling to believe that God's promise is real.

PRAYER: Generous God, may the witness of Abraham and Emma strengthen me in my own faith journey, especially when I find myself doubting your word. May my heart move with gratitude, love, and faithful service in your name. Amen.

The Pharisees believe they are following the right path. They give up much of their freedom to follow the letter of the law, believing that doing so will draw them closer to God. Thus they have difficulty comprehending the actions of Jesus who welcomes tax collectors and sinners at table with him, who speaks publicly to women, and who feeds and heals on the sabbath. His disregard for the law threatens all the Pharisees believe. The freedom with which Jesus and his followers live is incomprehensible to those bound by a myriad of rules and regulations.

The Pharisees had sacrificed so much to get closer to God. Yet Jesus states, "I desire mercy, not sacrifice"—a radical way of thinking to the Pharisees. Being merciful means more than following the letter of the law. It requires a lifestyle change. And how does one measure mercy? At least with the law, either a person obeyed or didn't, which was apparent to everyone.

We may find it easier to sacrifice some of our freedom—to follow a rule—rather than to be merciful to a person in need. Mercy requires that we give, love, accept, suspend judgment, forgive. Mercy means relating with compassion even when our heart feels hardened. It means recognizing that we are all sinners and at the same time are all welcomed at table with the Lord.

Is it a more difficult path to follow than the law? Perhaps. But in giving mercy we receive mercy and meet God in people we might have overlooked. What better way to grow into a full relationship with God?

PRAYER: **Guide of my life, I want to follow you. May I both give and receive mercy as I live each day. Amen.**

SUNDAY, JUNE 5 • Read Matthew 9:18–26

The woman, who has been bleeding for twelve years, desperately desires healing in her life. In all likelihood she has lived as an outcast, considered unclean because of the hemorrhages. She must be tired, lonely, sad—and determined. This woman manages to find her way through the throngs of people surrounding Jesus and get close enough to touch the hem of his garment.

Perhaps she thinks of Jesus as her last hope. Or maybe she trusts so deeply in his promise of healing that nothing will prevent her from getting close to him. Regardless of her motivation, she makes the journey, touches the hem of the healer's cloak, and then hears the remarkable words, "Take heart, daughter; your faith has made you well." She believes those words and is instantly healed, the promise fulfilled.

Oh, to have the kind of faith and trust that bleeding woman had in Jesus' promise for healing and wholeness. Trusting Jesus' promise in the midst of the isolation of illness, the pain of death, the bewilderment of betrayal can require a leap of faith for those of us who have more experience with promises broken than fulfilled. It is all too easy to crawl into ourselves and ignore, or even push away, the healing hand of God that longs to caress us.

The gift of faith has been given. The healing power is present. The promise is fulfilled. Will you trust enough to crawl out of yourself and through the crowd to touch the hem?

PRAYER: Gentle Healer, open me to the healing I need in my life. Help me to trust in the promise of your healing presence and in your word, which is fulfilled as it is spoken. Amen.

Saying Yes to God

June 6–12, 2005 • *Charles O. Butler*[‡]

MONDAY, JUNE 6 • Read Psalm 116:1-2, 12-19

The psalmist exults in the Lord. God indeed has heard his cry for help. Gratefully he declares what he will do: he will call on the Lord's name, pay his vows in the presence of the congregation, and take thanksgiving gifts to the altar.

Why is the psalmist so grateful? Did he win a victory on the battlefield? Did he survive a serious illness? We do not know. We do know the psalmist is overjoyed, praising God for intervention on his behalf. He promises faithful obedience to God.

What moments of profound gratitude do you recall? What praises did you offer to God when you realized how wonderful God had been to you?

I remember a time when my heart leaped for joy. All through my high school years I struggled with the question, "God, what do you want me to do with my life?" No clear answer came. But in July 1946, as an army private stationed at Fort Benning, Georgia, I experienced a growing, inner conviction. I knew that God was calling me to be a missionary overseas. Great joy! I had a purpose for my life. With the psalmist I could sing, "I love the LORD because [God] has heard my voice!"

Take a good look at your life, past and present. Recall the significant moments of decision. Praise God as one present when you were least aware of it. Discover anew how God has worked in the minute details of your daily living. Let each day be a grateful *yes* to God!

PRAYER: God, I thank you for hearing my cries for help. May I not take your love for granted. Help me to live daily in joyful obedience to you. In Jesus' name I pray. Amen.

[‡]Retired United Methodist pastor; formerly pastor-missionary to the Republic of Panama; living in Rochester, Minnesota.

TUESDAY, JUNE 7 • **Read Genesis 18:1-5a**

Can't you see Abraham sweltering in the heat of the day, praying that God might send cool breezes his way! Abraham looks up and is amazed to see three strangers standing nearby. He runs out to greet them and begs them to stay a while. The three men accept Abraham's enthusiastic invitation. Abraham asks Sarah and a servant to bring food to nourish and water to quench thirst and refresh dusty, tired feet.

Abraham does not recognize these three strangers as heavenly beings. He sees persons who must be hungry, thirsty, and exhausted. Abraham's hospitality knows no bounds.

But is Abraham's kind of hospitality advisable for us folks of the twenty-first century? We live in a dangerous world. To open the door to a stranger might invite robbery—or even murder!

But on the other hand, dare we disobey God's word? This passage is not an isolated biblical word concerning hospitality. Matthew 25:31-46 declares that whenever we reach out to someone in need we reach out to Jesus. The writer of Hebrews commands us not to neglect hospitality to strangers; they may be God's angels (13:1-2).

What then must we do? First, we can practice hospitality to strangers in safe surroundings, like welcoming new persons to church. Or we can visit hospital patients or inmates in prison—persons who long for contact with folks on the "outside." Second, we can seek God's guidance. As Christians we have all experienced times when we recognized a deep, inner impulse to reach out to someone in need. Looking back, we knew for a certainty that we had responded to a genuine cry for help and had spoken an obedient *yes* to God.

PRAYER: O God, help me to discern the needs of others. May I respond in love. I pray this in Jesus' name. Amen.

This Genesis passage focuses on our need to respond hospitably to others. This is what Abraham did when he became aware of the three strangers who stood nearby.

As I reflect upon Genesis 18, I examine my past. I discover my sin to be twofold—failure to be hospitable to others and refusal of hospitality extended to me by others. In either case, I say no to God.

In the spring of 1987 I went with an Iowa "Witness for Peace" delegation to Nicaragua. The people of that country were caught up in a contra war, planned and financed by the U.S. government. (Seventy thousand Nicaraguans died in that war.) Our group of twenty went as concerned Christians.

The delegation spent a night and day in a rural community near the Honduras border. Early in the morning we formed small groups and accompanied our Nicaraguan hosts to their work. I joined a group of four men who dug fence postholes in hard terrain. We took turns using a dull shovel.

One of the Nicaraguan men went to his home and returned with a tin plate laden with black beans, rice, and tortillas and offered me some of the food. Since the leader of our Witness for Peace group had cautioned us against accepting locally cooked food, I declined the offer.

Miguel, one of the Nicaraguan men, turned to me and said, "We do not have much to give, but what we have, we offer in love." I could not resist such an invitation. Four pairs of eyes watched me intently as I broke off pieces of tortilla and, using them as spoons, dipped the pieces into the beans and rice and ate.

Then it happened! I experienced an unanticipated Holy Communion moment. Time stood still as divine mercy drew the five of us together in a deep awareness of our common humanity under God. Thanks be to God, my no became a clear, unmistakable yes!

PRAYER: Dear God, help me say a clear, unmistakable yes to you in both receiving and extending hospitality. Amen.

Saying Yes to God 171

Sheep are a fearful lot. Growing up in Alabama, I remember well the time when our sheep were brought down from a wooded, mountain pasture to the barn lot. The night before, stray dogs had attacked the sheep. I was with Dad; our family dog accompanied us. We walked down to look at the sheep. One ewe, focusing her attention on the approaching dog and remembering the attack the night before, keeled over dead of a heart attack!

In the Bible sheep symbolize fearful, defenseless human beings. What in the crowds that day caused Jesus to see the Palestinian folks as "sheep without a shepherd"? Did he see the helplessness of the Jews struggling under Roman military power? Or the plight of the common people as they endeavored to comply with the detailed, religious laws imposed by the Pharisees?

Who might Jesus consider to be the helpless and harassed in today's world? Would he have in mind the thousands of refugees who flee their homelands or inmates in crowded U.S. prisons or anxious parents struggling to survive economically?

And what good news of the kingdom would Jesus declare today? Would he bring peace to troubled minds? Would he direct refugees to a secure and safe abode? Would he offer prison inmates interior freedom as they await release from prison confinement?

We must ask ourselves: How can we become God's yes in the midst of a world where harassed people lack purpose and vision for their lives?

PRAYER: O God, show me how I can best respond to those in need. Grant me an alert mind and a sensitive and compassionate heart. I pray this in Jesus' name. Amen.

Jesus instructs the twelve disciples. He tells them their task: Proclaim the good news to the "lost sheep of the house of Israel." Jesus gives his disciples divine authority to cast out evil spirits and to heal those who are sick.

Jesus provides specific travel instructions for the disciples: "Take no cash with you, no luggage, no extra pair of shoes or change of clothes." Secondary concerns need not distract the disciples. They must focus on the task at hand, that is, proclaiming the good news!

Sometimes we lose sight of the centrality of our mission as we journey through life. We pastors, for example, may be so enthralled with new computer systems and spend so many hours exploring their possibilities that we get sidetracked and lose sight of the primary task at hand: to proclaim the good news of Jesus Christ. Both pastors and laity may spend so much time in planning and organizing for future programming that we leave no time to follow through on our central task.

Today's scripture offers the needed corrective: We must take seriously Jesus' command to focus on the immediate task at hand, a command that establishes priorities in terms of our use of time—whether with the computer or time spent in organizing and planning. These tasks are not to impede or detract from the central task of making God's word about Jesus Christ and his redeeming love clearly heard. Relying constantly on Jesus' ever-present guidance, may we all be so disciplined that secondary concerns do not encroach on that which is primary—obedience to the living God.

PRAYER: God, help us to trust in you and only you. May we allow your Spirit to lead, impelling us into the lives of others. May the seeking of your will be our primary intent. In Jesus' name we pray. Amen.

SATURDAY, JUNE 11 • Read Matthew 10:16-23

In this passage Jesus informs the disciples that the life of a disciple will not be easy. He warns them that they will be handed over to government authorities. "Do not worry about those difficult times," says Jesus. "I will be there with you to tell you what to say!"

In early April 1997, while participating in a protest gathering on the capitol steps in Washington, D. C., I learned about my own nation's training of Latin American soldiers at the School of the Americas (SOA), located at Fort Benning, Georgia. While the school purports to stress human rights awareness in its programs, I learned that many of these soldiers returned home to engage in brutality against their own people. I then resolved to join others in the intent of trespassing onto the military base the following November. We hoped our protest would alert the U.S. Congress to our urgently felt need to close the SOA.

Because I had been arrested twice for trespassing (November 1997 and November 1999), I went on trial with eight others at the federal courthouse in Columbus, Georgia, on March 10, 2000. Each one of us stood before the judge to declare our reason for trespassing. I experienced personally Jesus' promise to his followers centuries before when he said: "When they hand you over, do not worry about how you are to speak or what you are to say; for what you are to say will be given to you at the time; for it is not you who speak, but the Spirit of your Father speaking through you" (Matt. 10:19-20).

When we struggle and speak out on behalf of those who have no voice, we discover the reality of Jesus' promise. Holy-Spirit strength enables us both to witness and to act.

PRAYER: God, help me to trust your word. May my confidence in you erase all fear as I seek to witness to you in times of crisis. Amen.

How do we say a big yes to God? We can do so by placing God at the center of our lives. In these verses Paul states that when we reach out to God in faith, we receive the peace of Christ. When suffering comes our way, it will not throw us off course. As we suffer, we endure, grow in character, and discover a hope that is robust and alive.

As Christians we struggle for a deeper understanding of suffering. Sometimes we blame God, accusing God of placing suffering in our paths. Sometimes we may surprise ourselves by deliberately choosing to suffer.

The nine of us who protested the U.S. military training school located at Fort Benning, Georgia, opted for a special kind of suffering—that of going to prison. Ours was an act of solidarity with suffering brothers and sisters in Central America.

Imprisoned for only three months, I still got to know fellow inmates and connected with them in the name of Jesus Christ. While deprived of freedom, I suffered minimally. Through my action I endured, grew in character, and discovered a genuine hope.

Voluntarily going to prison is not an option for everyone. You may not be able to choose the suffering that comes your way. But if you are open to God and seek God's guidance, your suffering will produce endurance, character, and hope. Your suffering will become an instrument in God's hands. Your life will be a big, affirming yes for God!

PRAYER: Dear God, we thank you for this adventure of faith. May we be hospitable to others, and may our compassion for others grow. May our personal sufferings meet the needs of others and glorify you. This we pray in Jesus' name. Amen.

Discipleship: A Pain-full Process

June 13–19, 2005 • Christina M. B. Carrasco[‡]

MONDAY, JUNE 13 • Read Psalm 86:1-10, 16-17

The best light show I ever saw happened in Timbuktu, Mali, West Africa. After a full day of sweltering heat, the cool of the evening was a welcomed relief. I laid out my blanket on the sand and collapsed onto it, exhausted. Glancing upward, I noticed unexpectedly that the light show was about to begin. God, the director, opened with a shooting star across the sky, which left a green trail for a few seconds before evaporating into the darkness. The stars shone like never before so far from human lights and noise. In the stillness, a wave of calm overtook me as the stars continued their spectacular production. Perhaps Annie Dillard was right. "You do not have to sit outside in the dark. If, however, you want to look at the stars, you will find that darkness is necessary."

Alone in the dark is probably how the psalmist feels when expressing Psalm 86. In the first seven verses, this individual cries out to God in a time of trouble and pleads for help. But the tone changes in verses 8 to 10. The cries of supplication turn into cries of praise, culminating in verse 10, "For you are great and do wondrous things; you alone are God." This is a common theme in psalms of petition: the cries of suffering turn into affirmations of faith. Perhaps part of the growth process of discipleship is that faith is often strengthened through the times of suffering that inevitably occur.

Perhaps the only way to see God's light shows is to lie out in the darkness. Perhaps the only way to verses 8-10 is through verses 1-7. Perhaps the only way to Easter is through the cross. Perhaps only in the darkest of nights do the stars shine brightest.

SUGGESTION FOR MEDITATION: Reflect on a dark time in your life. What stars, what glimpses of God, became visible to you through that experience?

[‡]Associate pastor, Westminster Presbyterian Church, Knoxville, Tennessee.

I put the harness on with some fear and trepidation. OK, a lot of fear and trepidation. I heard the carabiners snap onto it and then attach to the rope. *What have I gotten myself into?* a voice inside me screamed. It was my first time to rappel. I dangled more than one hundred feet in the air over the side of a cliff. The instructor told me to lower myself gently down by loosening my grip and letting the rope slip through the palm of my right hand. I put my feet on the rock and leaned back as instructed, but I could not let go of my grip. My knuckles turned white; my hand began to ache. Though my head told me to trust the teacher, my hand would not let go of that rope. I feared what would happen if I did let go.

Letting go is always a scary proposition, whether it's a rope as you dangle over the side of a cliff or a parent on the verge of slipping into the next world or a child ready to spread her wings as she sets off to college. Letting go is painful and implies a loss of control. For those of us who always strive to be in control, letting go is even more difficult.

Abraham also faces a scary proposition of letting go. Letting go of his first son whom he loves so much and the woman who has brought this son into the world. Letting them go into the wilderness with little sustenance. Where will they go? How will they survive? With unanswered questions, Abraham lets go of the rope and follows God's instructions. It is hard, painful. But it is part of his discipleship process, part of God's greater plan.

SUGGESTION FOR MEDITATION: What or who might God want you to let go of? What keeps you from following God's instructions? In prayer ask God for the courage and faith to let go.

Hagar has given up. She has nothing left, no hope. All is lost: her son, their dreams, their future. With her last ounce of energy, she lifts up her voice and weeps. God hears the voice of Ishmael, cast under the bushes, and sends an angel to Hagar. "What's wrong, Hagar? Why are you troubled?" the angel inquires. "Do not be afraid, for I will make a great nation of your child." Then God opens her eyes, and she sees an abundance of water nearby. From that time on, Hagar and Ishmael remain in the wilderness, living on the resources provided by God through nature.

God didn't open her eyes to see a bustling city nearby where she could get a job, rent an apartment, and find a good daycare center. In fact, God doesn't change her circumstances at all. Hagar and Ishmael continue to live in the wilderness most of their lives, finding some way to survive.

So many times in difficult situations, I pray for the circumstances to change: for that obstinate person to see things my way, for healing of body from illness, for a result I want or for a process to go quickly and smoothly. So few times do I pray for God to open my eyes to the resources that will help me deal with my life circumstances. Seldom does God change circumstances. Instead, God changes us in the midst of our circumstances.

God will not abandon us in our wilderness times. In fact, God is often closer than we can imagine, ready to open our eyes to the people and the resources around us that will carry us through those times of difficulty. God will give us "a future with hope," as Jeremiah reminds us, no matter what wilderness we find ourselves wandering in.

PRAYER: Open our eyes, Lord, that we might recognize your rich resources of sustenance in the midst of the wilderness. Amen.

In my growing-up years, I decided to be a pianist. I took lessons for several years and advanced quickly from the basic material to more complicated music. But as I got older, I developed other interests: sports, school, friends, and church. My dedication to piano waned; practicing became more of a struggle, and I eventually gave it up. I had decided to become a pianist, but only through a lifetime of practice and dedication would that vocation come to fruition.

Perhaps Christian discipleship is similar. Becoming a Christian begins with a decision at baptism or confirmation that then must be developed as a way of life. It will never come to its full fruition without a lifetime of practice and dedication. Paul follows this line of thought with the argument that if we are dead to sin through our baptism, how can we go on living in it? Rather, our baptism initiates us into a newness of life, which then involves us in a continual process of becoming the ones God has created us to be.

Yes, as human beings sin will always be a part of our lives. But we strive to be "worthy of the calling we have received." Hopefully, day by day, we can become a little more Christlike. The decision to follow Christ is just the beginning. How we live out and live into that decision will determine what we will actually be when we grow up.

PRAYER: Though I stumble and fall so many times on the road of discipleship, help me to do my best day by day to follow you. May my external living reflect my internal believing. Amen.

Paul writes, "So you also must consider yourselves dead to sin and alive to God in Christ Jesus." Those words took on new meaning for me when I read *The Dark Night* by Saint John of the Cross. In Book Two, Chapter 10 he describes the process of fire consuming a piece of wood, using it as an analogy for the spiritual life.

First, the fire dispels all the moisture from the wood. Fire purges all contrary qualities that the wood holds. Second, the wood turns dark, sometimes even emitting a bad odor. The work of the fire can reveal the ugliness in the wood and all its bad qualities. Finally, the fire transforms the wood and makes it beautiful. Who hasn't noticed the glowing embers left over after the campfire has died down? The wood now contains the same qualities of the fire; it glows, gives off heat, and even produces sparks. The transformation is complete.

In order for the fire to burn even brighter, the wood has to die. Wood cannot become fire without giving up its qualities. Humans cannot become alive in Christ without dying to sin. We too must be purified and transformed by the fire of the Holy Spirit so that Christ may continually burn within us. We must die to live, yet another paradox on the Christian journey of discipleship.

SUGGESTION FOR REFLECTION: **What needs to die in my life in order for Christ to burn even brighter?**

In the cartoon movie *Monsters, Inc.* monsters of all shapes and sizes receive training in how to scare little kids. Ironically, the monsters themselves are scared of the children. Fear plays a big part in our lives from our earliest childhood memories. Who hasn't been afraid of monsters under the bed or in the closet that sneak out at night? Unfortunately for some, those monsters are real. We fear the monsters of failure or loneliness. We fear not fitting in, physical pain, or the uncertainty of the future. There is much we fear if we are honest with ourselves.

Perhaps that is why the phrase "Do not fear (or do not be afraid)" appears over and over again in the messages of the angels and scripture as a whole, calming and soothing our fears. Even in our short lectionary passage, Jesus reassures his disciples three times to have no fear, at least of the people or things of this world. Rather, we should fear God. The good news is that this God we should fear, this God who created the heavens and the earth, cares for the lowliest of the birds. This almighty and all-powerful God knows us so intimately that even the number of hairs on our heads are counted. This amazing God of love sent God's son to live and die and live again for us.

There are many fearful things in this world, many monsters real and imagined, but as Christians we know of an even greater love in this world that can cast out all fear. When the world's monsters seem out to get you, take heart and take refuge in the God who values you so much more than sparrows, so much more than you can ever hope or imagine.

PRAYER: God of life and love, may I not get so wrapped up in the fears and concerns of this world that I forget how well you know me and how much you love me. Amen.

SUNDAY, JUNE 19 • Read Matthew 10:34-39

The theologian Kermit the Frog once lamented, "It's not easy being green." Well, Kermit, it's not easy being a Christian either. It never has been, never will be; and it was never meant to be. From its inception, Christianity has been countercultural and a danger to society. We preach community not individuality. We believe in generosity instead of getting as much as we can. We talk about forgiveness instead of revenge. We even bring up the notion of loving our enemies as opposed to killing them.

Jesus alludes to bringing not peace but a sword. He states that he has come to divide families, and he insists we must lose our lives and take up our crosses. I don't like this passage much, and I understand it even less. Then again, there is much about God and life in general that I don't fully understand.

Regardless of whether I like it or understand it, Jesus makes it clear that being his follower is costly. He makes it clear that we must love God with our *whole* heart, not just a part of it. This passage sums up this week's emphasis. The cost of discipleship is a pain-filled process and may even cause us to choose God over our families or our own desires. Discipleship asks us to trust the process, take up our crosses, and live our lives in the way of Christ. Christian discipleship is not always logical. We may not always understand in the midst of difficulties or see the road ahead or know where we are going. But we are asked to trust in the God who sees the forest, not the trees, and who loves us more intimately than we could ever imagine.

So it all comes down to this: Is Christ more important than everything else in your life? Does the way you live your life give testimony to your answer?

SUGGESTION FOR MEDITATION: **Become still for a moment, and breathe deeply. Reflect on the two questions above. End with prayer, asking God to reveal ways you can become a better disciple.**

Faith Alive

June 20–26, 2005 • *Pavel Prochazka*[‡]

MONDAY, JUNE 20 • Read Romans 6:12-14

Throughout his epistles, the apostle Paul emphasizes that everything required for humankind's reconciliation with God has already been accomplished in Jesus' death and resurrection. Yet we are meant to become a part of the divine process that moves us from reconciliation to sanctification.

According to Paul, God's work, which begins in us with baptism and continues by faith, involves our acceptance of certain imperatives. To follow Christ means to enter a new life under a new lordship. Sin can no longer be allowed to "exercise dominion" over us. This is a profound change in our value system, like being "brought from death to life." Freed from the temporal chains of our old selves, we no longer live "under law." Having died and risen with Christ, we are subject to an eternal measure and live "under grace."

After the Communist takeover in Czechoslovakia, many teachers were forced to choose between their career in education and their Christian faith. Policy in the new regime left no place for Christians in the teaching profession. Though they truly loved their profession, to continue in it meant teaching the spirit of Marxism and atheism. Presenting themselves "as instruments of righteousness," many courageous Czech educators refused to abandon their faith and had to leave their positions.

Although eternal life in Christ is a gift God gives freely, it is a gift to be acted upon. It pits us in a constant struggle with sin. Yet "under grace" we receive the assurance of redemption that will sustain our faith, a faith alive.

PRAYER: God, give me strength to be an instrument of your righteousness. Give me courage to be yours. Amen.

[‡]Associate professor, Matej Bel University, Banska Bystrica; United Methodist Church superintendent, Slovak Republic.

Christians' efforts receive reward when they gain acceptance in the name of the Lord. This acceptance may show itself in many ways: an open door, a visitation, a heart open to help. The disciples understood that when people accepted them, they accepted the gospel message of Jesus as well. If they accepted Jesus, they were reconciled with God. In this way, the disciples received their utmost joy—their faith reward.

The communist government in Czechoslovakia nationalized Methodist Church property in Plzen, including the sanctuary and the pastor's apartment. The former church and parsonage were turned over to the Technical University. For many years church leaders appealed in vain to the authorities for the return of the property. Meanwhile, the pastor had to rent a flat, and the diminished congregation met in the Hussite Church.

In 1986 a young pastor was appointed to Plzen. He began an intensive search for another building to house the church. He received one hundred thousand crowns from church headquarters in Prague—not a large sum. One day the young pastor found a suitable house in a good location. What a surprise when the owner said she was asking one hundred thousand crowns!

But the story didn't end there. At that time the state secretaries for church affairs had to approve all property transactions, and these officials were instructed not to grant permission. However, the official in Plzen, at considerable personal risk, made the property transfer possible and expedited the process. This state secretary for church affairs later accepted the Lord.

God found a way to give the church what was necessary, and the young pastor experienced the joy of his faith reward.

PRAYER: Guide me, Jesus, that my work in your name will lead others to union with God. In that will be my faith reward. Amen.

We do not like to think about God putting us to the test during our faith journey, but how would we react in the circumstances facing Abraham? The three-day journey to the land of Moriah must have seemed endless, as thoughts swirled in Abraham's mind: *How had it come to such a trial? Was God truly the God of peace and not of evil?* What a gripping test of faith!

Some parts of eastern Czechia experienced devastating floods in July 1998. Our family property was badly damaged as the waters eroded the house and destroyed all that surrounded it. The damage was twofold—we not only lost property but also a place linked to lovely memories. Afterward, someone asked, "How can you see God in that difficult event?" Oh, we could! The person who posed the question had no idea that our family had left the place just two hours before the flood began. For some inexplicable reason we decided to shorten our holiday and leave earlier than planned. Had we stayed just a little longer, our lives would have been endangered. We believe that God was at work in our actions that day.

Faith in God is dynamic rather than static—that is, God works with us. Complacent, self-centered persons completely miss God's dynamic work in their lives and thereby lose the meaning of being created in God's image. Like Abraham, it is imperative that we hold a dynamic faith, a faith strong against all odds, lest we stagnate or fossilize.

Today's scripture gives a vivid picture of what dynamic faith means. God asks Abraham to sacrifice the beloved Isaac, the clear evidence of God's favor, the ground of innumerable future generations. Abraham is to give up the son for whom he had longed for twenty-five years, the one in whom God's promises would begin to be fulfilled. Abraham is asked to surrender Isaac, the symbol of blessing for the nations. The future hinges on Abraham's faith dynamic—his unflagging obedience to God.

PRAYER: Lord, for real hope in you against all odds, I pray. Amen.

Human freedom is one of society's most discussed and controversial issues, a subject of debate for both the general public and professional anthropologists. Faith freedom is God's intent for each human being, a gift to be accepted and enjoyed. Acting on that freedom, however, is not always an easy or simple matter.

From time to time, clergy working under the communist regime in Eastern Europe took part in international conferences held in the "free West." Not one of them ever emigrated during those trips. On the other hand, tourist travel provided the general public a good opportunity to stay in the West. Buses often returned to Eastern Europe with empty seats. Many communists remained abroad as well.

Church workers returned home to communist rule despite the oppression. They returned home even though the communist leaders would have welcomed their staying abroad. The authorities even provided for their escape by allowing wives to accompany the traveling clergy. The church leaders, however, decided to return in accordance with their deep conviction in faith freedom, having "become obedient from the heart to the form of teaching to which [they were] entrusted." Faith freedom led them back to Christ's work, of which they were a vital part.

Faith freedom, according to the apostle Paul, means making decisions on the grounds of God's love and in solidarity with God's people. We receive righteousness of supernatural origin through God's grace. Freedom through grace does not direct us to go wherever our natural heart leads us. Rather, faith freedom moves us to avoid sin and spiritual death. Such freedom points to the possibility of serving righteousness and sanctity, whereby we receive God's gift of everlasting life. Faith freedom requires active participation in our sanctification by living our lives in Christ.

PRAYER: Liberating God, deliver me from the bondage of sin. May your reign be my real happiness. I want to experience your freedom in the power of your Holy Spirit. Amen.

Urgent faith questions that express both anguish and down-heartedness are not far from each believer: How long must I suffer? When will God step in to help me? Why do you keep silence, my God?

I belong to a group of people who have lived much of their lives under communist regime. Communist ideologists disseminated a theory of a dying church. The church would die out with the aging generation, they claimed. In the late sixties, it seemed to us aged believers that the ideologues might be right. Many people left the church: some did not value Christian faith; others gave up active church membership in order to stay in their professions; some loved the life of the world more than the life of the Spirit. Churches remained half-empty, overwhelmed by communism's specious success. Looking at the church rolls, some within the church lamented like the psalmist, "How long, O LORD?"

The fourfold repetition "How long, O LORD?" testifies that the psalmist sought help everywhere—even to the four corners of the earth. Where is the hidden God? When enemies triumph, the suffering one laments: "Eli, Eli, lema sabachthani?" that is, 'My God, my God, why have you forsaken me?'" (Matt. 27:46)

When a multitude of enemies arose against the psalmist, he understood it as their way to thwart God's work. And here a new hope begins: There comes a time when God will intervene, but human impatience does not dictate God's timing.

The faith that laments is not yet a faith lost. What is important is not to be lost in despair. Some instances in life we cannot help ourselves. However, no situation is hopeless for God. Faith lament is therefore legitimate so far as we recognize God's supreme might over our situation and we trust in God's assistance.

PRAYER: Almighty God, be with me and keep me from despair when I see no human help. Amen.

SATURDAY, JUNE 25 • Read Psalm 13:4-6

Following the faith lament, comes joy. The psalmist does not give up under the clear superiority of his enemies. Even in dire circumstances, he is not without hope. He does not succumb to the temptation to look for ultimate help through people. The psalmist knows that God holds the right to the last word.

In 1982 a small group of clergy began to publish a daily devotional guide by Czech and Slovak Methodist pastors. Aware that the communist censors read the texts carefully, we wrote in a manner we assumed would be acceptable to them. It worked. However, at some point, censorship of church publications became the task of a young graduate of philosophy. He was extremely diligent but had no understanding of the Bible. He constantly raised questions and demanded changes. One verse he chose to censor was Romans 3:23: "All have sinned and fall short of the glory of God." The censor did not like the word *all* and wanted us to change it. He argued that we couldn't speak for all people, only Christians. He did not think the verse should include unbelievers for whom the Bible had no meaning. Therefore, the young censor suggested we substitute "all Christians" for the word *all*. Of course, we couldn't alter scripture, and like the psalmist, we trusted in God's steadfast love even when God seemed to be absent, even when our enemies said, "I have prevailed." The joy of our faith was complete when the text finally remained unchanged. The young censor did not remain in his post for long.

The psalmist emphatically states his steadfast hope in God's mercy and remains faithful and pious in spite of circumstances. The original Hebrew text makes it clear that the psalmist trusts in God alone: God causes things to go well. Faith and joy come from fellowship with the One who "first loved us" (1 John 4:19).

PRAYER: Thank you, dear Lord, for the wonderful gift of full joy of faith given to me through your care. Amen.

The angel of the Lord called to Abraham: "Do not lay your hand on the boy." Because of Abraham's absolute trust and obedience —his faith orientation—God saved the beloved Isaac, and Abraham called that place "The Lord will provide."

The communist regime in Czechoslovakia meant hardship for the religious community. How were we to see the fulfillment of promise if current conditions demanded sacrifice? The bloated bureaucracy did not allow churches to expand their staff, resulting in greatly overworked employees. The Methodist Church headquarters in Prague had only one employee to care for all church finance and administration. For years the state denied permission to add even one more employee.

One day, the Ministry of Culture sent an auditor to the church headquarters to carry out an in-depth inspection. All paperwork went through his hands as he reviewed the administration's accuracy and effectiveness. The auditor determined that the present arrangement did not sufficiently support procedures of the headquarters. "What will you do if your only employee gets ill?" he asked. That opened the way in the forthcoming review of the auditor's report with state authorities. The state soon approved a new employee for the church headquarters: God had provided for a better future. Czech and Slovak Methodists have become aware through personal experience "that all things work together for good for those who love God" (Rom. 8:28).

Abraham received the strength to say, "Here I am." He willingly obeyed God's voice. Abraham's respect and reverence before God's way of handling the situation oriented him toward complete obedience. So it must be with us as we mature in our faith orientation: the Lord will provide.

PRAYER: Lord Jesus, lead me away from religious action other than that based on your sacrifice. Amen.

Faithfulness in Prayer

June 27–July 3, 2005 • Jane E. Vennard[‡]

MONDAY, JUNE 27 • Read Genesis 24:34-38, 42-49

Genesis 24 is devoted to the single story of finding a wife for Isaac. Hidden among the named characters is the anonymous servant sent by Abraham to select a suitable woman for his son. This servant, in addition to being obedient to his master, is a man of prayer. The servant prays for help in the midst of his journey. He uses common language, explaining to God exactly what he hopes will happen and trusting that he is being heard. When his prayer is answered he bows his head in gratitude for God's blessing and God's presence in his life and the life of the family he serves.

The servant models the integration of prayer into daily life, and his example challenges us to do the same. Imagine participating in an ongoing conversation with God as you go about your daily tasks. You might ask for guidance as you walk into a meeting or make a phone call. You might breathe a prayer of gratitude when things go well, when beauty breaks into your awareness, or when you witness simple acts of hospitality and kindness.

In this story God answers the servant's prayer before he "had finished speaking in [his] heart." My prayers seldom receive immediate answer. I often hear silence when I've hoped for a reply. But answers are not the point of prayer, for the essence of true prayer is attention to God without expectation. Daily, ongoing conversation is one way we can attend to God in our lives, recognize God's presence in the ordinary, and draw closer to God.

SUGGESTION FOR PRAYER: Talk to God in your heart as you go through your day. Practice praying in conversational language and trust that God hears, even if God does not seem to answer.

---

‡Ordained to a special ministry of teaching and spiritual direction in the United Church of Christ; senior adjunct faculty in prayer and spirituality, Iliff School of Theology; author; living in Denver, Colorado.

I had been single for fifteen years and had made peace with my solitude. Then a man with two small children walked into my life and soon after asked me to marry him. I said "I will," just as Rebekah responded when asked if she would go with the servant to marry the master's son. And as Rebekah's family blessed her as she prepared for her journey into the unknown, so too my family and friends blessed me in my decision to marry. Separated by thousands of years, both Rebekah and I said yes to a gift presented to us. We turned away from our familiar lives toward the unknown and the offered blessing.

Jesus tells us that when we ask, we will receive; when we knock, the door will be opened. But what of those times when we have not asked or knocked, but God offers a blessing anyway? In these situations God is not answering our prayers but giving us an opportunity to which we must prayerfully respond.

I did not answer my invitation as quickly as Rebekah seemed to; I needed time with God to sort out whether this offer of marriage was a blessing or a distraction. As I opened my heart to God's guidance I did not receive explicit instructions, but I did receive the assurance that whatever I decided, God would be with me. So I said yes and, in fear and trembling, turned toward the blessing. In the years since, gratitude has been my prayer—gratitude for the blessing offered and gratitude that God so often knows what we need and want without our ever asking.

SUGGESTION FOR MEDITATION AND PRAYER: **When has God offered you a blessing without your asking? Pray in gratitude for all you have received.**

As you read Psalm 72, a prayer for the guidance and support for the king of Israel, you may feel a tension between the words of the prayer and what you know of the behavior of Israel's leaders. Often they did not rule with justice or judge with righteousness. They did not provide deliverance for the needy when they called and had no pity on the weak and the poor. They looked to their own interests and schemes, ignoring God's longing for justice and peace.

You may feel that same tension as you witness the decisions and activities of today's leaders—world leaders, national leaders, church leaders, leaders of local communities. Experiencing that tension, I can become cynical, despairing, or hopeless—quick to anger and eager to point the finger of blame. But if I step back and remember my times in leadership positions—in my family, in a classroom, on a civic committee, or in the church—I know that I have not always made choices that reflected the love and mercy of God. These reflections make me realize how desperately I need the prayers of others when I serve in any position of leadership. Our leaders, all of them, need our prayers.

Psalm 72:15 says, "May prayer be made for him continually." These few words tell us what we must do. They call us to faithful and unceasing prayer. Rather than attending to the disparity of the words of the psalm and behavior of those who lead, let us attend to God on behalf of our leaders and cry out for them to remember that they are the servants of "the LORD, the God of Israel, who alone does wondrous things."

SUGGESTION FOR PRAYER: As you hear, read, or think about today's leaders, offer a brief prayer that they may be filled with the love, mercy, and wisdom of God.

The woman arrived for our spiritual direction session, sat in the chair, and adjusted the pillow at her back. She sat quietly for a moment, then blurted out, "I'm not doing my morning prayer." She paused and then said, "I don't know why I don't do it. I know how it sets the tone for my day. I know that I am more grateful, recognize more blessings, and treat others with more compassion when I begin my mornings with God. But I still don't do it. Why do I do what is not good for me rather than what my soul longs for?"

I asked the woman whether she was familiar with Paul's letter to the Romans in which he expresses the same dilemma. She did not know the passage, so we read verse 15 together: "I do not understand my own actions. For I do not do what I want, but I do the very thing I hate." "Paul wrote that?" she exclaimed. "I guess I'm in good company."

We talked about how Paul addresses a universal problem of inner conflict: how we struggle to do what is right and still do what we know to be wrong; how this dilemma appears in our physical, emotional, intellectual, and communal lives, as well as in our spiritual lives. "Not only are you in the company of Paul," I assured her. "You are one with humankind."

When we turned our reflection back to the woman's initial issue of not praying in the morning, she said, "I felt as if I had fallen off the prayer wagon and was sitting in the dust while all the faithful pray-ers went on without me. I just need to remember to get on the next wagon as it comes along."

"Exactly," I responded. "As a wise person once told me, faithfulness in prayer is the willingness always to start over."

SUGGESTION FOR MEDITATION: Where in your life do you experience Paul's dilemma? Ask God to help you choose to do what you desire rather than what you hate.

FRIDAY, JULY 1 • Read Matthew 11:16-19

Have you ever been confused about what is true or wise? Have you been called to celebration or mourning but did not join in? Have you ever believed what someone else said about a friend and did not stop to discover truth for yourself? This passage challenges us to listen for God's guidance in our lives, to turn to God and pray for discernment when confronted with ambiguity and confusion.

I used to think of praying for discernment as problem solving with a spiritual dimension; we simply included God in the process of rational decision making. I have since realized that discernment is not an activity we undertake but a gift we receive, a gift from God.

Praying for discernment requires no set prayer, no outline for the process, no formula for assurance. When we pray for discernment we simply express our willingness to engage in a life process of listening for God's desire in our lives. We listen with all of who we are for what is true and wise and loving. Praying for discernment becomes a stance in life, a way of being, a readiness of heart that calls us to live with senses awake, hearts open, and hands unclenched ready to receive God's gift.

Usually the gift I receive does not come suddenly or on command. Rather it comes as a prompting, an intuition; through a dream or the casual words of a friend. Only in retrospect do I realize that God has answered my prayers for discernment.

SUGGESTION FOR MEDITATION AND PRAYER: Remember times in your life when you received the gift of discernment. Thank God for those experiences; ask God to give you the courage to become still, open, and willing to receive again.

Jesus often withdrew to quiet places to pray, to deepen and strengthen his intimate relationship with his Abba. But in this passage Jesus prays out loud in public with the intent that those around him hear his words.

Jesus' prayer expresses thanksgiving and praise for the gifts of wisdom given to those who are open and willing to hear. In his prayer, Jesus encourages those who are set in their ways and attached to a rigid definition of truth to open their hearts to God's revelations.

Jesus then goes on to proclaim his own intimate relationship with God. He calls God his Father and claims to be God's son. Some interpret verse 27 to mean that Jesus is the only way to God. However, this verse also challenges the hearers of ancient times and the readers in this day to wonder about their own relationship with God.

In Paul's letter to the Philippians he writes: "Let the same mind be in you that was in Christ Jesus" (2:5). If we are to become one in mind and heart with Jesus, then we need to avail ourselves of the intimacy he experienced with God. Through prayer—silent prayer and verbal prayers in private or prayers of thanksgiving and praise in public worship—we can all deepen our relationship to God.

All our prayers begin with God, who initiates this holy relationship. God calls each of us to intimacy, encouraging us to claim ourselves as the beloved sons and daughters of God. God, through Jesus, urges us to let go of rigid understandings of who Jesus is and who we are in relationship to God and invites us into a life-giving relationship.

SUGGESTION FOR MEDITATION AND PRAYER: Reflect on how Jesus Christ reveals God to you. Thank God for what you have received and the loving relationship into which you have been invited.

We can rest our bodies in many ways. But Jesus speaks here of a different kind of rest, a rest for our souls. We might expect our soul's rest to come from Jesus' relieving us of our heavy burdens. But he promises rest for our souls when we take on his yoke. To take on the yoke of Jesus links us to him in all we do.

A friend of mine experienced the rest that comes from taking on Jesus' yoke last summer. She and her family were on a trail ride in Utah when her horse began to buck. She held on for a few seconds, was thrown to the ground, then was kicked by the flying hooves. The blows crushed her sternum and broke her ribs; her lungs began to collapse.

As my friend's older son rode back to the stables for help, my friend huddled on the ground in shock and pain, struggling to breathe. "As I lay there finding it almost impossible to catch my breath," she told me weeks later, "I thought of all the people in the world who were, at that very moment, fighting to breathe. I became one with them—breathing, breathing—and instead of being overwhelmed by their fear and pain, I felt my own burden lift. I rested in that grace until the helicopter arrived with medical help."

We do not have to experience trauma to take on the yoke of Jesus. All we need to do is turn to him in prayer, find him beside us, and trust that when we take on his yoke, we will find rest for our souls.

PRAYER: Give me the courage, gracious God, to take up the yoke of Jesus, to walk with him in partnership, and to discover rest for my soul. Amen.

Getting the Birthright Right

July 4–10, 2005 • *Peter Santucci*[‡]

MONDAY, JULY 4 • Read Genesis 25:19–26

Babies dominate the book of Genesis. Genealogies abound by way of birth lists, and the book is built upon the oft-repeated phrase, "These are the generations of. . . ." Because of this focus on begetting, the struggle to have children is also one of the prevailing themes of Genesis, the book of beginnings.

After the decades-long faith struggle that culminates in Isaac's birth, another struggle arises in the next generation. Isaac and Rebekah cannot have children, and, like many who wrestle with infertility, Isaac turns to God in prayer. We aren't told how long it is before the answer sought is given, but the very next sentence in scripture tells us that "the LORD granted his prayer, and his wife Rebekah conceived."

Things are looking up. But Rebekah has such trouble with the pregnancy that *she* turns to God in prayer. She receives both good news and bad. She will have twins: two nations will arise from one birth, a cause both for pride and consternation.

First, there will be the pride of having not just one nation arise from you, but two. But it will cause consternation as well. As the Lord says to Rebekah, "Two peoples born of you shall be divided; the one shall be stronger than the other, the elder shall serve the younger." Two nations create division within the family; *disunity* will be the word at the end of the day, as well as an inversion within the relationships.

God's blessings are almost always accompanied by a certain amount of turmoil.

PRAYER: Lord, I take from your hands both the good and the bad. For I trust you to work all things, even those I don't like, into a means of your grace in the lives of others and possibly even in my own. Amen.

[‡]Pastor, First Presbyterian Church of Lebanon, Lebanon, Oregon.

As a kid in Sunday school, I heard this scripture as a Jacob-is-good and Esau-is-bad story. But as I grew older, I heard preachers turn that presentation upside down and reframe it as Jacob-the-deceiver and Esau-the-deceived. Somehow, both versions seem correct, yet a bit too simplistic.

While my Sunday school teachers approved of the outcome of the story (Jacob gets the birthright and the blessing), they weren't so keen on Jacob's methods of getting what would by custom have gone to his slightly older twin brother, Esau. And they were right on both accounts. Yes, Jacob rightfully longed for the birthright and blessing, for they had a strong connection to a close relationship with God. Yet Jacob's means of acquiring the birthright (in today's passage) and the blessing (Gen. 27) are more than a bit sketchy. They are downright deceitful, and the family splinters because of the deceit.

Yet despite Jacob's deceitfulness, when it comes to trading his birthright for some of "that red stuff," Esau willingly falls prey to deception. Although he later regrets his decision, Esau is both open-eyed and willing when he "despised his birthright."

In Galatians 4:4-7, Paul dwells on our new family status as children of God. (Several translations use the word *sons* instead of *children* because the passage has to do with inheritance, which only sons received in that cultural context.) He writes, "But when the fullness of time had come, God sent his Son, born of a woman, born under the law, in order to redeem those who were under the law, so that we might receive adoption as children. And because you are children, God has sent the Spirit of his Son into our hearts, crying, 'Abba! Father!' So you are no longer a slave but a child, and if a child then also an heir, through God."

PRAYER: Father, you have called me your child. I want to live fully as your child, with all of the rights that you offer me and all the responsibilities that you ask of me. Fill my heart with your Spirit as my birthright, marking me as your own. Amen.

Christians have been called "people of the Book" because of the Bible's centrality to preaching, praying, and practice. Psalm 119 praises God for the gift of scripture, a world of God's self-revelation.

Psalm 119 is both wonderful and exhausting. It is wonderful in that it is full of wonder. The psalmist stands in awe of God's self-revelation through scripture. For 176 verses, we read of the joy, devotion, gratitude, praise, and indignation (at sin) that arises from those who have Word-shaped hearts. God does not stand aloof or rule from a distance. No, God has spoken, making known the divine will and intention, as well as how we might live in relationship with God.

These 176 verses are grouped into 22 octets: eight verses for every letter in the Hebrew alphabet. Each verse starts with the letter in which section it is. The effect is to give us an *A* to *Z* (Aleph to Taw, actually) of the Word-shaped life. While the method is exhaustive, the effect can be exhausting. Because each verse stands alone without any narrative continuity between what came before and what follows, by the time the praying reader gets halfway through the psalm, he or she often has become the sleeping reader. That's why meditating on one octet at a time is more than plenty.

Today's meditations all begin with the Hebrew letter *nun*. The words for the revelation of God contained in these eight verses are, depending on your translation: *word* (105, 107), *rules* (106, 108), *law* (109), *precepts* (110), *testimonies* (111), and *statutes* (112). All these words represent different aspects of the role scripture plays in our lives.

PRAYER: Self-revealing God, thank you for the gift of scripture and for not standing aloof from us but revealing your many facets to us, especially in our Lord Jesus Christ. Amen.

THURSDAY, JULY 7 • Read Psalm 25

When things go wrong and especially when people seem to be out to get us, it's easy to turn inward in self-protection. Occasionally, an accuser enters into our lives, someone who has it in for us even when we've done nothing wrong. Our friends aren't always quick to listen, asking us what we did to bring this upon us. And maybe we do bring things down on us, but at times we feel falsely accused and harassed. In those times we understand Psalm 25.

Despite his torments, the psalmist refuses to turn inward. While reflective, the psalmist's inward look is always secondary to his upward look. He prays, "To you, O LORD, I lift up my soul." Instead of covering over his heart and protecting his soul, the psalmist lifts it up to God. The psalmist has learned to trust God in the past and turns now to God in trust again.

God's mercy is an overarching claim in the psalm's demonstration of trust. Constant indirect references to God's mercy appear throughout Psalm 25. Indeed, what can be more merciful than to "not remember the sins of my youth"?

In this psalm we discover the words of one whose condition calls for despair and yet, because of the sense of God's mercy, the psalmist continues to pray and to live in hope. Who among us has not felt such troubles of the heart? We all go through times in which circumstances create in us extreme anguish. The psalmist acknowledges that God knows his current situation and his sinful situations in the past and yet has been merciful toward him.

Mercy remains. Despair is not the final word. The psalmist knows one more thing: only God can help him. So he prays, "My eyes are ever on the LORD, for only he will release my feet from the snare" (NIV). Those are the words of one who has turned upward instead of inward.

SUGGESTION FOR MEDITATION: To whom do you look first when in a sticky situation? Do you turn inward, outward, upward?

In Romans 7, Paul presented his amazing rhetorical description of the uselessness of trying to achieve any sort of righteousness on our own. The law (that is, the Jewish Torah) outlines the requirements for living in right standing with God. But instead of bringing the life that it was supposed to bring, in Paul's opinion, the law brought death. Why? Because it showed the gap between God's righteous requirements of us and what we can actually do.

Paul gives us the bad news: we are spiritually incompetent. But thank God for the next chapter. Here we get the good news: "the law of the Spirit of life in Christ Jesus has set [us] free from the law of sin and of death." The law of Torah observance (the law of bad news, since it points out our sinful nature) has been superceded by a greater law: the law of the Spirit.

In John 3:14-15, Jesus tells Nicodemus, "Just as Moses lifted up the serpent in the wilderness, so must the Son of Man be lifted up, that whoever believes in him may have eternal life." In that story (Numbers 21:4-9), the Hebrews have rebelled against God, and God has sent snakes to bite and kill them—not so much a vindictive punishment as a living parable. Their rebellion is killing them. So, God has Moses lift up a serpent (the animal associated with rebellion in their imagination) on a pole so that the people could look at it, see their rebellion symbolized, repent of it, and be healed. Jesus told Nicodemus that the same sort of thing would happen when he, the Son of Man, was "lifted up" on the cross.

Paul agrees. He writes that "God has done what the law . . . could not do: by sending his own Son in the likeness of sinful flesh . . . to deal with sin." Looking to the "lifted up" Christ heals us of the sin and death of the law and opens us to a new and wide-open life in the Spirit.

PRAYER: Jesus, thank you for becoming like us to free us from the law of sin and death so that we may enjoy an expansive new life in the Spirit. Amen.

Over the past few years, our family has accumulated a fairly large set of wooden toy trains and tracks. From time to time, they sprawl all over our family room floor.

As each of my children has grown into playing with the trains, each has hit a period of frustration with them. Beyond the difficulty of getting the track systems to work out, their first frustration has to do with the trains themselves. Magnets at the front and back of each train piece makes them easy to connect and disconnect. But two-year-olds don't understand how magnets work or why an end piece will connect to only one end of another piece. While watching my son try to put two negatives together might cause me to laugh, it's no laughing matter to him.

Paul reminds us in today's passage that we can go about living in one of two ways, and neither is compatible with the other. In fact, like the poles of a magnet, they repel each other.

Two chapters earlier, Paul had written these words: "What shall we say, then? Shall we go on sinning so that grace may increase? By no means! We died to sin; how can we live in it any longer?" (Rom. 6:1-2, NIV). He continues by stating that at our baptism, we died to sin so that Christ could raise us to new life.

The word that defines that old way of living is the *flesh* (which the NIV glosses as "sinful nature" to avoid confusing "flesh" with "body"). The way of the flesh is contrary to the new way of living that Christ has raised us to, life in the Spirit. Just like the repelling magnets of the trains, the flesh-life and the Spirit-life cannot connect: "You are not in the flesh; you are in the Spirit, since the Spirit of God dwells in you."

SUGGESTION FOR MEDITATION: Paul writes, "Anyone who does not have the Spirit of Christ does not belong to him." How do you define your Christian experience?

PRAYER: Spirit of God, I want the new life that you bring, not my sinning, to define my life. Amen.

My wife is a gardener. She has dirt in her blood. I'm just a dabbler. I don't even like dirt under my fingernails. But even though I only dabble, I have gained an appreciation for what gardeners and farmers do.

When I was a kid, I thought that all soils were created equal. I have since learned that each soil is unique, creating different conditions in which things grow with vigor or hardly at all. Jesus knows this and so do his hearers as he tells them the parable in today's passage.

Jesus tells the parable in two parts. He tells the parable of the sower to a large group of hearers, while telling the interpretive part to his disciples. Jesus tells the parable to separate the real gardeners from the dabblers.

In today's reading Jesus mentions four types of soil, implying that there are four ways of hearing and receiving the message of God's reign. Although there are many soils, only one allows the reign of God to take root.

These are hard words to hear, for us as well as for the original audience. For if we honestly assess ourselves, the soils of our lives are often mixed. As much as I would like to say that I have done an expert job in cultivating the soil of my life to ensure its receptivity to the Word, I know there are beaten pathways and rocks and thorns, just as in the parable.

Although we cannot create the sun or rain or seeds—the conditions for life and growth—we can cultivate our soil with hoe and rake and spade, making our soil as receptive as possible to receive what God broadcasts our way.

SUGGESTION FOR MEDITATION: How would you describe the soil of your soul right now? last year? What tools are you using to prepare it to receive Jesus?

PRAYER: Lord, help me plow the soil of my life in preparation for what you choose to plant in it. Amen.

Searched and Known

July 11–17, 2005 • Sarah Parsons[‡]

MONDAY, JULY 11 • Read Genesis 28:10-19a

Jacob dreams his great dream of a ladder to heaven as he sleeps on the ground, using a stone for a pillow. This unusual detail creates a vivid image. Jacob has apparently stopped for the night in the middle of nowhere; only in a barren place does one use a stone for a pillow. Yet on this stone in the middle of nowhere Jacob dreams his dream of God's vibrant presence. Here, of all places, he finds "the gate of heaven" (Gen. 28:17). Before he leaves, Jacob blesses the stone, the same stone he may have so begrudgingly laid his head upon the previous evening.

In the harsh and barren places of everyday life, we find our own stones; and sometimes we set them down bitterly, saying "This will have to do for my pillow." But Jacob's story demonstrates that we never know what will evoke a dream of God. Maybe, in some cases, such a dream is made possible by a hard, cold surface under the head. And when the dream of God arrives, it changes everything. God's entrance makes the ordinary extraordinary; it makes even the hard, cold surface sacred.

Pain is never something we seek out, and we should not be expected to enjoy it. But, as Jacob discovered, pain and barrenness can bring us into close contact with God. In a barren place, where we are out of our normal routines, where we find ourselves uncomfortable and in between, a slightly wider opening may appear in our awareness. Circumstances are not what they have been or what we want them to be—we do not want this stone for a pillow—but when we lie down on it and God speaks, suddenly even the stone is sacred to us.

SUGGESTION FOR MEDITATION: Consider the hard, cold places in your life. How might God be making them sacred?

[‡]An Episcopal laywoman, teaches English as a Second Language course to Kurdish immigrants; living in Nashville, Tennessee.

God is with us everywhere, in happiness and sadness. The idea that we cannot wander away from God is a familiar one in Christian thinking; even young children grasp the notion that God sees them and stays with them. I often take comfort in the idea that God sees all of me, even the parts of which I am ashamed. God knows all of it and chooses to stay in relationship out of love.

Psalm 139 describes yet another aspect of God's relationship with us: we believe ourselves to be walking in darkness and believe that God walks with us, but there's more to the experience than that. For God, our darkness is not even darkness. For us, the darkness seems all too real; sometimes we sink so deep into sadness, depression, grief, or despair that the darkness stretches on endlessly. Even so, God does not experience our darkness as darkness. There simply is no darkness to God.

The psalmist's beautiful insight is that our mental states are not necessarily God's, that God's consciousness and perspective differ radically from ours. God walks through our walls as if they do not exist, because, for God, they do not. And if our darkness is not truly darkness, then our sadness, depression, and grief are not so defining or all-encompassing; they do not have a fixed reality that we must battle. They are just states of our human minds—*real* feelings, yet simply feelings that pass through us. They deserve our attention, but they do not have ultimate power over us.

Thus, viewing our darkness from God's perspective transforms it. We are God's, and "the night is as bright as the day."

SUGGESTION FOR MEDITATION: Imagine seeing your experience through God's eyes, as the psalmist does. How does it look different when viewed from such a perspective of light, love, and forgiveness?

We are known by God, says the psalmist, thoroughly and completely. This fact can be both comforting and unsettling. All of us believe parts of ourselves are unattractive. Some attributes we even consider downright shameful. Psalm 139 seems to say that "we can run, but we can't hide," which might not be an altogether welcome message. We all like to hide things. We hide things even from ourselves: thoughts, insights, and traits we find too painful or disturbing to bear. And still, God knows all of it, "all [our] ways," "behind and before," thoroughly and completely.

Of course, God's knowledge of us goes far beyond a mere clinical assessment. Through the power of grace, we are not only known in our entirety, but God chooses and accepts us just as we are. God does not see us in our totality, get upset and disgusted, and walk away. On the contrary, God remains through every up and down, traveling into every dark place. And through it all, God chooses us, suffusing with love even those parts that we find disgusting.

Ultimately, the psalmist chooses to experience God's gaze, chooses to be known: "Search me, O God, and know my heart; test me and know my thoughts." Our awareness of God's permeating love can change the way we feel about our "shameful" parts. With the psalmist, we find that we can safely invite God in. We learn that our shameful parts are actually lovable, that true love is not only a possibility but a reality for each of us. We are entirely known and entirely beloved.

SUGGESTION FOR MEDITATION: Consider, insofar as you feel comfortable, a part of yourself that you tend to hide from others—an experience, attribute, fear, or insecurity. Then imagine that part known and suffused with a divine love that spreads through your whole being.

We know that the world has many problems; we see them in the news daily. Poverty, homelessness, lack of medical care, damage to the environment, violence—the list goes on and on. The creation indeed yearns and groans, waiting for salvation. But what if the creation is not merely waiting for salvation? What if it is waiting for us to do something? What if it is waiting "with eager longing for the revealing of the children of God"? If the creation awaits our help, then our responsibility is great.

Paul writes of a present suffering and a groaning throughout creation. Consider the larger context of the apostle's life. Imagine the ostracism faced by Paul. The old community in which Paul found security and identity turned its back on him when he experienced transformation on the road to Damascus. The new community suspected his motives. Yet notice the hope in Paul's words! Yes, we suffer in the present world, but today's suffering is "not worth comparing with the glory about to be revealed to us"! He lives with hope in Jesus Christ. He prays in that hope.

Reading the Romans passage again, I notice that no single one of us must do *all* the salvation-work. We are called to an act of self-revelation. As impossibly simple as it sounds, Romans says that we will help save the creation by being our true selves, by revealing our natures as children of God. This makes sense: by claiming our true identities and revealing them in the world, we naturally bring hope, light, and love. The salvation work is already going on; by being ourselves, we step into it and strengthen its flow. Each of us plays a unique role; to play the role well we simply claim the joy of God's parental love for us.

The vision of creation saved is almost too great for us to imagine, yet we are each called to be part of its greatness. We don't have to do it all. May we each find our unique answer, however small it may seem, to the creation's cry for help.

SUGGESTION FOR PRAYER: Ask to become a part of the creation's salvation by becoming your truest self, claiming your identity as a child of God and living in that hope.

Living "according to the flesh" means living by fear—a harsh idea but seemingly true. Living "according to the flesh" describes a state of being in which we take great interest in and even depend on material things. And, of course, living by the flesh generates fear: the flesh dies. All the material world will disappear—maybe soon, maybe in the distant future, but someday. I know this fact, whether I allow myself to think about it or not. So of course I am anxious when I find myself putting a lot of stock in things material. I worry at some level about when this will all be gone. When will I lose it, and what will I do then?

Romans says that God's gift to us is a leading by the Spirit instead of flesh, which means that ultimately we can relax. We have flesh, true; we also have Spirit, which will not disappear. This strange, unseen security, unlike the ones we can see and count on, is actually more secure than the things we see and touch, if only because it lasts. Although we naturally fall back into fear all the time, it's up to us to remember that we have received and continue to enjoy a deeper, lasting security. To use the scripture's imagery, it's up to us to remember that we are not slaves who stand to lose our homes and livelihoods in a sudden change of circumstance. Instead, we are adopted children of God, guaranteed a secure inheritance.

This passage asks us to hope for what we do not see, and it models this hope for us. It demonstrates the human capacity for enduring vision, a vision of spiritual safety. It calls us forward to an act of great imagination: to believe in the reality of a relationship, an identity, and a security that we cannot see or touch. May we allow such great imagination to form in us and learn to trust in things unseen.

SUGGESTION FOR MEDITATION: Use the image of adoption to envision your relationship with God. Imagine God's converting your status from slave to adopted child. Feel the security of this close, enduring parent-child relationship.

Jesus' parable reminds us of the inextricable intertwining of good and bad. In the world's approach, killing the weeds would also kill the wheat. On the one hand, this is bad news: evil is part of our world, and we're stuck with it.

I have heard it said that in order to feel happiness, we have to feel sorrow. Usually I rebel against that idea, because it trivializes sorrow, casting it as nothing more than an unpleasant foil to the experience of happiness that we all really want.

Jesus' parable does not claim that unhappiness exists to accentuate happiness or that the bad exists to highlight the good. It merely points out that the good sprouts and the weeds are part of the same whole. Thus it would seem that our sorrow and happiness, our pleasure and pain, also form part of a larger whole. Our sorrow does not exist so that we can recognize happiness; our sorrow simply is. For the time being, sorrow and happiness simply grow together in the same field. To experience earthly life is to experience both. This is our lot—weeds and good sprouts. While God did not intend the comingling, here it is as our reality. To live fully, we live this reality as it is.

Each person's pain is part of the world's pain. Christ knows that the world has pain in it; he prepares his listeners for the sorrow sewn into the very fabric of human existence. And he offers hope that one day the pain will be collected and bound for burning, leaving the good sprouts to be gathered in.

SUGGESTION FOR MEDITATION: **Imagine your own pain and the pain of those around you as part of a larger whole, as a field containing weeds and good sprouts. Further, imagine Christ tending the field, gently clearing the weeds away, allowing new, healthy shoots to grow freely.**

If I were a parent, I would find it hard to discipline my kids. I can imagine myself melting at the first tear, even though I know that kids need boundaries, rules, and consequences. The scriptural image of evildoers thrown into a furnace of fire, followed by "weeping and gnashing of teeth," also troubles me. It's not a pretty picture but one full of suffering and pain. I'd prefer gentler words.

Yet Jesus thinks it important to emphasize the difference between good and evil, and he also points out that God knows the difference. When terrible things happen in the world, God knows, just as God knows each of us through and through. God not only recognizes evil; but like any good parent, God sets limits and promises punishment. There is a noteworthy difference between good and evil, and Jesus' parable reminds us that pain will be associated with wrongdoing.

The good news of Jesus' parable is that we don't have to do the work of separating the good from the bad. We may have a sense, sometimes a very clear sense, that one action is good and another is evil. And we often find ourselves driven to judge, to punish wrongdoing and reward good behavior. To live in a reasonably stable society requires punishment and reward.

But in the ultimate sense, the Son of Man will take care of all judgments, deciding which parts of our world are of the kingdom and which are not. And it relieves me to have the burden of ultimate judgment taken away; I trust God and Christ to judge more than I trust my own limited consciousness. Therefore, I can let go of my grudges, my vengeful plans, even my anger eventually. It's a relief to do so. When I can let go of these things, I am free to love and enjoy my life, trusting that true justice, God's justice, is already at work in the world.

SUGGESTION FOR PRAYER: What burdens do you carry as a result of your desire to judge? Ask God to judge for you, so that you can be free.

How Can I Keep from Singing?

July 18–24, 2005 • *Chris Evan-Schwartz*[‡]

MONDAY, JULY 18 • Read Genesis 29:15–28

Laban deceives Jacob by switching his daughters. Jacob has worked seven years for the prize of Rachel (Laban's younger daughter); his love for her makes the time seem short. To Jacob's great surprise, Laban brings Leah in to Jacob instead of his beloved Rachel. Laban was in a bind. He had to marry off his older daughter Leah before giving away the younger in marriage. Perhaps Laban saw this act as the only way to honor the customs of his people, an opportunity to take control and follow the proper order.

I recently spoke with a brother and sister from India, currently living in the United States. Both will have their marriages arranged by their family "back home," with the brother needing to marry first. In their minds, this is the accepted and honored natural order. Laban's deception is the problem here, while Jacob himself was the deceiver earlier.

Deception is a recurrent theme in this troubled family and in our world. Things are not always as they seem. Others deceive us, sometimes with hidden agendas. We become "pretenders," answering others' queries with "oh, I'm fine!" A new position may not be accurately represented in the interview process. We may ask, as Jacob did, "Why have you deceived me?" On the other hand, we may play the role of deceiver, taking situations into our own hands, as did Laban. Our greatest deceptions may come when we deceive ourselves. To what degree do we rely upon God's wisdom, order, and guidance in our lives? How often do we find ourselves willing to step aside, listen, and discern?

PRAYER: Holy God, guide me with your love this day. Make me attentive to my impact on others. Amen.

[‡]Codirector of a state-funded early childhood program for children at risk, St. Paul's United Methodist Church, Cedar Rapids, Iowa.

God is trustworthy, a keeper of promises. The first part of this psalm sets the stage for our unceasing prayer and praise. God invites us to be seekers and to rejoice in that role as we form our identity. God gives us "holy exercises" to connect us within the stream of history:

- give thanks
- call upon his name
- make known
- sing
- talk
- glory
- rejoice
- seek
- remember

I remind my three children, "Remember who you are. Evan-Schwartzes don't _____." I fill in the blank with words most relevant to the particular occasion or leave-taking. I've created a boundary, while trusting in my children's good judgment after years of nurturing and presence. Memories create an identity for our family. Our memory of God's saving acts in history gives us direction.

Ever-expanding brain research tells us that our brains are most active when we teach others. We come to know at a deeper level that which we can articulate to others. The psalmist knew this and guided us in this direction thousands of years ago! Through active, "holy exercises," our belief is strengthened. Music is worship, a vehicle of praise. It also cements our connection to a loving God.

Our praises must ring through our lives, bringing God's love, peace, and justice to others.

PRAYER: I thank you for your works of grace and mercy, O God, and rejoice in your constant presence in my life. May I be your witness this day. Amen.

Jesus describes the kingdom of heaven through parables to subvert or to overturn the usual view; we gain a glimpse of his radical vision of God's reign. In these parables of the kingdom, Jesus calls us to see the world from a perspective that differs from the more common assumptions of vision based on power. The smallest of all seeds, the mustard seed, represents small beginnings, encouraging us to be open to possibilities and transformed by hope in God's loving purposes.

Often we notice the biggest first. We desire the "big splash." Numbers speak volumes in our competitive world. It is tempting to be caught up in results or the latest catchword being sown through mass media or the Internet. We emphasize church attendance statistics, counting every possible worshiper to get the greatest number. We judge and are judged by size—with bigger being better. We lose sight of the essence, the heart of our faith. Jesus teaches that God judges by a vastly different set of measurements. Mustard seeds and yeast remain insignificant by all standards, yet Jesus elevates them in these basic parables.

Jesus asks us to consider the potential in even the simplest action, the smallest portion. Our infinitesimal efforts may be the catalyst for phenomenal growth, to which the mustard seed and the portion of yeast described in Matthew attest. We may choose to sow seeds of good, which are nurtured and empowered by God's grace through the Holy Spirit. This is how God's reign continues to expands, though that expansion may seem slow by our hurried and often harried standards!

God creates miracles through those things we may consider unimportant, unworthy, or uneventful. By ignoring the seeds in our midst, we deceive ourselves.

PRAYER: God of the large and small, your kingdom is at hand. Help us recognize the signs of your reign. Work in us to act as yeast in the world, bringing your love, light, and joy to others. Amen.

As clergy or lay leaders in our congregations we face people's expectations of leading prayer, modeling praying, and even teaching others to pray. We deceive ourselves when we create a hierarchy of spirituality, putting on masks of competence or ascribing to others undeserved ranks of spiritual stature. As humble servants, we open ourselves to the leading of the Spirit, accepting our weaknesses.

Paul offers words of reality and freedom. "We do not know how to pray as we ought." Sometimes the words do not come. We have desert times. We don't have words to speak or we have times of not hearing God speak to us. We may even confuse the words of long-memorized prayers.

Paul helps us understand how our weakness in prayer becomes a gift. He reminds us in Romans 8:24-25 that in hope we were saved. "If we hope for what we do not see, we wait for it with patience." The knowledge of God's loving purpose sustains us. We trust that the Spirit will intervene for us, as we increasingly open ourselves to God.

We enter prayer intentionally, in a spirit of meditation. As we listen in the quiet, we open ourselves to the Spirit's intercession. God searches our heart. We accept our human limitations in praying. With patience, confidence, and faith, we trust that God hears and understands our "sighs too deep for words."

PRAYER: Loving God, expand our experience of prayer. Renew our attentiveness. Gift us with patience, quiet, and sighs beyond words that communicate our deepest desires. Make us listeners tuned in to your word. Amen.

At a time of spiritual searching, I was drawn to The Upper Room's Academy for Spiritual Formation. One of the many joys of participation comes in the opportunity to live in community with others who are intensely seeking God's will for their lives. I found meeting new friends and soul-mates a true blessing. Through deep relationships, often formed through sharing in covenant groups, open minds and hearts to God, I found a context for growth. Submitting to this model of spiritual formation transforms; it requires vulnerability, receptivity, and response. This spiritual connectedness moves beyond thought, far beyond "head" work to the depths of soul tending.

The Academy exposed me to the Quaker tradition of sitting in silence with others and the query process. This community silence moved me to new realms of prayer and the Spirit's intercession. Practicing "the presence," daily reflections, and sharing with others brought to me a new peace.

The practice of centering prayer exposed my heart to being searched. While sitting with others in patient openness seemed awkward at first, it became a time for which I hungered. I found myself drawn to contemplative practices and began to sense what it means to yield to quiet. Anxieties and concerns, often uppermost in my mind, furnished my self-talk. The refreshment of opening to God through contemplative prayer brought a new peace to my life.

I continue to be challenged to find the time and space for this heart searching. My openness to God has a direct connection to my purpose in this world.

Wendy Wright suggests that "God's will is not a puzzle to be solved, but a mystery whose contours emerge as we journey on." May we intentionally open ourselves to the mystery of God's transforming power and will for our lives.

PRAYER: Loving God, search my heart. I offer myself to you, yielding with trust and love to your formation. Amen.

One summer I directed a faith-based recreational program at my church for neighborhood youth. The activities provided middle-school youth with a desirable alternative to watching television, videos, or wandering the streets. Some families new to the neighborhood heard of the program as they attended a daily meal program.

The presence of young people who were recent refugees from Liberia and Sierra Leone blessed the workers. Youth and college-age helpers listened with intrigue to the vivid personal stories of those who had risked their lives to escape war-torn regions. One ten-year-old girl recounted waiting in a long line, day and night, to be "processed." She described her fear as she witnessed the questioning of the family ahead of hers. Words were exchanged, and, horrifically, the mother of this family was taken aside and beheaded. With fear and trembling, my young friend's family stepped forward, the next to be verbally drilled. They escaped alive—physically unharmed, yet emotionally scarred.

In hearing this story and others, I realized the deep trauma these families had experienced in leaving their countries. I wondered how they could sleep at night, and I posed that very question. "Oh, that's easy! We surround ourselves with Bibles and then we always feel protected!" These children literally created a boundary with Bibles and felt God's presence.

These who knew of hardship, distress, persecution, peril, famine, and tools of murder found their security and hope in God. "In all these things we are more than conquerors through him who loved us." Nothing can separate us from the love of God in Christ!

PRAYER: Holy God, we offer thanks for your constant presence in our lives. Heal us. Help us to trust. Protect all who live in peril, especially children. Amen.

Give thanks, acclaim God's name,
tell all that the Lord has done.
Make music and sing
the Lord's mighty wonders!
Revel in God's holy name
delight in seeking the Lord.
Look always for the power,
for the presence of God.
(International Committee for English in the Liturgy)

We have traveled through deception, illusion, peril, and persecution in this week's readings, journeying through the darker side of humanity: trickery, paybacks, and family dysfunction. We return to the steadfastness of God's love. Even in the depths of our lives, we seek and find the light of God shining.

We remember God's covenant as it has come to us. We delight in beds of iris blooming at a retreat center and remember bulbs planted and nourished in good soil. We smell bread baking and notice signs of growth, sometimes as subtle as yeast working in the loaf of bread.

We cry out to God through sounds and silences, asking that our feet stand on solid rock. As heirs and God's chosen, we remember God's works. We praise God and celebrate the wonders all around. In the words of a hymn by Robert Lowry:

No storm can shake my inmost calm
while to that Rock I'm clinging.
Since love is Lord of heaven and earth,
how can I keep from singing?★

PRAYER: Holy God, keep us radically attentive to your presence. As you have led generations through times of peril, guide us along paths of peace. Keep our songs of praise alive! Amen.

★"My Life Flows On," #2212 in *The Faith We Sing*

Encountering God's Mercy

July 25–31, 2005 • Eric K. C. Wong[‡]

MONDAY, JULY 25 • Read Genesis 32:22-24a

Having made an agreement with Laban, Jacob leaves his father-in-law to meet his elder twin brother, Esau, from whom he has fraudulently gotten the status of firstborn and received the blessing from their father, Isaac. Jacob, unsure of Esau's forgiveness, asks God to keep the promise of protection (32:9-12), while preparing for the worst by dividing his family, servants, and animals into two groups, lest all his belongings be destroyed. This is a helpful approach to difficulty: pray for God's help, while taking action.

Jacob remains behind alone, desiring some quiet time for himself as he prepares to meet his brother face-to-face. Two options probably come to mind: either Esau will accept him—or not. In the latter case, Esau may fight or even kill him.

By reading farther in Genesis, we learn that Esau forgives Jacob, inviting him to his place in Edom. Jacob humbly follows behind Esau at first but settles down in Shechem eventually. We learn later of the rape of Jacob's daughter in this foreign land. What a price to pay for previous wrongdoings.

Jacob chooses to live in a foreign place rather than in his hometown. We can imagine his worries about and fear of Esau. It was a lifelong burden. I remember a statement spoken by the former chief secretary of the Hong Kong Special Administration Region (SAR) when she tendered her resignation: "I have never done anything against my conscience throughout my years as a civil servant." How blessed is a person who has no wrongdoing weighing on his or her conscience.

PRAYER: Dear God, keep us from wrongdoing; heal us and give us courage to remedy our wrong deeds. Amen.

[‡]Professor, theology division, Chung Chi College, the Chinese University of Hong Kong.

While alone beyond the river, Jacob encounters God in the guise of a man who comes and wrestles with him. Before the man's departure before dawn, Jacob seizes the opportunity to ask for a blessing. The man does so and at the same time hurts Jacob's thigh. The story leaves us with many questions: How did God actually appear to Jacob? What did the wrestling mean, and why did it take the whole night? Why could God not simply wrestle down Jacob? Why did God have to leave by dawn? For all the questions, this story offers at least two lessons for us today.

First, in many developed countries, those who work and live in cities busy themselves with professions, friendships, family, and other urgent matters. Persons who live in cities experience a much higher rate of psychiatric problems than those who live in villages or in developing countries. Tight schedules damage physical health and spiritual relationship with God. When Jacob puts aside business for solitude, he opens space for himself as well as for God; God comes to him. Jacob's story reminds us to take time out of our busy daily schedule for ourselves—and for God.

Second, it is hard to say whether Jacob or the stranger wins the wrestling match: "When the man saw that he did not prevail against Jacob, he struck him on the hip socket; and Jacob's hip was put out of joint." Jacob seems to understand that the stranger is an unusual man, so he negotiates for a blessing, indeed a blessing of God. If we make the time, we will also encounter God in unexpected forms. Our aim: to seize the possibility for God's mercy and love.

PRAYER: O God, help us take time for ourselves and for you. May we seize the opportunity for promise and blessing! Amen.

WEDNESDAY, JULY 27 • Read Matthew 14:13-14

What would you do if your dearest teacher, one of your best friends, died? If the pastor who baptized me passed away, I would try my best to attend the funeral ceremony. If I received the news of the teacher's death after the funeral, I would allow myself a quiet time to recall him or her.

Jesus is no exception. Having heard about the death of John the Baptist, who baptized him, Jesus leaves his hometown. The cause of John's death was Herod's vow to Herodias's daughter on his birthday. Certainly John's criticism of Herod's immoral marriage with his brother's wife Herodias brought about his demise. A righteous man died because of injustice!

There is a time for sorrow. Jesus takes a boat and goes to a quiet, lonely place by himself. This is a personal and private matter. Somehow, actually rather surprisingly, people living in different towns know about Jesus' intention and destination. They have reached Jesus' "deserted place" by land before Jesus does. If I were Jesus in that situation, I would have left that deserted place for another one—if I had not gotten angry with the crowds for disturbing my privacy. What would you do if you found yourself in such a situation?

It normally takes some time to restore emotional equilibrium. Rather than think of his own personal and emotional needs, Jesus affirms God's mission. He has compassion for the large crowd, much more than for his own situation; he chooses to help those in need.

PRAYER: Jesus, grant us the wisdom to prioritize matters that surround us. Grant us the love to serve others and a willingness to sacrifice our time for others' needs. Amen.

Hearing that Jesus is nearby, the crowd has sought him out and laid their sick at his mercy. As he works his way among them, they forget about going home to eat, which is unusual for the people of an ancient time. Suddenly it is sunset. The compassion of Jesus, and his willingness to stay with them until the sick are healed, has distracted them from their physical hunger.

On Sundays I often hear my dear brothers and sisters in the faith criticize the sermon—its theme, its relevance to the scripture, its length, the adequacy of the pastor's preparation. I listen, concerned to improve my own sermon crafting, but I also wonder: *Does our criticism of the sermon leave room for the message of the scripture to feed our hunger?*

The crowd surrounding Jesus peacefully and quietly enjoys being with him, forgetting about the time. Jesus' disciples, straightforward administrators, inform their master of the sunset situation and ask him to discharge the crowd, over five thousand people, for their own provision. Yet despite the coming of darkness, the people themselves seem to hunger only for the provision of Jesus. Having both room and time for the message of his ministry, they seem instinctively to understand that "they need not go away."

Though our concerns about a sermon may seem sound, perhaps we, like the five thousand, should relax and allow Jesus to feed our many hungers.

PRAYER: O Lord, help us make room in our thoughts to listen to your words. Distract our attention from our daily concerns so we can acknowledge and enjoy what may lie beyond our sight and experience. Amen.

The coming of evening makes the situation of a hungry crowd a burning issue. What better solution than the one the disciples propose (dismiss the crowd and let them buy food in the villages) comes to mind? Yet Jesus responds, "They need not go away." He suggests that the disciples feed the people, even though they do not have food enough. Jesus continues to operate out of a sense of compassion, kindness, and mercy.

There are different explanations for the miracle of feeding the big crowd. We may never know what actually happened. Perhaps Jesus keeps giving the fish and bread again and again without emptying his hands until everyone eats and has enough. Or the crowd could have brought their own food but did not bring it out at first. Seeing Jesus break and give the food, they take out their own food. Or even, as some scholars further suggest, according to John's version (6:9), the crowd is moved by the young boy's offering of his five loaves and two fish, which spurs them to a generosity of spirit.

As a young child, I learned and accepted only the supernatural understanding of this miracle—an extraordinary work, the demonstration of Jesus' power over natural law. It took me some time to understand the more humanistic approach. The insight of the supernatural understanding concerns only the crowd's physical feeding. The humanistic approach asserts that if the crowd can overcome selfishness or be moved by the boy's deed to bring out their own food, then Jesus has fed people's thoughts and changed people's minds. I wonder if we cannot integrate the two understandings: Might Jesus overcome the law of nature, while at the same time convert people's minds and feed their imaginations and creativity?

PRAYER: O God, strengthen our understanding of your words. Broaden the horizon of our minds to appreciate differing interpretations of your words. Amen.

Some years ago, the first woman elected chair of the legislative council of the Hong Kong SAR donated a kidney to her daughter. Her decision and action were widely appreciated. I asked myself if I would do what she had done or if I would even consider donating an organ to an unknown person. Like many people who ask themselves similar questions, I discovered the limits of my willingness to sacrifice.

Paul expresses his willingness to sacrifice himself on behalf of the Jewish people, even if that means he will be "accursed and cut off from Christ." Obviously facing a great difficulty as he considers the means by which his "own people" may receive salvation, Paul feels "great sorrow and unceasing anguish" that God's promise to his ancestors, the Israelites, might be challenged, perhaps even made void.

Listing the blessings showered on the Israelites by God, Paul notes the singular honor for which God has chosen them—that "from them, according to the flesh, comes the Messiah, who is over all." Like the mother who donates a kidney to ensure the promise of a full life for her daughter, so Paul seeks to find a way to secure the fulfillment of God's promise to the descendants of the Israelites.

In his new life as a converted follower of Christ, Paul has become all the more aware not only of his deeply rooted Jewish heritage but also of the peril his people may face if they cannot accept the salvation offered them by God in Christ. Paul's willingness to be cut off from Christ on their behalf is a moving reflection of the depth of his love for them.

PRAYER: O God, grant us strength to face our old beings and to be transformed into new persons. Grant us vision to contribute to the reign of God. Amen.

SUNDAY, JULY 31 • **Read Psalm 17:1-7, 15**

Justice is a luxury for many Asians, who either live in countries where a fair legal system is yet to be established or have no chance for education about their rights as human beings. In contrast, citizens of developed countries cannot tolerate the conviction of an innocent person or the failure to prosecute a guilty person. The legal system of a developed nation is designed to avoid or at least minimize such situations.

As citizens and Christians in a developed nation, we may not often be directly involved in the justice system, although it frames our expectations on a personal level. We may experience, for example, a teacher's unfair grading, a supervisor's unequal distribution of the workload, or a colleague's envy. Our responses to such daily experiences are to a great extent reflections of our concept of justice and of our trust in a just God.

If I found myself in the psalmist's position, I might consult a lawyer. Having received legal analysis, I would have to decide whether to pursue a legal remedy. But the cost of obtaining justice is usually high. How much money, time, and effort would I have to expend to gain justice? And how many nights of sleep would I lose?

Psalm 17 is the prayer of an innocent person who suffers from injustice. Trusting that God will "see the right," the psalmist nevertheless notes that he has "held fast to [God's] paths," and his "feet have not slipped." Yet he does not invoke legal remedies or prescribe the type of justice he requires. Rather, he simply calls upon God, confident that God "will answer."

When we experience daily injustices, we can follow the example of the psalmist, opening our hearts to God to be tried and tested and trusting that God will "wondrously show [God's] steadfast love." Ultimate justice is granted only by the One who knows our hearts fully.

PRAYER: O God, incline your ear to us; hear our words. Comfort us when we face social and personal injustice; let your eyes see the right. You are our judge and our comforter. Amen.

Our Generous, Saving God

August 1–7, 2005 • *Elizabeth T. Massey*[‡]

MONDAY, AUGUST 1 • Read Genesis 37:1-4

The story of Jacob's family is fateful for the fulfillment of God's promise to Abraham. Yet the themes of this passage do not augur well for the family's immediate future. As the story opens, teenager Joseph serves as a helper to his older brothers, the sons of Bilhah and Zilpah, an appropriate status in the family hierarchy. But Joseph brings to Jacob's attention a critical report about these brothers. Perhaps with the sense of invincibility that comes with being a teenager and almost certainly with a degree of naïveté, Joseph sets the stage for conflict.

Jacob clearly demonstrates his greater love for Joseph than his other sons, which suggests that the youngest, not the oldest, will be the chosen one of God's promise to Abraham and his descendants. Jacob's gift of a coat with long sleeves—possibly an indication of royalty—potently symbolizes his paternal favoritism and signals an overturning of the hierarchy. The coat stirs Joseph's siblings to uncontrollable jealousy. Unable to speak civilly to him, the brothers shun him.

This portrait of a dysfunctional family rings true. Sibling rivalry, disregard for status, thwarted expectations, and inappropriate gifts of favoritism continue to wrench families. Where today's families may seek counseling to restore healthy relationships, Jacob's family is left to its own devices to work things out, apparently without seeking God's guidance in the process. Thus far the story has no heroes, no villains—only flawed individuals.

PRAYER: Dear Lord, when family conflicts threaten to divide, help us remember you are the author of wisdom and reconciliation in the very home where our life with you began. Amen.

[‡]Lay Episcopal chaplain; social worker, family and children's agency; course coordinator, St. Luke's Church School of Prayer and Healing; living in New Canaan, Connecticut.

Jacob's love for Joseph seems to have blinded him to the extent of his other sons' jealousy and hatred of their brother, while Joseph continues to be naïve and trusting. That is one reading of why Jacob would send his youngest son out to visit his brothers to check on their well-being. That he asks Joseph to bring back a report once again indicates how out of touch Jacob is and how much faith he has in this son. The language points to a still deeper meaning. In response to Jacob's command to go, Joseph replies, "Here I am"—Abraham's response to God's call. The language suggests that a dramatic turn of events is about to happen.

When the brothers see Joseph approaching and decide to kill him, they act without seeking God's guidance. At the crucial moment, the timely intervention of those brothers who do not wish to hurt their father or have Joseph's blood on their hands saves his life. Joseph is saved though his history of insensitivity to issues of power and status have almost resulted in his death. Thwarted in that action, his brothers instead sell this spoiled child into slavery.

Do we recognize God's generosity and mercy that rescues us from situations we have gotten ourselves into through insensitivity, irresponsibility, or a lack of compassion? If we are honest, we can remember times when we have lauded it over others in our church families, at work, or at home because of our view of ourselves. Isn't it also true that at these times we have been out of touch with God?

PRAYER: Dear Lord, help me to see my own insensitivity, overeagerness to show off my gifts, or aspiration for more than I can handle. Let me learn from your example that a humble, tender heart is what you ask of me. Amen.

Instead of fussing that life is too busy to be thinking about God at every turn, why not try an experiment? In one day, see how many ways you can find to seek God's presence continually.

I am an evening and late-night person. Workday mornings I struggle out of bed at the last moment, dress hurriedly, scarf down my breakfast, grab my lunch, and head out the door. Driving to work, I ordinarily strategize client sessions. In the office I rarely have a moment to myself.

But then I stop and think of my opportunities to look for and remember God in the daily whirl. I imagine saying, "Bless you, God, for opening my eyes to another day." When I take the time to seek God's presence, I ask the Lord's guidance before I sit with a client or lead a group. I remember that my most difficult client, who suffers beyond measure, is God's child also. As I look out the window by my desk, I can praise God for the vista of neat homes, freshly mown lawns, and the blue Long Island Sound in the distance. As I work out at the gym, I marvel at the miracle of my body's endorphins as the stresses of the day disappear. As I walk from the barn where I park my car, I look up at the century-old sugar maples towering over the farmhouse and see God's handicraft. Cutting up brilliantly colored vegetables for dinner, I thank the Lord for creating beauty that also gives pleasure in the eating. At the end of the day, I can say the intimate words, "Guard me sleeping and guide me waking."

The more the habit of seeking God grows, the more I feel God's presence breaking through in a flash of joy, wisdom, comfort, sustenance, or challenge. Praise be!

PRAYER: Creator God, help me to look for you in all things. Let me keep the thought of you close to my heart so our relationship deepens. Amen.

The individuals God selects as leaders in Hebrew scriptures and in the New Testament are entirely human in their frailties. Joseph was no exception. Yet God chose Joseph to be the saving instrument of Jacob's line, fulfilling the promise made to Abraham and his descendants. Before attaining this honor, however, Joseph first needs training.

As a slave in Egypt, Joseph suffered pain and ignominy while "the word of the LORD kept testing him." Plucked out of his family system and on his own, he had to learn the right use of his gifts as a dreamer. His childish pride in the visions he dreamed gave way to a compassionate responsibility for his rare gift, and in time "what he said came to pass."

Joseph's wise use of his gifts as a dreamer and as a perceptive interpreter of dreams led to his favor with the king of Egypt, who "set him free" and made him "ruler of all his possessions." But more than freedom and wealth, the king rewarded Joseph with the power "to instruct his officials" and "to teach his elders wisdom." The youthful dreamer, grown up and having passed God's testing, received the full benefits of God's saving generosity.

The gift of dreaming dreams that foretell the future can be, as Joseph learned, a deadly serious business. Another dreamer, Martin Luther King Jr., had a vision in which God's justice and mercy would be realized in a more open, free, fair land of opportunity. Though King's dream cost him his life, his death proved that the dream is more powerful than the dreamer. Long after wise dreamers like Joseph and King are gone, inheritors of their visions may marvel, "What he said came to pass."

PRAYER: God, whether we are waking or sleeping, speak to us. Fill us with a vision that continues to celebrate your glory in the hopes and dreams of others, long after we have passed your testing. Amen.

We make incessant demands on our clergy and lay leaders. We expect them, like God, to know each one of us intimately yet respect our privacy. We require our ministers always to celebrate each Communion as if it were as fresh for them as for us, to preach each sermon as if our very lives depended on it. The hymns they choose must touch our hearts; the funeral homily must evoke smiles and tears of recognition.

Our lay leaders must instill a love for Jesus in our children; organize hospitable coffee hours; and visit homebound parishioners, bringing them the latest news. And yes, the operating budget must balance; the broken window in the bathroom be fixed; and a classroom be repainted and refurbished by parishioners. So much to do; so little time in which to do it.

Above all, we expect our spiritual leaders to be prayerful people, touched daily by God. Jesus, the exemplar of spiritual leadership, withdraws alone to a mountaintop where in nature's quiet he can pray. He needs and seeks this solitary prayer time, even to the point of sending his disciples out into the tempestuous world on their own. Perhaps we should grant our clergy and lay leaders—and ourselves—the time and solitude to do likewise, to "recharge" for ministry and the tasks at hand.

What occurs during prayer may be uncertain, but we do know that when we pray from the heart, something always happens. We may be restored to peace of mind, filled with a sense of joy and wonder, or find the needed words to soothe an irate family member or friend. Let us encourage one another, brothers and sisters in Christ, to find that time of solitude for prayer that refreshes our spirit for leadership.

Suggestion for prayer: Using the words Jesus taught us, say the Lord's Prayer slowly, reflecting on the meaning of each phrase in your life this day.

To the people of Jesus' time, the stormy sea with its unleashed power represented the forces of chaos, ever threatening to break loose and destroy the civilized order. The story of Jesus' walk on the water implies God's ability to surmount tumult as Jesus goes to the vulnerable, tempest-tossed boat that carries the disciples, the nascent church.

The forces of chaos are equally present today: conflict between Israel and Palestine; civil wars, famine, and the HIV/AIDS pandemic in Africa; turmoil in Iraq and Afghanistan; nature's unpredictable storms and earthquakes continually remind us of ever-present possibilities for mayhem and destruction in life. Yet God's generous power to bring order and mercy to humankind still works to build faith, healing, and reconciliation. But do we always believe that?

At times we all experience doubts that God's goodness will prevail. Like Peter, we too would like to have concrete proof that God will save us. Yet even with that proof, we can falter when we focus on the tumultuous waves around us rather than on the steadfast presence of Jesus. With mercy and understanding God sees both our faith and our weakness, forgiving us our doubts while stretching out a strong arm to steady us.

Like the disciples, we may find Jesus in unexpected places when life's vicissitudes challenge us most. But like Peter, who did, after all, get out of the boat and approach Jesus, we must have the courage of our faith to reach for that strong, outstretched arm wherever we find it. Even if we waver, God's grace will prevail and bring us to safety and peace.

PRAYER: Jesus, help me to keep the eye of my heart on your presence, even in moments when the stresses of life seem overwhelming and I am beset by doubts. Guide my faith journey that I may face the world strengthened and renewed. Amen.

What Paul says we need in order to be saved seems so simple: to have faith in our hearts that we also speak aloud with our lips, proclaiming that we believe in the one Lord of all. God has been faithful to God's promises down the centuries, showing righteousness. Can we show righteousness by doing our part?

Angelia was a lovely, sensitive, only child, born to a Jewish mother and Greek father. Although both are thoughtful, cultured people, they did not bring up their daughter in either faith tradition. She surprised them when, at age thirteen, she announced she was going to become a Christian. She told them that she had been searching for a spiritual home and had found it, close at hand. Her questions about the mysteries of life were being answered nowhere else in the big city where they lived. This young girl had the courage to proclaim her budding faith, and her baptism brought an awakening to her parents also.

How often are we presented with opportunities to speak out about our faith? Do we seize these moments or let them pass by, anxious about how we might be received? It is one thing to recite the creed on Sunday in church. It is another to reach out to a friend, neighbor, coworker, or stranger with faith-filled words that welcome respectful conversation. Yet if we are shy about offering, imagine how reticent someone will be to ask—even at a time of great spiritual need.

God's generosity brought us all, the peoples of this world, into being, and God's word is there guiding us to find ways to speak these truths from the heart.

PRAYER: God, you have created me with the capacity to respond to your love and to live according to your promises. I want to be eager to share what you mean to me so that others may come to know you. Grant me this gift so I may be generous as you are. Amen.

Reunited!

August 8–14, 2005 • *Steve Harper*[‡]

MONDAY, AUGUST 8 • **Read Genesis 45:1-15**

Estranged, *separated, at odds, divided*—these are all terms to describe broken relationships and damaged emotions. No matter what the reasons, we experience a feeling of sadness when we hear words like these; we feel that it should not be this way. Today's reading recounts the healing of the long-standing estrangement between Joseph and his family.

Joseph, separated from his family through no fault of his own, is clearly a victim. At times we too feel victimized by others, perhaps through words or actions, a one-time experience or sustained over many years. Everything within us bears the pain of undeserved suffering. Why should we attempt reconciliation, especially when no such effort is forthcoming from those who have wronged us?

And yet . . . and yet, our hearts are sad. How we wish things might have been different! We continue to live with a heart that longs for reunion. Then, one day, like Joseph, we realize we have an opportunity to make things different. Sometimes Joseph's story is our story. If anything is going to change, we must initiate the change. And in such moments, an amazing grace is given—grace to let our broken heart, not our wounded spirit, speak. Setting aside justice and pain, we take the first step. The longed-for reunion occurs because we refuse to be a victim and let God lead us to be a healer.

PRAYER: God of the victims, come to our assistance. Protect us from evil, while helping us see opportunities to make things different. And when we see them, give us grace to extend forgiveness and the hope of reconciliation. We ask this in the name of Jesus. Amen.

[‡]Vice President and professor of spiritual formation, Asbury Theological Seminary, Florida campus in Orlando; living in Winter Springs, Florida.

The victim has been given grace to become the healer. But this grace-filled healing did not result from a snap decision. The process that led to the reunion extends beyond today's selected passage. It begins back in chapter 37 when his brothers cast Joseph into the pit. Perhaps Joseph remembers his brother Reuben's sparing of his life and the plan intended by Reuben to result in his rescue rather than his slavery.

Perhaps the dreams and impressions combine to let Joseph know that God intends to use his life as a means of grace, rather than as an agent of destruction. Clearly Joseph understands Egypt's abundance to be for other nations (41:57), which sets the stage for a willingness to apply his generous spirit to his own family members.

Thus, by the time his brothers stand before him and plead for assistance (chapter 42), Joseph is already predisposed to extend mercy and help. He can move beyond the past and do the right thing in the present.

To his brothers' credit, they display signs of genuine improvement. Judah's intercession for Benjamin (44:18-34) moves Joseph deeply (45:1). God has led Joseph to the place where he can see past his own experience and offer life to the very ones who had conspired to take it from him.

For those today who have moved beyond victimization to reconciliation, this story bears powerful testimony to the transforming grace of God in our lives. We do not have to be forever victims; we can become wounded healers, people who extend mercy and forgiveness to those who desperately need it—perhaps even to the people closest to us.

PRAYER: God, give us grace to move from being victims to being healers. Our world needs people whose primary motivation is not to "get even" but to get life back to the way you intend it to be. We cannot do this without deep grace. We ask for it in Jesus' name. Amen.

Judaism gave birth to Christianity, and many of the first believers converted from the Jewish religion. A look at Christian practices reveals a connection to similar ones in the Hebrew Bible.

That being so, it is not unusual for us to ask, "What about the Jews?" Every generation has raised Paul's question; we still ask it today: "Has God rejected [God's] people?" Because Paul's response—"by no means"—is a strong one, we must not pass over these readings quickly. They contain a great lesson in our theme of reunion.

The lesson is this: God is at work, even at the deepest level of rejection. Paul's heart breaks for his fellow Jews who, rather than accepting Christ, have turned away from him. Perhaps Paul takes comfort in recalling the story of Elijah.

At the time of Israel's deepest apostasy, a remnant still remained. Paul likely saw the new Christian community as the "remnant" in this particular case, or perhaps he knew those who remained Jews, in the truest and finest sense of that word. Either way, the point is the same: God is never completely absent in a people. No matter how total or final someone's (even a nation's) separation seems to be, God has not abandoned them. God is at work in them. God will keep promises made concerning them.

Paul takes great hope in this affirmation, although his confidence never eliminates all the questions or the mystery that surrounds this particular issue. Likewise, our belief that God is always at work may not answer all our questions or make a mystery absolutely clear.

In this particular case, the Jews' rejection gave rise to a new option: the inclusion of the Gentiles. Even the problem gave time and space for God to do something new. And on similar occasions, it may be so for us and for those we love.

PRAYER: God of all people, we will never completely understand how you work, but may we never falter in our conviction that you are at work—in all people everywhere. Amen.

It is almost impossible to take the historicity out of this chapter. The situation to which Paul refers is so full of "Israel," it connects to the past, present, and future. Today we focus our meditation on the plain fact that God's desire to reunite what is divided may include nations, not just individuals.

Who of us can say with certainty that God will not do something to restore Israel to a depth of faith that Paul perceives the nation has lost? And all the more so, if God somehow has a hand in the "hardening" of people's attitudes (vv. 7-8) so we Gentiles get the opportunity to be saved. Wouldn't it be just like God to act on behalf of the Jews to restore them in a way that would, in the end, include a belief in Jesus as the Messiah?

Paul calls it a "full inclusion" in verse 12. John Wesley, commenting on this verse, said, "So many prophecies refer to this grand event, that it is surprising any Christian can doubt it." To be sure, it takes the theme of reunion into a new domain and to a new height. But, why not? In today's reading Paul says, "The gifts and the calling of God are irrevocable."

If in any sense this is so, then we can never write anyone off or rule anyone out. God can reunite divided nations and races. God can work through the divisions and differences in your life and mine. Why not?

God's ability does not cancel out human responsibility and the necessity of faith, as the opening of chapter 12 clearly shows. Most scholars agree that Israel's "full inclusion" does not necessarily mean 100 percent. The basic principles of salvation have not been suspended, but nothing and no one is beyond the reach of reuniting grace—even a nation.

PRAYER: God of all nations, in praying for the Jews, we pray for ourselves. In praying for Israel, we pray for our country—that we may be included in the wonderful story of your desire to reunite all things to yourself. Amen.

Our greatest need for reunion occurs within ourselves. Jesus says that to live as a divided self results in "defilement." Ironically, the Pharisees best illustrate this danger. They have developed two selves—a public one and a private one. On the outside, they appear righteous and respectable. They carefully monitor and meticulously maintain every outward action. They use the "correctness" of their actions as a means to measure and judge others.

But the Pharisees' private self behaves quite differently. Hidden from view are evil intentions, murder, adultery, fornication, theft, false witness, and slander. Some scholars believe that Jesus' list actually names things the Pharisees listening to him have done. The deep danger comes in this separation of inner condition and outward conduct. God created people to be one self, not two. Living divided lives imperils the soul.

We too live in a culture contaminated with "secret sins"— those committed away from public view. Hardly a week goes by without someone being exposed for "hidden faults." Our society bears witness to the tremendous need to experience the reuniting of a divided self.

The word *salvation* means "wholeness." Elsewhere Jesus refers to it as a "healthy eye" (see Luke 11:34). By contrast, he frequently refers to the hypocrite—the "play actor" whose public face is not the real face. Two-faced living will destroy us.

But grace abounds. Jesus clearly shows in this Gospel lesson that he can both detect and cure this disease. There can be a grand reunion of separated selves, resulting in our no longer needing to practice secrecy but rather experiencing the joy of being "one self" both inwardly and outwardly.

PRAYER: Creator God, restore to us the singular life, so that who we appear to be is who we actually are. We ask this in Jesus' name. Amen.

The passion of the Canaanite woman's heart provides a strong contrast to the pretense of the Pharisees in yesterday's reading. Their cry of "offense" contrasts with her plea for "mercy." She could have taken offense at Jesus' words to her; instead she seizes the moment to draw near, rather than draw back. This encounter generates hope—hope that those deemed "far away" from God can, in fact, be reunited with God. This passage also contains a stinging irony—that those deemed "far away" from God can actually end up closer than those who think they are near!

This story reminds us that the reunion we seek must occur in the core of who we are. External assessments (Pharisee equals good; Canaanite woman equals bad) cannot determine the true state of things or the potential for change.

Perhaps Jesus' reference to the woman as a "dog" is less a statement of fact than a test: "Are you going to let what people say about Canaanites (or your own self-image) keep you from the table of grace?" The woman's reply reveals what is going on inside her, just as Jesus' words about the Pharisees in verses 18-20 showed what was happening in them. The Pharisees turned away "offended." The Canaanite woman leaves with "mercy"— the healing of her daughter. Even those deemed far away—those thought of as dogs—are candidates for reunion with God.

Today may be a good day to ponder your heart to see how you respond when the risen Christ reveals your weakest characteristics. If your heart is "offended," watch out. But if it cries for "mercy," pay attention. The reunion we all need with God is not automatic, and our public image is not the predictor of reunion's likelihood. Only our deep inner response to the approach of Christ determines the outcome.

PRAYER: God, make haste to help me. Make speed to save me. My heart cries for mercy, for even the "dogs" can eat the crumbs that fall from your table. And one crumb of grace will heal my weakness and reunite my soul to you. In Jesus' name. Amen.

The sign of reunion with God is unity with one another. This week we have pondered the theme of reunion in a reconciled family, a restored nation, and those on the margins. In each case, people allowed God to work in their lives, and in so doing they came closer to one another in a "very good" and "pleasant" unity and a cause for celebration in the public worship of God's forgiven and reconciled people.

Dorotheos of Gaza, a sixth-century monastic leader, realized that the monks' devotion to God was not bringing them closer to one another. He concluded that the quest for God could never reach its full potential without a corresponding effort to grow closer to one another. He viewed the relationship this way:

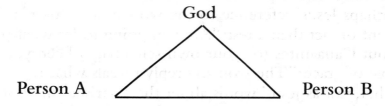

We live in an individualistic culture, but we are not the first to do so. Today's reading implies that unity among the people of God is not an abiding or automatic reality. Dorotheos of Gaza's experience further confirms the truth, always with the same warning—"independent" religion is dangerous.

In worship the presence or absence of unity is clearly seen. We gather week after week desiring the thing God most wants to give—"life forevermore." But we sometimes fail to realize we will never know that life fully or genuinely without "life together." But God is working to restore and establish unity. Our reunion with one another creates the environment in which God can provide the "oil" and "dew" of blessing.

PRAYER: Dear God, as we worship you today, may we do so in the spirit of unity that allows "life forevermore" to be real in us. Wherever we lack that oneness, help us move toward reunion with our brothers and sisters in the faith. Amen.

Faithfulness

August 15–21, 2005 • Monica Jefferson[‡]

MONDAY, AUGUST 15 • Read Exodus 1:8-14

Today's text reminds us that the "a new king arose over Egypt, who did not know Joseph." The people of Israel live under the authority of a government and culture that does not know the faithfulness of Israel's God. Egypt and Israel share a history of God's provision during a time of famine, which gives both peoples an opportunity to celebrate the goodness of God together. The shared history of provision and faithfulness is lost and replaced with the fear that one group would control the other.

We live in a culture where the history of God's faithfulness and provision is unknown or reduced to sound bites, epic movies, videos, or silence. Our lives often reflect the social, political, and economic norms of the day. The stories of how God provides and remains faithful through unlikely circumstances such as the connections between Joseph, Egypt, and Israel go untold even in our churches. We too must look for the places where we share a common history of God's faithfulness and model that faithfulness in a world starving for love, peace, justice, and a relationship with God. Like Joseph, we must use our God-given gifts and talents for the benefit of all people in all situations.

Our charge is to proclaim and live in such a way that the world knows that God is still in control. Through Jesus Christ, we share a history and a future where we need not fear one group of people over another. God delivers us into a new reality that replaces fear with faith.

PRAYER: Dear God, help me to remember your faithfulness and provision in times when I choose fear over faith. Help me take every opportunity to share your witness in a world that hungers for your love. In Jesus' name. Amen.

[‡]Area Staff Coordinator for Urban and Intercultural Ministries, The United Methodist Church, St. Louis, Missouri.

Out of the water

I live in a city sandwiched between two great rivers, the Mississippi and the Missouri. Channels, reservoirs, and gates regulate the flow of these rivers to provide smooth traffic flow and safety. Yet, these human-engineered structures cannot always prevent these mighty bodies of water from overflowing. The powers of the rivers are greater than the power of human desire to contain and control them.

Pharaoh gives the order to kill the baby boys of the Hebrew people to prevent the growth of the Hebrew population. Out of the Nile River, worshiped as life-giving among the Egyptian people, Moses' mother floats him into a new life of safety. The order of destruction becomes the channel through which life is given. The palace of the Pharaoh will become the home of the baby boy Moses, whose name means, "I drew him out of the water." Moses floated into God's plan for deliverance of Israel and all humanity.

Saving Moses' life through the protection of his enemy, Pharaoh, demonstrates the reconciling power of God. We, like the midwives, are to say no to worldly powers. We offer our sons and daughters to God for protection like Moses' mother. And we, like Pharaoh's daughter, choose to protect the least among us. God uses the circumstances of the oppressor and the oppressed to offer deliverance for all. Jesus' death and resurrection are God's rescue plan from oppression and death into eternal life.

PRAYER: Dear Lord, forgive me when I try to regulate and channel your power for my selfish desires. Give me a God's-eye view of the world so that I may be a part of your plan for deliverance, liberation, and transformation. In the name of Jesus I pray. Amen.

On our side

The psalmist gains a new revelation of God's faithfulness and power as he acknowledges that "if it had not been the LORD who was on our side," Israel's enemies would have defeated them. This revelation moves the psalmist to a new level of understanding of personal power and God's power. The psalmist can rest in the security of God's power to overcome any enemy, circumstance, or situation.

My mother-in-law, Mother Jefferson, had strong opinions about most every subject. She was a leader in her local church and in the Jefferson family. Prayer, study, and mission work were a part of who she was not what she did. She approached every activity with the attitude of "let's pray" or "let's ask the Lord." She prayed and anointed people with oil as a sign of the healing presence and power of God.

Two years ago I watched as diabetes, kidney failure, and a weakened heart ravaged the body of Mother Jefferson. When asked how she could face sickness with a positive attitude, she replied, "The Lord is on my side. Sickness is my enemy; each new day I praise God, who defeats my enemy." Her profession of faith encouraged others to believe in Jesus Christ and find peace in their hearts. She never stopped letting people know in times of blessing and challenge that the Lord is the source of power.

PRAYER: Dear Lord, maker of heaven and earth, I submit my life to you this day. Forgive me when I think I am operating out of my own power. I need your help to face the challenges and blessings of this day. I pray that you find my thoughts, words, and actions pleasing today and forever. Through Jesus Christ our Lord. Amen.

Living sacrifice

Paul begins chapter 12 of the book of Romans with an appeal to the followers of Jesus Christ to stay focused on God—a difficult undertaking for a newly formed group blending Jewish and Gentile traditions and practices. Yet Paul encourages this young community of faith to be a unified body of believers in Jesus Christ at work in the world, presenting themselves as a "living sacrifice."

Understanding that the new follower of Jesus Christ is full of expectation, Paul instructs the new believers in Rome to focus their hunger for learning on being "transformed" so that they "may discern the will of God." Paul knows that their continued growth in the faith will involve worship, prayer, study, service, and fellowship; he urges them to be "one body in Christ" in these pursuits. Though their individual gifts and talents will vary, they "are members one of another."

Balancing the responsibilities of family, work, school, and countless other activities fills our days and discourages the excitement we once felt as new followers of Jesus Christ. Worship and spiritual discernment are consigned to the to-do list of each day. But Paul teaches us that we must integrate the secular and spiritual in our lives, making ourselves "holy and acceptable to God" in all we do. That, says Paul, is our "spiritual worship."

Perhaps it is time to renew your relationship with God through Jesus Christ and the power of the Holy Spirit. As you go through the day, pray for the old hunger you knew as a young believer. Balance your priorities in new and surprising ways. Allow the gifts of others to be a guide to understanding, and give your full attention to God in every moment.

PRAYER: God, I present myself to you today. Forgive me for taking you for granted. Help me to be worshipful and holy, a living sacrifice in the world. Amen.

Our help

The Christian life sometimes puts us right in the path of our enemies. For reasons known and unknown, persons disagree with us, despise us, or seek to destroy us. Our faith does not prevent us from encountering enemies, but the psalmist assures us that God will not allow us to be "prey to their teeth."

Faith is a choice not for the faint of heart or spirit. Even when our personal lives are balanced and secure, the world is a battlefield. Strife within families and among friends, in churches and communities often threatens our security like a flood that would sweep us away. On the world stage, today's friends may be tomorrow's enemies. War, crime, and violence are born of anger that can be "kindled against us," not in spite of our faith but because of it.

"Blessed be the LORD," who is "our help." The psalmist invites us to speak a blessing to God in stressful times. God "who made heaven and earth" offers the security of God's power and peace to a world in need of help and healing. As Paul advised the young church at Rome, so the psalmist advises: stay focused on God. Though our enemies are poised to attack us and the raging waters threaten to overwhelm us, God will deliver us. We will escape "like a bird from the snare."

SUGGESTION FOR MEDITATION: **Stop several times today and say, "Our help is in the name of the LORD, who made heaven and earth." Use this phrase to help you focus or refocus your day on the power of God.**

PRAYER: **Lord, forgive my dependence on self. I give my day and myself back to you. In the name of Jesus, I pray. Amen.**

Who do you say that I am?

Knowledge is often best imparted by spending time with or studying a subject. Human beings learn from other human beings. Some persons learn best visually, while others prefer experiential or auditory learning. Geography, family, and cultural norms all affect how and what we learn. All learning takes time and relationship. Wisdom and understanding occur in time and space. Faith lessons pass from one generation to the next.

The book of Matthew emphasizes Jesus' teaching and stories with their foundation in the writings of the Hebrew Bible. Peter, as a Jew, knows the stories of the coming Messiah. His life of listening and learning culminates with his response to Jesus' question "Who do you say that I am?" When confronted with the reality of Jesus' presence, Peter recognizes Jesus as the Messiah.

People invite others to know Christ personally. Family, friends, children, programs, events, positive or negative experiences become the channels through which people grow in personal knowledge of Jesus Christ. Some people grow up hearing the narratives of God's faithfulness, while for others the stories are new. The telling and retelling of the stories of Jesus Christ with excitement and integrity prepares followers and seekers to recognize Jesus in our world. If you want to know Jesus, spend time with Jesus through study, prayer, worship, and service—the Holy Spirit will take care of the rest.

PRAYER: God, I pray to know you better. Give me the wisdom and the insight to recognize Jesus so that others may recognize the Jesus in me. In Jesus' name, I pray. Amen.

I will build my church.

Simon Peter, nicknamed the "rock," would not have been most search committees' choice for the founding pastor of a new church start-up because he was a man of extremes. When he was right in his interpretation and analysis, he was very right, such as the recognition of Jesus as Messiah in the text. At other times we find Peter sinking after walking and Jesus questioning his faith, "Why did you doubt?" (Matt. 14:31). Yet Jesus looks past the flaws of this ordinary man and invites him into service in the new community we call the church. For the Jews the Jerusalem temple and the stone upon which it was built were considered the center of the known world. Through Jesus, a new community forms that centers the world on a relationship with God that will break down all barriers.

Peter will hold the keys to heaven, becoming the imparter of authoritative teaching. Jesus, who has taught with authority, now gives Peter authority to teach in his name. As the leader of the church, Peter will apply Jesus' teaching to concrete situations in the everyday life of the church.

This new community called the church is part of God's continuous plan to bring people into right relationship with God. The church and its purpose in the world are of God's design, and the "gates of Hades" cannot prevail against this community. The text makes it clear that Peter the "rock" will be the person to start this community, but God will build and give this community its power to grow. The building of the church from diverse groups of ordinary people is divine in nature and eternal in scope.

PRAYER: Gracious God, thank you for building your life-giving church for the healing of the world. In Jesus' name, I pray. Amen.

The Call

August 22–28, 2005 • *Roberto L. Gómez*[‡]

MONDAY, AUGUST 22 • Read Exodus 3:1-10

Moses, having grown up in the court of Pharaoh, has run away from his past, his home, and his people. He hides in the mountains of the Sinai desert. If Egyptian army units search for Moses, they will not find him. Moses hides well.

Instead, God finds Moses. What a surprise for Moses! Moses ran and hid, but still the Lord God found him. In discussions with people about their call to ministry, I have discovered that running away and hiding are common initial responses. When God called me to the ordained ministry, I literally ran away. To my surprise I ran right into God. I saw no burning bush, but I certainly felt God's presence and warmth.

Interestingly enough, prior to the burning bush incident, nothing indicates that Moses is a religious, pious man. Moses is aware of his Jewish heritage, but we do not know of his religious practices. Since an Egyptian princess adopted Moses, might we assume that Moses learned to worship as an Egyptian?

Moses, a man far from God and a murderer to boot, discovers himself found and called to lead the Hebrew people out of Egypt. One of God's virtues is the ability to overlook past indiscretions, failings, flaws, shortcomings, and errors. God touches a person's life and transforms that person for service. So it is that God calls Moses to return to Egypt and deliver the Jews from slavery, leading them to a land flowing with "milk and honey."

SUGGESTION FOR MEDITATION: How might God be calling me to ministry? How am I running away, attempting to hide from God? When God finds me, how will I respond?

[‡]Pastor, El Mesias United Methodist Church, Mission, Texas; faculty member, Spanish Conference Course of Study, Perkins School of Theology.

The call to minister and serve strikes deep into the core of our being. When God calls, we often ask, "Who am I to be called by God? I am not equipped for ministry. How could I possibly be in ministry?"

While in my teens, I met a pastor who was sight impaired. Forty years ago, our society was less accepting of people with physical challenges. Yet, this man, with his wife's help, served as an effective pastor. When God called, he could have responded, "Who, me? I'm blind; how could I be a pastor?" Instead, he responded in faith.

Another young man answering the call to serve God struggled to take required religious courses while also studying for the GED (Graduate Educational Development tests, the equivalent of a high school diploma). Finally, he concentrated on completing the first step, the GED. Then he returned to the religious course work, which required great sacrifice and hard work. He became qualified as a local pastor. Through God's grace and guidance, he is doing good work as a beloved pastor.

Moses too struggles as he responds to the call to lead his people out of Egypt. *Who am I?* he wonders, *to do such a task?* The story of God's calling of Moses reminds us that that God both calls and equips us. When I felt the call to preach, I did not speak well or clearly. At moments I despaired. I did not have an Aaron to speak for me.

I took speech courses and a speech therapist helped me. With prayer and practice, my speaking improved. One day, I was asked to say a pastoral prayer at a sister church. To my amazement, a man with a drinking problem responded. I then knew that God had called me and prepared me and would use my speaking to help others. When God calls and you respond, the grace of God will bless your ministry.

PRAYER: Lord God, when you call me to ministry, bless me with your loving presence so that your grace may flow through me to be a means of grace to those in need. Amen.

Psalm 105 encourages its readers to tell others about God's deeds and wonderful works, reminding them that God sent Moses and Aaron to the Hebrews and that through these two men, God did wonderful things on the sojourn from Egypt to the Promised Land. The Christian church journeys toward the kingdom of God, and part of its ministry is to tell the world about God's deeds and wonderful works.

I once pastored a congregation in a lower-income Hispanic/Latino neighborhood in a large Texas city. The church had a kindergarten program, annual vacation Bible school, and outreach programs to youth during the summer. We had Sunday morning and evening worship as well as a women's meeting on Monday nights. Tuesday evenings we had a prayer group, and Wednesday was church meeting night. Thursday evenings we held Bible study. We in the church felt so proud of our church activities and outreach to the neighborhood.

To improve our evangelistic outreach, a group of church members decided to visit house to house in our church neighborhood. As we visited, we realized that we had not done an effective job of sharing the good news of Jesus Christ. We learned that one block from our church location, people knew we were a Protestant church. Two blocks from us, people knew we were a Christian group. Three blocks from us people thought we were a community center; and four blocks away, people did not know we existed, although we had been in the same location for almost thirty years!

Sadly, this story repeats itself too often for many congregations. We need to pray and then put into action Psalm 105. "Make known his deeds among the peoples . . . tell of all his wonderful works."

PRAYER: Father, thank you for our many blessings. May we share our blessings and "make known [your] deeds among the peoples." Amen.

Today's scripture lesson presents a plan for living as a follower of Jesus according to the apostle Paul. The recommendation, while simple, presents a huge challenge.

For over twenty years I have taught a pastoral care course for persons studying to be pastors. Students in the class present experiences and case studies of their pastoral work. In the first ten years of the course, students rarely presented incidents of violence in the family, neighborhood, or city. However, in the last five years the increasing number of violent incidents involving church members that the students report in their case studies has troubled me. If violence is on the rise among members of the church community, imagine the increasing violence among persons with no relationship to a faith community.

Paul's list of ethical behavior offers a code of living in a spirit of love: "Let love be genuine; hate what is evil, hold fast to what is good; love one another with mutual affection; outdo one another in showing honor." When we learn to abide by this Pauline code, surely our world will be a better place.

As followers of the Lord Jesus Christ, we gather weekly for worship and fellowship. We scatter to serve in his name. Yet, as we go out into the world to work, play, and rest, we may become disconnected from the lifestyle we are called to live in the spirit of Jesus Christ. With God's help, we need to hold fast to our new life in Christ and stay connected to the Christian lifestyle. Perhaps that is what John Wesley meant when he said that the work of the church was to "spread scriptural holiness across the land."

PRAYER: Creator of all people, keep us close to you. Guide our thinking and doing that we may be connected to your fellowship and bring you honor and glory. Amen.

Empathy is an important concept in counseling. A counselor helps a person by acknowledging his or her situation, feelings, and thoughts in a caring and supportive way. Empathy is a wonderful therapeutic skill that helps those in need of emotional and personal support. In ministry, empathy carries the added benefit of God's love.

Paul instructs the young church at Rome in the practice of Christian empathy. Christians help the happy rejoice and the sad weep. They enjoy the company of all, and they do not consider themselves wiser or more important than anyone else. But their behavior toward their enemies is what truly marks the Christian community. Christians are not to curse their enemies but to bless them; they are not to seek revenge on their enemies but to "live peaceably with all." In fact, Christians are to help their enemies in need, thereby "overcom[ing] evil with good."

In his book *The Love Command in the New Testament*, Victor P. Furnish suggests that in Paul's thought, love is the primary motive for living. This insight helps us to see the power and significance of today's scripture. If we take Paul's words to heart and allow the Holy Spirit to empower us, then our way of living will include empathy not only for those we love but also for our enemies. If love is our primary motive for living, we will "take thought for what is noble in the sight of all," showing care and support not only for those who love us but for those who despise us.

PRAYER: Father God, let Jesus, the Prince of Peace, rule over us in our hearts, minds, and actions, that love for our neighbor will be a principle of our living. Amen.

I attended a music concert of a rising Christian singer who had an amazing number of people in her entourage: band members, backup singers, sound technicians, bus drivers, a publicist, and other personnel. All these people depended on her. Her inability to sing for a lengthy period would threaten their livelihoods. They hope the singer will make it big, because when she does they too will prosper.

Such is the case for Simon Peter, his brother, and friends. They do not number themselves among the rich and powerful of their time. Then they meet Jesus, an amazing and gifted rabbi who can preach, teach, and do miracles better than any other rabbi. Thousands follow him. The disciples began dreaming that when Jesus becomes the new king of Israel, he will install them as his helpers. They dream that with Jesus they will become rich and powerful.

One day, Simon Peter, inspired by the Holy Spirit, proclaims Jesus as the Son of God, the expected Messiah. Surely Jesus will become king. At that moment, Jesus tells the disciples that he intends to go to Jerusalem, where he will be killed and on the third day be raised to life. The disciples are stunned, shocked, bewildered. Their dream of wealth and power is dashed into a thousand pieces. Simon Peter challenges Jesus but to no avail. Jesus has set his course. In time the disciples will also pay a high price for following Jesus.

Sometimes when we respond to the call to discipleship, we anticipate a glorious, exhilarating journey of promise and success. More realistically the journey will also include tears, pain, disappointment, frustration, and failure. As we follow Jesus we learn that the road to Jerusalem and Golgotha is still there and that we cannot avoid it. Discipleship exacts a high, personal cost.

PRAYER: Lord Jesus Christ, help me understand that the call to discipleship is not one of wealth, power, and success but rather one of obedience and faithfulness to your cause. Amen.

Jesus' words to his disciples about the cost of following him are straightforward and sometimes harsh. Following Jesus had its price then, and it has a price now.

My road to following Jesus included attending college and majoring in church history. One of the required courses on my journey was the history of the music from the Medieval and Renaissance periods. I liked music but lacked formal training in music. I studied hard and felt that I had put forth good effort to prepare for the first test. The professor played several notes and asked me to identify the composer, composition, and historical importance. My mind went blank. To make matters worse, a gifted music student sat next to me and wrote and wrote in her exam book. I felt like I might be bearing a cross on the road to seminary that I could not carry!

Finally I calmed down and wrote briefly about the music. After the class I went to the professor and asked for help. He gave me good advice: I would have to deny some fun and social activities and spend more time in the music library.

The crosses we bear are different for each of us. For me in college, music history was a type of cross (a burden to bear). Sometimes, others see our self-denial and know the crosses we bear. However, at other times only the individual and God know the challenges of self-denial and cross bearing. What fruit might come from the crosses we bear? The crosses can keep us focused, humbled, and prepared to follow Jesus. We deny ourselves and carry the cross, not for ourselves, but for his honor and glory.

PRAYER: Dear God, keep me humble and give me the courage and strength to deny myself and to carry the cross of discipleship. Amen.

All Is Possible

August 29–September 4, 2005 • *Victoria Obedkoff[‡]*

MONDAY, AUGUST 29 • Read Psalm 149

As Snoopy, the cartoon character, says, "To live is to dance—and to dance is to live." When rushing from La Guardia to the JFK airport to make a close connection, I collapsed onto the shuttle bus and the driver proclaimed, "Ma'am, welcome to my dance floor!" I just looked at him. This was no time for dancing—he needed to step on it! The driver started weaving in and out of the traffic to pumped-up music. He tangoed and two-stepped and waltzed for a bit with a big truck, flirted with an SUV, and turned on a dime to lose a limo so skillfully and gracefully that he could dance me to the end of love, as Leonard Cohen puts it. Grinning and tapping, we arrived on time, more human and more alive than when I had boarded.

"Let them praise [God's] name with dancing." God will surely feel praised at the Rochester Thanksgiving contra dance weekend, hosted in the grand old Salem United Church of Christ. God will surely feel praised as we do-si-do to the fiddle and the old banjo. Our biblical faith dances us beyond our stresses, shyness, and isolation into community and joy.

I have a friend who is sad and angry that loved ones die and lousy things happen in this world. He is unwilling to dance in a broken world. Yet, through the dancing we shed our stress and isolation, and our mourning makes way for joy. The One who calls us to dance delivers us from our past into the power of *now*, the power of connectedness, the power of *all is possible*.

PRAYER: Dance me, God, into being your graceful partner in all I do! Amen.

[‡]Minister, St. James United Church, Toronto, Canada.

I came to hear baroque music at a Toronto concert but couldn't take my eyes off the conductor. He worked with his whole body. I feared he would fall off the riser each time he would rock back, then rise up to follow the baton. When I thanked him after the performance for his expressive style, he grinned and said, "I studied at the Fred Astaire school of conducting."

How good it is to pour our whole selves into our work, until worship and work are one! Psalm 149 calls us to uncompromised praise—until verse 6 causes a double take. "Let the high praises of God be in their throats, and two-edged swords in their hands, to execute vengeance on the nations and punishment on the peoples." Our throats constrict and our feet are leaden when ugly feelings have us in their grip. How can we sing and dance our praises to a God of singular goodness, yet be poised to execute vengeance?

Singers know that the voice box in the throat does not produce good sound. Full, authentic sound comes from lower down, from the very "diaphragm" of our being, the "drumskin" that resonates as we breathe deeply. We must go deeper into ourselves and pray that God transform rather than bless our primitive urges for revenge and punishment. Our God is a whole and holy God of vibrant life, not a double-edged God who blesses the two-edged Christianity that would have us bomb foreign peoples or cut off a close friend who has disappointed us.

Let us repent of doubletalk, and practice loving our enemies as Jesus requires us to do, until this work becomes a dance of praise to the One through whom all is possible.

PRAYER: O God, may we unite in love and creative response to the world's problems and in all things offer undivided praise to the source of goodness who blesses the pure in heart. Amen.

Bring to mind a situation in which you feared not getting your share. Perhaps you and a friend wanted the same thing, making you feel tight and anxious. We seldom express these uncomfortable feelings and try instead to be fair.

Roger Fisher, negotiation and conflict resolution expert, tells a story about two people and one orange. Each person wants the orange. With admirable restraint, they acknowledge that each desires the orange. Being fair-minded people, they divide the orange in half. The first person goes home, peels her half, throws away the peel, and eats the fruit she has been longing for. The second person goes home, peels her half, ignores the fruit, and uses the peel she wanted to bake a special cake.

As author Thomas F. Crum puts it, often we are so intent on doing the "fair" thing that we fail to realize what we actually need or desire. What if we shared our needs and wants with one another, honoring the possibility that "whatever [we] bind on earth will be bound in heaven"? Avoiding conflict makes no one happy. Faith invites us instead to authentic communication with one another, working together in faith to find agreement.

We have been given the promise that "where two or three are gathered in my name, I am there among them." When we "agree on earth about anything [we] ask," we are cocreators with Jesus. The One through whom all is possible empowers us to create solutions we have not yet imagined.

PRAYER: Magnificent God, help me choose to act from faith in abundance rather than fear of scarcity. Help me risk communicating my authentic needs and wants and be open to a novel solution. Bless me with what I truly need. Amen.

THURSDAY, SEPTEMBER 1 • **Read Romans 13:11-14**

The scriptures call us to cast off the works of darkness and conduct ourselves honorably as in the day. As I write in December of 2003, my country is in an uproar over the deportation of Maher Arar, an Ottawa computer consultant, from a New York airport to ten months of torture in a Syrian jail. Human rights groups in both Canada and the United States describe his case as a symbol of post-9/11 excess. It appears that Canadian officials passed Arar's name on to U.S. officials because of an accidental connection to someone who might have known someone who was linked to a possible terrorist. Given "six degrees of separation," any one of us could be "disappeared" for "rendition," a political euphemism for torture. Even language can be appropriated to mask what is really going on.

The language of scripture is itself problematic when it equates "darkness" with bad works. Let us remember that without darkness, nothing comes to birth. Without darkness, the stars would never be seen, nor our sleep be sound and restorative. God comes to us both in darkness and in light. Living in Christ calls us to align our thoughts, words, and works with right conduct, showing justice, fairness, mercy, compassion, and respect for the mutuality of our human relations. Living in Christ requires that our works be visible and accountable to the One in whose image we are created.

PRAYER: God of the new day, wake us up to what is really going on. Shine your light upon our works of national and international affairs. Empower honest scrutiny of all our complicity in the mess the world is in today. Align our thoughts and works with your will for humankind, that you may be pleased to dwell in our midst. Amen.

Sometimes we don't feel like getting up, especially when it's a dark, frozen, winter morning in northern Saskatchewan. Accepting an invitation in August to guest preach during Advent was one thing. Rising at 6:00 AM to drive a few hours north on the appointed day was another. Fortunately, for ninety-nine cents, a person could book a wake-up call and sleep like a baby.

The phone rang, shattering a deep sleep. I put on my best falsely bright voice and thanked the operator. I lay immobile, my mind drifting to the car I had to dig out of the snow and then let myself slip away. Ten minutes later, the phone rang again. "You're not up, are you?" the same operator accused. She had my number, all right. I thanked her for going the extra mile. Now I would too. I was on the road to one of my best days in ministry.

Sometimes we need a little help to wake up and move on. Sometimes what we hear or see or read wakes us up to reality as it is—and what yet could be. Sometimes it takes caring confrontation with a close friend or spouse. And sometimes the God of Advent comes to us through the operator, going beyond the call of duty to reach us. The Spirit moves through conscientious folk who will aid us if we ask for help. Our lives depend on it!

PRAYER: O God, who calls us to wake up to living fully, to showing up fully ourselves, to sharing our gifts, to spending ourselves in love, thank you for this day of making a difference. Amen.

In August 2003 a grade 6 firestorm hopscotched through neighborhoods in Kelowna, British Columbia, passing over one home while destroying the rest of a block. We find it hard to deal with such randomness.

The Exodus passage instructs the Israelites to smear the blood of sacrificial animals on the doorposts of their homes. That night God will kill the firstborn of Egypt to punish "all the gods of Egypt," while passing over the marked doorposts. The religious festival of Passover is still celebrated, yet its meaning has evolved. The twentieth century brought the horror of the destruction of both the innocent and the transgressors. Faithful eyes must learn to see God in the reconstruction rather than the destruction of life.

What's inspiring is that the Israelites go on to live; they respond gratefully and faithfully to being "passed over." The Israelites built a more compassionate and just society, practicing Jubilee through debt forgiveness and land redistribution. Kelowna people are rebuilding a friendlier, more compassionate, and unified city. Walls went down as well-off suburbanites fleeing the fire zone relied on the kindness of strangers who welcomed them into their modest homes.

Has the seeming randomness of cancer, fire, war, or other circumstances caused you to wonder for what purpose you have survived while others have fallen? Eighty-year-old Toronto citizen Cyril Howes, Royal Air Force veteran of World War II, survived D-Day in Normandy and missions to Arnheim. To keep faith with his fallen comrades and the ideals that led them into wartime service, Cy now fights economic globalization through campaigns to keep our fresh water bodies and universal health care system in public hands and to stop the militarization of space. This is how Cy lives out being "passed over." How do you?

PRAYER: Liberating God, you lead us through difficult times to make a difference with our lives as cocreators with you. Amen.

Your heart is broken. The love and trust that you had so carefully tended and nurtured has been shaken to its roots. The very thought of having to see that person again creates feelings of anger and apprehension. Yet you long for his or her continued presence in your life. What do you do?

In its original context, this passage was related to discipline within the body of Christ of those who had strayed or offended. These verses outline a type of "checks and balances" for repairing relationships and restoring offenders to Christian community, as well as protecting the ones who initiate the difficult conversation. The closer the relationship, the harder it may be to rally from hurt in order to risk a caring confrontation.

It rests with each of us to accept the responsibility of making the first move toward repairing a relationship. We do so intentionally and prayerfully rather than recklessly. We give the other party the opportunity to hear us and to make amends. If that effort fails, we ask for a meeting and have two or three witnesses present. The witnesses may be persons skilled in mediation and conflict resolution. They also provide a safeguard in the event that the differences are not resolved. If the matter goes to the larger community and still finds no resolution, then we must detach from that person and move on with our lives.

Do not fear initiating a difficult conversation if you have prayerfully prepared and bring an open heart instead of blame. Take the next step of involving witnesses; embrace the opportunity for authentic relationship by speaking truth with love and readying yourself for transformation through the process of resolution. The love and grace of Christ will accompany you for the sake of peaceable community and the well-being that God desires for us all.

PRAYER: God, strengthen my faith. All is possible through you. Amen.

In Honor of the Lord

September 5–11, 2005 • Grace Bradford‡

MONDAY, SEPTEMBER 5 • Read Exodus 14:19–31

What do I do now, God?" I can hear Moses asking when he learns that Pharaoh's army is in pursuit of the Israelites. At times he hasn't known which way to head or what to do next. Now his people have given in to fear; they prefer to go back to Egypt and suffer under Pharaoh's oppression rather than starve and die in the wilderness. But Moses has established a pattern of looking to God for answers.

Moses has learned that God will not leave him alone. He knows that God will protect the Israelites; God's angel moves between them and their enemy during the night. When Moses obeys God and stretches his hand over the Red Sea, God separates the waters; the Israelites walk through on dry land. With another stretch of Moses' hand, their enemies are swallowed up by the returning waters, and "not one of them remained."

How often have we been lost on a busy highway or tormented by a seemingly dangerous pursuer or unable to find our way out of a pressing problem? The easiest route was to give in to fear and to await whatever would come. Or perhaps we thought to fight back in anger. Certainly we felt alone.

Jesus prayed in the garden of Gethsemane, knowing his enemies were crowding in on him. We can almost hear him ask, "What do I do now, God?" Yet knowing he would not be left alone, he submitted his will to God, leaving us with the same assurance that was given to the Israelites at the edge of the Red Sea: "The LORD will fight for you, and you have only to keep still" (NIV).

PRAYER: Jesus, help me to replace the daily fears of my life with your assurance that you are always with me. Amen.

---

‡Lay speaker; Covenant Discipleship member; Class Leader, Asbury United Methodist Church, Washington, D. C.

Even while the Israelites were pursued by Pharaoh's army, God had a plan. Now, at the edge of the Red Sea, the Israelites have no escape from the mighty Egyptian army. They turn to Moses who, as always, turns to God for a plan.

God's angel and the pillar of cloud, which have led the army of Israel through the wilderness, now move behind the Israelite camp to stand between Pharaoh's army and the people. While the Egyptians wait through the dark night until they can continue their pursuit, the Israelites cross the Red Sea, which God has "turned into dry land." At daybreak the great army of Pharaoh rushes after the Israelites, only to realize too late that there is one more miracle in God's plan. Moses stretches out his hand a second time, and "the entire army of Pharaoh" perishes.

God shares the plan with Moses, who trusts and listens to God and does what he is told to do. The Israelites' escape from their Egyptian pursuers happens as God knew it would. And the people, miraculously delivered from a mighty and persistent enemy, understand that indeed "the Lord is fighting for them." Having seen with their own eyes God's "great power," they put their trust in [God] and in Moses [God's] servant" (NIV).

During dark times when our faith is tested, we often tell God what to do, how to do it, and when to make it happen. Or because of our limited human understanding we may, like children, continually appeal to God, asking what to do next. God uses such times as opportunities for our spiritual growth, but we first have to accept the presence and power of God's protecting love between us and our fears. Then we can watch God's plan unfold—that all will know the power of the Lord.

PRAYER: Father, I want to do your will. Thank you for your faithfulness to me, and help me to be faithful to you. When there is darkness in my life, help me to remember you will bring the light. Amen.

What's your song for today? When the Israelites safely reach the other side of the Red Sea, they, as a gathered community, take the time to sing a song of thanksgiving. They recall what they have endured and how God has guided them each step of the way.

Can't you picture the joyous celebration of singing and shouting praises to God? Can't you feel the rhythms of Miriam leading the women in dance as they shake their tambourines and sing, "Sing to the LORD, for he has triumphed gloriously"? Can't you hear the sounds of their stomping feet and clapping hands?

Our daily blessings of recuperating from sickness, receiving a long-awaited pay raise, a child's favorable report card, reuniting with a friend, or completing a difficult task are all worthy of sharing and celebrating with others. God moves mysteriously in our lives every day. Bringing family and friends together and telling our stories to them, especially the children, gives us the opportunity and the joy to spread the good news, give thanks, and "sing to the Lord." God triumphs gloriously in our lives every day.

Have you sung your song today? Take the time to think about it, smile about it. Give words and melody to your song as you sing your thanks, for God is worthy.

PRAYER: Father, I know that you are with me all the time. Help me to acknowledge, record, and tell others of the blessings you bestow every day. Help me also to rejoice in the stories of others that praise your good works. Amen.

A friend of mine keeps a record, proudly reporting that he never forgets mean things done and said to him, as well as the praises he *didn't* receive from years back. When children say, "I'm sorry," we hug and continue to love them. Even when they do not say it, we love them and soon forget the misdeed. When adults do not apologize, we often hold it against them. Yet Jesus tells us to love our enemies; forgiveness is an act of love.

Peter asks Jesus, "How often should I forgive?"

Jesus answers, "Seventy-seven times."

Seven times is a lot of forgiving; seventy-seven times seems incomprehensible! That's a lot of forgiving, though we aren't going to count. And that's the point of Jesus' reply: counting means we haven't actually forgiven. Counting means we're still keeping track, holding tightly to these hurts.

Forgiving others releases them from guilt. It frees us from the collage of unpleasant words and deeds pasted in our memories, and from the burden of anger that we carry against others. It also helps us to become more aware of times when we have trespassed against someone and didn't apologize.

Jesus provided the ultimate model of forgiving, when on the cross, with nails hammered into his hands and feet, he cried out, "Father, forgive them; for they do not know what they are doing" (Luke 23:34, NIV).

PRAYER: Forgiving God, help me to be more like Jesus. Give me the words and courage to say sincerely to others, "You are forgiven!" Help me also to ask for forgiveness from you and from those against whom I have sinned. Amen.

Jesus tells the story of the king whose slave owes him ten thousand talents. Wanting to settle accounts, the king tells the slave that he plans to sell him and his family since he hasn't repaid his debt. The slave falls to his knees, begs forgiveness, and promises to pay if given another chance. In truth, the debt is such an amount that the slave can never repay it, making the king's subsequent forgiveness of the debt all the more dramatic.

Leaving the king, the slave comes upon a fellow slave who owes him money. He demands payment at once. The fellow slave falls to his knees and begs forgiveness, but he finds that the one to whom he is beholden has a hard heart. How quickly a king's softened heart and a debt forgiven are forgotten.

Which model do we follow? In our daily activities at our workplaces, on the highways, in our homes we may encounter people who ignore us, speak harshly to us or even become aggressive toward us. Some persons may owe us a favor or money. Can we forgive them, and continually forgive them seventy-seven times, as Jesus told us to do?

The good news is that we don't have to carry around unpleasant remembrances in our hearts and minds. When we recognize our debtors as forgiven children of God just as we are, we can project thoughts of love toward them. God's forgiveness teaches us to behave toward one another with patience and compassion in times of misfortune that inevitably befall us all. As Jesus says, "Forgive your brother and sister from your heart."

PRAYER: Loving Father, please forgive me for being unforgiving toward others. Soften my heart and help me to remember the love that Jesus modeled. Teach me to forgive so that I am free to love fully. Amen.

The nations of the world at times seem to grow apart, rather than together. They take sides, choosing enemies and friends and making little effort to understand one another's languages or customs. Even Christian denominations judge other ways of worshiping God, condemning the music of some churches, the style of preaching, and the methods of prayer. Consequently, we often do not acknowledge other people as our sisters and brothers in Christ. We judge them for what we decide are their sins.

Our eating habits often differ: some eat meat; some do not; others fast regularly. We observe the sabbath on different days, often accepting only one way of worshiping God—our way! We allow these small differences to cloud the real issue of whether we glorify God in our worship and daily living.

Paul, in his words to the Romans, addresses some deeply held convictions among the members of the faith community. They, like us, have differing customs and cultural issues. He begins by considering the matter of dietary laws: some support the restrictive approach of the Jews; others eat meat sacrificed to idols. Whether eating vegetables or meat, each position makes a strong statement about the believer's fundamental convictions. How could one be reconciled with the other? Paul goes on to discuss the observation of special days: some treat all days alike; others regard some days as sacred.

For Paul, the new age inaugurated by Christ sets aside all previous injunctions about food and worship. God welcomes all, and as Paul states in verse 6, whether eating or abstaining, observing sacred days or not, the important fact is that all is done in honor of the Lord.

If we err in our understanding, God will forgive us and continue to work in us according to our individual needs. God accepts the way each of us glorifies God's name.

PRAYER: O God, help me worship you with all my heart, soul, and mind in the way that is best for me and to respect the worship ways of others whose cultures and convictions may differ. Amen.

SUNDAY, SEPTEMBER 11 • Read Romans 14:7-12

This scripture reminds us that we do not live or die alone; we live and die to the Lord, while growing in our relationship with others. Our greatest spiritual growth takes place when we are with others. We can withdraw for a period into a monastery, retreat area, or our home to meditate, evaluate self, and affirm Jesus' teachings and God's laws, but the practice and living of these takes place when we are in community with others.

In our neighborhoods, workplaces, churches, malls, and even in our homes, there will always be persons who worship, pray, and serve God in ways that differ from ours. Thus there is the potential for conflict, for we are all human. But as Christians living for our Lord, our focus must be on the choices we make for the Lord, not the choices others make.

We are not in these communities to preach, scold, or be passive. We are there to be a blessing and to recognize one another as members of God's family. God calls us to be Christ in action by what we let the Holy Spirit say and do through us. We receive love to pass on even in the most difficult of times. At the end of each day, we can look back on our activities and ask ourselves, "Was I a blessing or a hindrance in this situation?" Jesus lived, died, and lives again for us now and calls us to live and die for him.

The Lord says, "As I live, every knee shall bow to me, and every tongue shall give praise to God. So then, each of us will be accountable to God."

PRAYER: Dear God, right now we need your blessings. Forgive us all for allowing conflict to enter this gathering; may your love show through in all that we do. Amen.

Is God Enough?

September 12–18, 2005 • *Robert L. Wise*[‡]

MONDAY, SEPTEMBER 12 • Read Exodus 16:2-7

The Israelites find themselves in the middle of a barren desert because they have trusted God's guidance. Now they have nothing but empty grocery sacks and growling stomachs. They want an accounting from God, Moses, and Aaron before the bar of justice as they ask the age-old question: Can God provide enough to meet our needs?

We probably wouldn't put the issue in quite the same terms, but we get equally upset with our leaders when matters don't turn out as we'd expected. We know what it is to grumble against God when the stock market goes bad and the economic indicators turn sour. The issue? We trust only what we can see!

Assembling in the desert, the Israelites see only sand, heat waves, and barrenness. Maybe God is only a mirage. Egypt had been difficult, but they had had enough to eat. Yet they completely miss God's point: humanity does not live by bread alone; God offers a new basis for security.

The Israelites would learn to see with the eyes of trust!

Yes, our leaders will make mistakes. Yes, national economic ups and downs will affect us. Yes, at times it will appear that we don't have enough. Yet these circumstantial factors should never lead us to despair because our God continually stands in the shadows, holding all matters in divine hands.

Resolve to change. Rather than grumble, put your trust in the God who always provides.

PRAYER: O Lord, forgive me for failing to believe you will accomplish what I cannot see at this moment. Please give me eyes of trust. Amen.

[‡]Bishop of the Communion of Evangelical Episcopal Churches, living in Oklahoma City, Oklahoma.

TUESDAY, SEPTEMBER 13 • Read Exodus 16:8-9

While we generally don't think of ourselves as being overheard when we complain, this story makes it clear that we are *always* heard by a most unexpected source. The omnipresent God of the universe stands at the door listening.

When we sit quietly in our church pews we are convinced the Almighty is paying careful attention to us. But when we sit at the kitchen table at home, God is nowhere in sight. We quietly confide our doubts to each other. Moses' response warns the Israelites that at such moments God stands listening. What was the issue for them and us? We can't trust what we can't see.

As the Israelites struggle in the barren desert, they see no alternative to eventual starvation. During their time in Egypt they had looked out at the night campfire to see pots of meat cooking. In their new situation all they can see is sand. Their conclusion: they will perish.

We too don't trust what seems intangible. Oh, yes, we say we believe in God, but we have few written reports of what God looks like. On the other hand, we can instantly identify a five-dollar bill. We've seen financial statements and bank accounts. We can carry stocks and securities in a briefcase. We grumble when these symbols of affluence disappear.

After nearly four thousand years, we find it painful to admit that we struggle with the same problem the Israelites had. We must place our ultimate confidence in a God we will never see with our eyes. Is God enough? To those who see with the heart, the Almighty always is. Let's stop complaining.

PRAYER: O Lord, please heal the blindness of my heart that I may see with faith. Grant me the capacity to trust you far more than I do the tangible securities on which I so willingly base my life. Amen.

The passing of the centuries has not diminished the power of the story of manna and quail. The Israelites offer grumbling, and God responds with an abundance of grub. As the days go by, the supply from the hand of the Lord does not diminish. God's answer is a never-ending abundance.

In the mornings and evenings after that first provision, what must the Israelites be thinking? Are they repentant and remorseful? The stories that follow in the book of Exodus don't paint that picture. We keep meeting a stiff-necked people who never get the lesson. Despite the lavishness of the Lord's provision, they quickly seem to forget.

What was the problem? Scripture repeatedly tells us that these people had memory problems: they forgot what God had provided in the past!

The Israelite problem seems absurd when we read about it in the Bible. We can easily stand back and lament the people's lack of awareness—as long as we don't think about our own. But let's put the shoe on the other foot. How often do we reflect on what God has given us? Consider our common issues: health, provision, housing, employment, opportunities, and material blessings. When we look at all we have, can we say that God has ignored us? Do we believe that the Almighty has removed a divine hand from our life?

Truthfully we all have a hard time remembering everything God has given us. Our lives, so full of abundance, often do not reflect our acknowledgment of God as the ultimate source of all blessing.

Why not stop right now and thank God for all that you have received? The Lord Almighty remains our provider.

SUGGESTION FOR PRAYER: Use this time to thank God for all your blessings and provisions.

Consider how the Israelites forget the wonderful things God does for them during their time of desert wandering. But the psalmist knows the significance of remembering. He calls the people who worship God to stay in touch with the many ways God's sufficiency covers them. Memory can make the difference.

Time has not changed the importance of remembering that God is enough. These six verses suggest three ways to keep the importance of God's work clearly in mind.

First, "glory in his holy name." God gives Israel the means of knowing the holy. Calling on God's name is like having God's telephone number. No longer are the Israelites a frightened people howling in the wind—they have an intimate relationship with God.

Second, "seek the LORD and his strength" reminds the Israelites they can depend on God to support them regardless of their difficulties and trials. God is the source of their capacity.

Third, "remember the wonderful works" admonishes the Israelites to stay in touch with the fact that God cares for the people. God has intervened in desperate moments. Those who had watched the waters part and Pharaoh's chariots disappear in the flood would know the difference this provision could make.

Here are three words for us to live by today: *Call. Seek. Remember.* Rather than allow yourself to obsess when the tide isn't flowing in your direction, stop and practice these three small disciplines. They have the power to put your life in a divine perspective and grant the capacities to meet today's needs. Memory can make the difference!

PRAYER: O Lord, I know memory can change my attitude of indifference. Today I want to know, look, and remember! Amen.

Last night I received an urgent phone call. A close friend and former staff member had just had a stroke. His wife was frantic, the situation desperate. The odds of his survival were slim. At such moments, the stakes reach their highest level.

Is God enough when we stand at death's door?

Sooner or later every person in the universe must face this question. The sands in the hourglass are about to run out. What can we believe at such a frightening moment?

Paul offers an unexpected answer to the Philippian church when he states that no matter what happens he will be in fine shape. In fact, he will gain the most by dying! What a surprising answer!

Paul's perspective has changed since his earlier confrontation with Christ, alive on the other side of the crucifixion. No longer is the issue keeping a heart beating or brain cells alive. Death has been defeated. The new question becomes how to serve this Christ who has given us so much life. How can we most effectively serve Jesus Christ?

As I stood with the phone in my hand, thinking about my good friend's fight for life, I recognized again that the most pressing issue did not revolve around his continued breathing. The pressing matter was how he would serve Christ. Here or there? And that was true for me as well.

Is God enough when we come to the end of the journey? Paul answers clearly, "You bet!" Today our task is to keep on the journey faithfully, serving Christ up to the moment we finish our time in this world.

PRAYER: O Lord, setting aside even my ultimate fears, I have one desire today: please help me to serve Christ effectively. Amen.

Once we have settled the question about death and we continue living, what other significant problems do we worry about? We have gotten beyond the number one fear of all humans. Should there be any other issues?

Paul knew that every day of our lives engages us in a spiritual battle that has the capacity to diminish our characters, our effectiveness, and our ability to serve God. This struggle does not usually come in some heroic moment of dramatic proportions. Most of the time we face the battle by what we say, do, and decide to be. It happens most often in the little things.

Paul's encouragement to the Philippians would serve us well: "Live your life in a manner worthy of the gospel of Christ." Paul put one foot in the first century and the other foot in the twenty-first century, telling time and eternity that it makes no difference in which age we live. The issues remain the same. Are we living a life worthy of the gospel?

Worthiness is about how I fight this spiritual war that erupts around me each day of the week. Instead of hate, I must give love. Rather than allowing my heart to fill with animosity, I must cultivate joy. When all hope is gone, I must recover the optimism of God demonstrated in the cross of Christ. Should pain come, I can remember what a privilege it is to suffer for Christ's sake. The closer I come to Christ, the more I will face the struggles of this battle with evil.

I already have the answer for all of these conflicts. God is enough! God will provide what is needed, not only to endure but to ensure our victory.

PRAYER: O Lord, I want to live a life worthy of you. Help me push back all other considerations and concentrate on worthiness. Amen.

This week we have explored the question of whether God is enough to meet our needs. From the Israelites' desert experience to Paul's certainty, the affirmation has been clear: God is.

In today's parable, Jesus reminds us of the importance of staying faithful to the one who has called us. Within the folds of this story resides both a promise and a warning.

The promise? The men and women God calls into service receive compensation for their efforts, provision according to the terms of God's agreement with us. At the end of the day, we will be paid at the pleasure of the master of the field.

At times we worry about the promise's fulfillment. It may appear unlikely that our heavenly Father will keep God's word. However, the story reminds us that regardless of the circumstances God's promise will be kept!

The warning? In the last line of this story, Jesus tells us the parable's meaning: "So the last will be first, and the first will be last." His play on words warns that the people who should be first can end up last! Because of envy and the fear of being shortchanged, they may actually negate God's generosity.

While other people may seem to do better or to be more blessed, we gain nothing through questioning God's justice. God remains sovereign and moves through the world in mysterious ways. Our task is to cling to the promises made to us and to put our confidence in God's provision. The promise is sure.

God will fulfill God's word. Count on it. God remains true.

PRAYER: O Lord, thank you for speaking your word to us. I will put my trust in what you have said and remember you are always enough. Amen.

Water from the Rock

September 19–25, 2005 • *Carol Birkland*[‡]

MONDAY, SEPTEMBER 19 • **Read Exodus 17:1-7**

Wilderness ahead
Weary and thirsty people
Taste God's miracle.

The Israelites stand around Moses, thirsty and demanding water. They grumble, doubt, and demand. As before, Moses turns to God for guidance. God instructs Moses and Moses obeys. The water pours forth from a rock, an inanimate, lifeless rock.

We can read the story and say God provided for the Israelites and performed a great miracle, but there is more to this reading. We can look at the children of Israel and see ourselves in this story. We wander through the wilderness of our lives, sometimes with direction and great purpose, sometimes not—or perhaps we try to ignore the direction of God's leading. We are often thirsty in a way, thirsty for the answers that will give our lives more meaning. We thirst for the knowledge that will increase our faith or for the insights that add meaning to our lives.

If we go one step further and think of the metaphor of Christ as the Rock from which the living water of eternal life flows, we can take comfort in the fact that we will thirst no more if we believe in Christ as Savior. God provided water from a rock in the desert for the Israelites. Through Christ our Rock, God has provided living water and salvation for all believers.

PRAYER: Gracious and giving God, quench our spiritual thirst. Fill our hearts with the knowledge that you are always present as we wander through the wilderness of life. Help us to share that belief with all who thirst. Amen

---

[‡]Journalist/editor; former director of Christian education, writer of Christian education curriculum; member, United Church of Christ; living in Cleveland, Ohio.

TUESDAY, SEPTEMBER 20 • **Read Psalm 78:1-4**

Give ear and listen
Words for all generations
Wonders of the Lord.

The psalmist reminds us of the miracle God performed in the wilderness, which in turn reminds us that God is always present in our lives to meet our needs. God continues to guide us. We are asked to listen and bend our ears to God's words. But the psalmist says that God's words will come in a parable, suggesting that we will have to listen carefully and consider what the meaning might be. The message will relate to things that we already know, that our forebears have told us. The psalmist goes on to say that the generations will be taught from these words and that God's great deeds will become apparent.

What cryptic words. This psalm has been referred to as the riddle of rebellion. It does not belong to the basic types of psalms such as hymns or laments but stands alone as a challenge to the reader. So what does it mean?

The psalm, a call to listen, perhaps is intended to pique the interest of those who waver in their beliefs. It serves to remind us that the law has been given to Israel and suggests that the precepts of the law need to be told to the generations so that all may learn and obey God's commandments.

The psalmist asks us to "give ear" and hear of the wonders God has made. It is difficult, in our cluttered lives, to find time to listen, but we might try to find the time to pause, to sit in silence and listen for the will of God.

PRAYER: Gracious God, open our hearts and ears. Help us take the time to look for and hear your wonders. We are ready to be your witnesses; we want to tell all generations of your glory. Amen.

O glorious deeds
God calls water forth from rocks
Unfaithful believe.

In these verses the psalmist tells us that God has not only given the law to Israel but also has redeemed its people by bringing them safely through the wilderness. He calls us to remember that God led the people by day and night and that God caused water to flow from a rock. The psalmist establishes God as both guide and provider.

Is the riddle of yesterday's reading solved by the facts presented in this second section? Is the psalmist calling us to belief and faithfulness by recounting God's guidance and sustenance in our lives?

Finding God in our daily lives can be difficult. We have no cloudlike spirit to lead us by day, no fiery light to guide us home at night. Our water pours from a faucet usually with no thought of God at all. Our wilderness is crammed full of distractions and realities that keep us from seeing God before us or by our side.

Yet the psalmist says listen, God's words have been with you for generations. They have been a riddle to your thinking, and God has sent signs along the way. Perhaps we need to look for the guiding hand of God; to notice the gifts, like water at the kitchen sink, that sustain us. This psalm calls for our awareness of God's daily miracles in our lives and encourages us to tell the generations about that presence.

PRAYER: Gracious and giving God, open our ears to the words of faith that have been spoken to us. Help us teach others about your years of guidance in the lives of your believers. May we always look for the signs that remind us that we are ever in your care. Amen.

THURSDAY, SEPTEMBER 22 • **Read Philippians 2:1-10**

Christ above all names
Now every tongue confessing
The glory of God.

The apostle Paul exhibited great skill in writing encouragement to the early Christian churches. Today's reading exemplifies his zeal for the followers of Jesus to remain faithful to their beliefs. His words carry meaning for Christians of the twenty-first century as well.

In this epistle to the church at Philippi, Paul reminds the readers that Christ has given the faithful the encouragement to love and to participate in the joys of the Spirit. He instructs the congregation to love others as Christ loved. Paul talks of absolute love, love that is without selfishness or conceit. He says that believers are to love others more than themselves. Today, as then, Christians have trouble living up to these expectations. Bombarded with societal affectations, employer demands, temptations to meet our own needs before helping others, few of us find time to do what we must to survive, let alone turn our love and attention to others.

As Christians we gather to worship; pray for others; give of our time, talents, and wages to help the less fortunate; and strive to love others as Christ has loved. Often, however, we remain unconnected from others, and we end up wondering if our efforts were enough. What else does fulfillment of the obligations of our faith require? Paul might tell us that we can find encouragement as we turn to God in prayer, as we confess Jesus as the Christ. As we join with other believers, we enter the journey that is our calling.

PRAYER: Gracious God, help us to love others as Christ has loved us. Help us to see the image of Christ in the faces of others, so that we may learn to love all people for Christ's sake. Amen.

FRIDAY, SEPTEMBER 23 • Read Philippians 2:11-13

Always obey God
Look to your own salvation
God's at work in you.

Paul tells the faithful to "get to work"! Previously, he encouraged members of the congregation to model themselves after Christ. Now he states, "work out your own salvation." It seems an odd choice of words. But the idea here is not to do good deeds in order to be saved; rather it is a mandate to make your life an example of your beliefs.

There's a tall order. Monastic Christians and other Christian sects have taken this edict to heart and have cloistered themselves away to be faithful to their beliefs, but most Christians live out their faith in the society of others.

Practicing our faith in a way that points to God rather than ourselves can be a big challenge. We may begin by recognizing that God is within us, enabling and encouraging us to act and react toward others in a just, humane, and loving way. In our basic kindness toward others we pass on God's love.

Recognizing our salvation and the grace of God that it represents can empower us to leave thoughts of self behind as we interact with others. This can be easy when we interact with pleasant, kind people but nearly impossible with others who test our patience. Paul's words encourage our best attempts at loving and caring for others. They remind us that God is at work in us and that God intends that we succeed in passing on divine love.

PRAYER: Gracious God, fill us with your Spirit that everyday we may go out into the world knowing that you love us. Give us courage to pass your love on to others. May our hearts be open to serve you through our actions and to show love to others in the name of Jesus. Amen.

SATURDAY, SEPTEMBER 24 • Read Matthew 21:23-27

Pointed questions asked
Jesus amid the teachers
Authority shown.

Matthew relates an incident in which Jesus' authority is challenged. While throngs of people had welcomed Jesus as Messiah earlier in the week, the church patriarchs confront him as he enters the Temple and question his authority.

The chief priests and elders ask, "Who do you think you are?" They want to know by whose authority Jesus acts and teaches. Jesus quickly answers their question with one of his own regarding the authority of John the Baptist, which requires them to take a stand on the role of John and to acknowledge God's authority in the lives of prophets.

In those times, people widely recognized John's ministry as a commission from God. If the men questioning Jesus deny that God gave him authority, they would be going against the popular view regarding John's authority. While the chief priests and elders want to discount Jesus' authority, they do not want to deny that God does give authority to prophets. After a discussion, they choose to tell Jesus they do not know the answer to his question. Jesus then replies that if they cannot name the authority by which John acted, then he will not tell them the source of his authority. However, the answer is implicit.

Jesus points to God as the ultimate authority for his actions. God is also at work in our lives, ever available as we seek to live our lives as role models of Christ.

PRAYER: Gracious God, help us recognize your authority in our lives as you prompt and encourage us to love and respect others. Amen.

Two sons, two answers
One big question yet remains
Who has done God's will?

Jesus describes the responses of two sons. The father asks each son to perform a task. One says no to the request but later goes to work in the vineyard. The other says yes but does not do the will of his father. Jesus then asks the chief priests and elders which son did the will of the father.

This Gospel reading presents many challenges. While biblical commentaries disagree over the exact wording, as noted in various translations of this text in the different Bible versions, all agree that the allegorical message of text has to do with Jesus' challenging the authority of those questioning him and their obedience to God's will. In this way he turns their challenge back on them.

Jesus suggests to the chief priests and elders that while they believe they are doing God's will, perhaps they are deceiving themselves. He tells them that the marginalized people of society, which at that time were the tax collectors and prostitutes, have a better chance of entering the kingdom than they do. These people believed the words of salvation and were baptized by John.

We need to consider these words in reference to our own lives. Most of us listen to the word of God, have been baptized, and seek to live responsibly as Christians. However, at times God has called us, and we said no, perhaps repenting to do God's will later. Or perhaps we have said yes to God's calling and strayed from our good intentions. We all feel at some time in our lives we have failed to respond to what Jesus calls the way of righteousness. Luckily for us, God is forgiving.

PRAYER: Gracious God, may our answer to your call always be the one you wish to hear. Forgive us and help us to move toward better understanding and acceptance of your will for our lives. Amen.

God Continues to Speak

September 26–October 2, 2005 • Marilyn W. Spry[‡]

MONDAY, SEPTEMBER 26 • Read Exodus 20:1-4, 7-9

As leaders of a marriage communication retreat, my husband and I defused an intense moment when a young woman expressed frustration to her husband: "Are you listening to me? How am I supposed to know you or what you are thinking?" We asked the couple to face each other, hold hands, and look into each other's eyes as they talked. The resulting sense of connection amazed them.

Sometimes we think that God neither listens nor speaks to us. How are we supposed to know who God is or what God values? This week's scriptures reveal different ways that God speaks to us when we give God our full and undivided attention.

Today's verses make a claim on our life, indicating the importance of a loving relationship with God. It is as if God says, "I am the only God. I am the one who loves you and has acted to deliver you and lead you to new life. I want your attention and love." Such a relationship will take time, focused attention, and wholehearted desire.

In marriage retreats, couples often receive an assignment to spend time each day listening and giving each other full attention. Once a week they are to go on a date and spend a longer time sharing dreams and longings. They remember the love that brought them together. God asks that we nurture our love and relationship with the divine, giving God central place.

SUGGESTION FOR MEDITATION: Sit for a moment in silent and loving companionship with God. Remember how much God desires a relationship with you. Listen with your heart. How is God speaking to you today?

[‡]Pastor, First Christian Church, Downers Grove, Illinois; pastoral counselor, retreat leader, spiritual director; teaching pastor/supervisor, Divinity School of the University of Chicago.

Carol approached her fifth-grade Sunday school class with anticipation and excitement. The class had been studying the Ten Commandments. When she asked the students what they remembered from their last meeting, Becky waved her hand eagerly. She could not remember the specifics, but she knew it was when God acted like her mom and gave us all the no-nos!

Too often we get stuck in thinking that God speaks mostly to us in terms of no-nos. We feel that God's main intent is to limit our freedom. In reality, the commandments represent God's way of guiding us into positive, life-fulfilling relationships. Our faith is not simply a private experience with God. Jesus makes that clear when he summarizes all Ten Commandments by saying we are to love God with our whole heart, mind, soul, and strength and our neighbor as ourselves.

Our loving covenant relationship with God automatically relates us to all the people God has made and loves. Far from restricting us, the commandments provide a way to live with others that does not cause pain but rather builds up relationships instead of tearing them down. The assurance that the commandments are a positive plan for living resides in God's promise to show "steadfast love to the thousandth generation of those who love me and keep my commandments."

Our attitude and actions toward those we can see serve as a good barometer of our love for God whom we have not seen. We cannot love God while acting in hurtful ways toward others. The two are inextricably bound together.

Prayer: O God, may my attitudes and actions toward others speak clearly of my love for you and all your children. May your perfect law bring with it true freedom. Amen.

WEDNESDAY, SEPTEMBER 28 • **Read Psalm 19:1-10**

Two wonderful days lay ahead of me as I began my first spiritual retreat in a beautiful area called Vision of Peace. The hermitage overlooked the powerful Mississippi River, whose rhythmic flow would calm my frenzied spirit. A lush forest with enticing trails surrounded the area.

I had come here looking for peace and a closer relationship with God. My spiritual director had suggested that first I might take a nap to give my tired body rest, then go for a walk, taking my time to look and listen carefully as I absorbed the beauty around me. He was sure that I would hear the voice that "is not heard" yet "goes out through all the earth."

I headed down the steep path that led me into the cool darkness of the forest. A delicate web brushed my face, and when I stepped back, I saw the sun glistening on a spider's intricate artistry that completely blocked my path. Overcome with awe at the complex wonder of God's creation, and not wanting to disturb such beauty, I backed up and went another direction.

My retreat began with questions and anticipation about God's direction and plan for my life. I didn't expect that God would speak to me through the work and patience of a tiny creature. But with the psalmist, I came to understand that indeed "the law of the LORD is perfect, reviving the soul." The commandments of the creator of the glorious handiwork that is Earth are "more to be desired . . . than gold" and "sweeter also than honey."

SUGGESTION FOR MEDITATION: Take some deep breaths; become aware of God's creative energy flowing through you. Allow God to revive your soul through the wonder of creation.

In the Chicago area where I live, it is not uncommon to hear on the evening news another horrible story about the abuse of children. Today six children were found shut in a basement, living in filth with no heat or food. The story appalled me.

I recently talked with some parents who seldom get their children to Sunday school or worship. When I expressed concern about the children's Christian education and process of growing in faith in Christ, they stated their belief in letting their children make their own faith decisions. They did not want to force anything upon them. I asked them to consider how their children would be equipped to make those decisions. While these children were materially privileged and not physically abused, I believe they were experiencing spiritual deprivation.

How will our children come to have faith? How will they know the ways to make decisions that please God? How will they learn about God's love and forgiveness as they begin to face their own sin and responsibility for life? When we fail to teach and provide guidance for our children in the ways of God, that is a form of neglect!

Today's psalm calls us to give praise and thanks to God for caring for us enough to give us the law to guide us. Far from being oppressive, the law revives the soul, makes the simple wise, and causes hearts to rejoice! Through the law we receive enlightenment and understanding that is enduring and dependable. We are often blind to our own motivations and hidden faults. We depend upon God's guidance through the words of scripture and the movement of God's spirit to help us.

PRAYER: O Loving Parent, how grateful we are that you do not neglect or leave us on our own to figure life out and find our own way. In thanksgiving, may we also lead and help our loved ones to find the way that is acceptable to you and brings new life. Amen.

We laugh when we hear the comedian Rodney Dangerfield spouting his trademark line, "I get no respect." But it is no laughing matter when God continues to speak to humanity and is ignored over and over again.

According to the Gospel of Matthew, Jesus tells this parable at a crucial moment in his life. He has come into Jerusalem in what we often call the triumphal entry just before the Passover. He knows that while the people hail him as a king, they are looking for a political savior; they have not been listening to his message centered in humble service.

Jesus enters the Temple and cleans house, showing his frustration and anger with leaders who are more interested in making a profit than in providing a place of worship. They are more interested in challenging his authority than in trying to hear the truth as he teaches.

Never giving up, Jesus tells today's parable and, in so doing, holds up a mirror to the faces of the chief priests and Pharisees in an attempt to help them see the truth. The parable of the wicked tenants reminds them of the many messengers of God who have been ignored and abused. Even the son of the landowner is rejected and killed.

As we read the parable, we may wonder how the religious leaders could ignore and reject such a persistent message. Perhaps the judgment and the hope come to us when we realize that having heard the gospel taught and preached many times in our lives, we must take special care that we not be deadened to its message. We must approach it as if we had never heard it before in our lives, as if we hunger and thirst to know and apply its meaning to our lives.

SUGGESTION FOR MEDITATION: What good news am I missing because I think I already know the story or believe that it is meant for someone else? Could it be that I need to hear it again as if for the first time?

PRAYER: O God, open my ears that I may hear. Amen.

The first activity of the seminar involved getting acquainted with several people through sharing information. The room was abuzz with chatter for several minutes. Then the leader asked us to think about how we had identified ourselves. The list included names, family background, schooling, and degrees earned. We also shared job titles, roles, and credentials.

As participants reflected on that experience, we realized that most of us identified ourselves and established our sense of worth by our accomplishments and vocations. Our sharing almost had a "can you top this" quality. The next time we did the exercise, the leader asked us to share qualities about ourselves, our beliefs, and what was really important and valuable to us. What information would help someone to know us better as a person? What really gave us a sense of worth? Many of us found this harder to do.

The apostle Paul understood this tendency to look at the outward credentials in order to establish our worth and value. He could do it with the best if them, and he had quite a list. But Paul shares this list, not to brag but to show that if we are looking at worldly credentials as a criteria of our worth, his are as good as or better than most!

However, we also know how quickly all of those "bragging rights" can disappear. The loss of our health, a job, a marriage, or the exhaustion that makes it hard to keep pushing are all known to us. Paul confesses that outward success is worth nothing when compared to knowing Christ Jesus as our Lord. God speaks powerfully to us of our worth through the death and resurrection of Jesus Christ. Through faith, God's mercy and grace welcomes us home with the assurance that we belong to God.

PRAYER: O God, thank you for giving me the best credential of all. I am your child, saved by faith through Jesus Christ. Amen.

At times, Paul seems to contradict himself. On the one hand he feels fulfilled and complete because he realizes that his worth and success have already been accomplished by Jesus Christ. His faith in Christ relieves his anxiety about his status. On the other hand, Paul talks about the vision and goal that he still sees and for which he continues to work and strive.

A satirical TV comedy called *Scrubs* takes potshots at the egos and manipulations that take place in the medical world. But the theme song for the show contains a telling phrase: "I can't do this all on my own," a confession of reliance and interdependence.

Paul can have every confidence in his worth and daily witness because he knows that he lives by the forgiveness of Christ, which allows him to leave the weight of the past behind. His oneness with Christ gives him the strength for the present challenge and task because he leans on Jesus Christ. He can still be future oriented and live with hope of finally reaching the prize of God's call because Jesus Christ has gone before him and overcome death.

We also know that Christ walks beside us as we move forward. Our vision and hope can give meaning to our present struggles. This week's scripture affirms that God never stops speaking to us. This anonymous statement was found in a church in Sussex, England, and was written around 1730:

> A vision without a task is a dream.
> A task without a vision is drudgery.
> A vision with a task is the hope of the world.

SUGGESTION FOR MEDITATION: Spend time listening to God. What vision or goal is God giving you? How will God help you as you move toward this goal?

What Will the Children Think?

October 3–9, 2005 • Christine Claire Archer[‡]

MONDAY, OCTOBER 3 • Read Exodus 32:1-8

Can you imagine what the Israelite children are thinking as they watch their parents eating, drinking, and rising up to revel? How quickly children catch parents in moral and spiritual inconsistencies. No doubt, these same children have been fed and edified by the telling and retelling of the mighty saving hand of the one true God—how God rescued the people from the bondage of slavery in Egypt.

Yet when Moses tarries longer than expected, the parents, anxious and impatient, turn to Aaron for a quick fix. Aaron colludes with the people, melting their little ornaments into one big idolatrous ornament. The golden calf not only assuages their fears but demands nothing from them spiritually or morally. The parents then give into an indulgent revelry, while their children watch, some with envy, some with disillusionment, and all with confusion.

Many of us live in the United States, a country based on Judeo-Christian values but rife with self-absorption and materialism. We try to live our commitments to worship, read the Bible, and pray with our families. During tough times, do our children see us turn to these true sources of strength, or do they see us run to our golden calves—malls, bars, gyms, television, Internet, refrigerator? The faith of the present generation and all those to come depends upon our choices.

PRAYER: Lord, thank you for loving us with a love that is jealous when we worship things other than you. Give us the humility to see what these things are and the desire and strength to root them out of our life. Amen.

[‡]Clinical social worker; parent/family educator and advocate; layperson, Manchester First United Methodist Church; living in Manchester, Tennessee.

God created, nurtured, and delivered God's beloved children, Israel, supplying them not only with their needs but also God's constant presence. I am reminded of the many single mothers I work with who have sacrificed much to raise their children alone—with little or no support from the children's fathers. They are the ones who sit for hours at the kitchen table with one child working on third-grade math, with laundry in the dryer, and with a daughter's sixth-grade science project waiting in the wing.

One day, Mom is late or makes a demand or corrects or says no to the latest request, and then the teenager is stomping out the door to "live with Dad." Mothers and Yahweh feel the anger burning in the cracks of their broken hearts. Mothers and Yahweh want to pull out and be left alone. Anger tempts Yahweh to destroy the people. Moms often abdicate and give up—"Live where you want. Do what you want. I'm tired of fighting!"

But then with Moses' courageous intervention, God remembers God's love for these children. Moses wisely names a few (Abraham, Isaac, and Israel), and God sees them in God's heart. Moses reminds Yahweh of promises made to deliver these children and of Israel's enemies who watch to see if God will be faithful.

And as the mother flings herself on her bed, she sees the pictures of her child, gap-toothed, grinning, with birthday cake smashed on his or her face, and she remembers. "Can a mother forget the baby at her breast and have no compassion on the child she has borne?" (Isa. 49:15, NIV).

Yahweh and mothers cannot resist extending once again the hand of the second chance.

PRAYER: Lord, thank you for your seemingly infinite patience with us. We don't want to take advantage of the second chances you offer. Amen.

How many times has your family enjoyed sitting around telling its "signature" stories? The Archers have many such stories: the time our car "blew up, then burned up" on our way back from a dirt-cheap family camping trip; the Christmas of the ice storm when we went through Christmas Eve and morning with no electricity, no hot turkey dinner, and no eggs-and-bacon breakfast. Or worse still—no way to try out the new computer video games. We never tire of recounting these tales.

The psalmist doesn't either. Again we hear the "golden calf at Horeb" story, sandwiched between amazing songs of praise to the God who is always good and whose mighty acts always save. The psalmist retells the tale, not just to entertain but to further deepen the family bond of the people of Israel.

The psalmist tells the tale to establish the whole history of the people of God in the context of God's salvation. His tale both encourages and exhorts his listeners to continue in faithfulness and obedience to the same living God.

As we Archers tell the story of the camping trip, we always stress God's protection of our family (not a hair on any of our heads was harmed), the good Samaritan locals who provided roadside help and hospitality, and God's generous provision of alternative reliable transportation. We retell the "icy Christmas" as God's gentle turning of our family from the gift-giving frenzy back to the austerity of God's gift in the stable.

When we tell our family stories, we pray they locate our family in the continuum of God's grace-filled history.

PRAYER: Lord, we praise you for saving us from our enemies without and within and for your ever-present mercies! Amen.

What Will the Children Think? 291

We often interchange the word *rejoicing* with "making happy" or "having a wonderful time." Most of our images of rejoicing involve either sentimentality or self-satisfaction. But Paul's admonition to his beloved church at Philippi speaks of a rejoicing forged from a crucible of worldly persecution and discomfort. His rejoicing is a release from selfishness, pride, and fears of deprivation.

Our daughter Rosemary was a happy eighth-grader, secure in her friendships and her place in school. She was also tremendously insensitive to her little brother (who worshiped her), rarely apologized, and had an adolescent sense of entitlement when it came to getting her needs met. Though she had a relationship with Jesus, it was just budding.

Then our family moved. Rosemary felt ostracized by the girls in our new community. While not in a literal prison like Paul, Rosemary felt imprisoned by social isolation and rejection. She began to wither more each day, ultimately losing twenty pounds from her 5'1" frame. My husband and I dreaded picking her up at school, for we would see her face a frozen mask.

Our only option was to "stand firm in the Lord" (NIV). As a family we had to internalize Paul's exhortation to "not be anxious about anything, but in everything, by prayer and petition, with thanksgiving present [our] requests to God" (NIV)—every minute of every day. Our emptiness led us to celebrate Communion together in the morning before sending the children off to school. We called all the prayer warriors we knew. We found a helpful Christian counselor to aid us.

Rosemary slowly emerged from this prison with newly implanted gentleness. Her new strength, not strident as before, came from the peace of her connection with Christ. She became especially kind to her brother—to this day they are best friends.

PRAYER: Lord, we confess the presence of too much anxiety and too little gratitude in our prayers. May we find our trust and our peace in you alone. Amen.

Have you ever driven a car with a misaligned front end or driven with a flat front tire without realizing it? You experience an ever-so-subtle but firm pull—either to the left (into sure danger of oncoming cars or a concrete median) or to the right (normally to a safe shoulder).

As he begins his closing to his brothers and sisters at Philippi, Paul exhorts them to think about things that are true, honorable, just, pure, and so on. Paul knew intuitively then what neuropsychological research has shown—that what we choose to think about causes habitual patterns of thinking, which in turn alters our perception of reality and ultimately influences our behavior.

Back to our misaligned car. When unwholesome images and thoughts rule our thought life, there is always a pull to the left, the dangerous side of the road. There is a constant need to invoke our conscious willpower as we yank the steering wheel to the center. Latest statistics estimate that we (and our children) in the United States spend forty hours a week in front of screens watching television, playing video games, or surfing the net. How many of the images and thoughts evoked by this screen meet Paul's criteria: "whatever is true, whatever is noble, whatever is right, whatever is pure, whatever is lovely, whatever is admirable—if anything is excellent or praiseworthy—think about such things" (NIV). When we pray, read edifying material, and perform acts of kindness, our "car" will stay in the safety of the center of the lane without the necessity of dangerous overcorrection.

PRAYER: Lord, help! I'm bombarded by temptations that threaten to pull me into a head-on collision. Give me the desire to focus on the things of you. Amen.

This parable of Jesus is the capstone of the two preceding it—a warning to those in the earliest faith community and all those churches that will follow. God offers grace and redemption, a veritable feast, to all who respond to God's invitation. If the thrice-chosen invitees do not show up, they can expect severe consequences.

In the writer's time, those who eschewed the king's wedding feast were not only the many religious leaders but all of those who feigned faith but really worshiped their own pursuits and agendas. How ironic that they would prefer their "farm" or "businesses" to the joy of a royal banquet with everything provided. In a clear allegory, Matthew even describes how some of the chosen guests mistreat and kill the bearer of the invitation to the "good news." The king then throws his doors wide open and sends his servants literally into the streets to bring back anyone willing to come to the feast.

In my job with the school system, I teach an intensive twenty-hour-long parenting class for parents of strong-willed teenagers. Many of these teens have already been involved with the juvenile justice system, and most of the parents are at the end of their rope. Though the class is a veritable feast of strategies and support, it is amazing how the parents resist coming. It seems the higher the education and income level, the greater the resistance due to "more important business."

In contrast, in court a mother overheard me describing the class and approached me about attending. She was desperate for help. She drove an hour each way for six weeks to attend the program. She came early, made coffee, helped clean afterward, applied what she learned at home, and has turned her entire family around. She came from "the street" willing and hungry, and she has been "feasting" ever since. God can only feed those who know their need.

PRAYER: Lord, we want to come to your table. We need to be nourished and directed by your grace. Amen.

The writer of Matthew adds a troubling story to yesterday's parable, which underscores its spiritual message. When the king (God) comes in to greet the hurriedly gathered guests, he notices one man not attired in wedding clothes. Wedding clothes here symbolize being clothed in God's righteousness. We assume that the man did not come to the wedding with a true humility but with an air of prideful presumption. The king, all discerning, "sees" and confronts the man's lack of preparedness to receive. The man, instantly convicted, cannot utter a defense and is thrown into the outside darkness. The writer again warns of the destruction that awaits those who cling to their own righteousness and shun the gospel message.

In yesterday's writing, I described a mother who came to the parenting class receptive. On the first day of class, I also had a father who came to the class without his "wedding clothes" on. An executive at a local company, this man had been court ordered into the class due to his son's serious criminal involvement. Upon his arrival, the father pronounced loudly to the entire group that he was here against his will. He further announced that he knew everything about parenting and that his son's problems were all due to the ex-wife.

This man tried (unsuccessfully) to sabotage both my teaching and his small group's encouragement and sharing. At the end of every class he wrote on his evaluation form, "every minute I have to be in this class is hell." I sadly watched him refuse the feast and ultimately choose to stay in isolated darkness.

Matthew warns us as individuals, families, churches, and nations that Jesus will serve only those who know they need him and are humbly prepared to receive him.

PRAYER: Dear Lord, we come to you on our knees, knowing that only you can clothe us with righteousness. Hold a seat for us at your banquet table of grace. Amen.

The Friendship of God

October 10–16, 2005 • Mark M. Yaconelli[‡]

MONDAY, OCTOBER 10 • Read Exodus 33:12–16

Moses is unafraid to open his heart before God. He speaks to God in the way good friends converse, with words that reveal an intimate trust. He offers his uncertainty, anxiety, and yearnings, all the while insisting on the full attention and presence of the Holy One. God is a friend to Moses, a listening friend who willingly shares the loneliness of Moses' struggle.

What would it mean for us to enter into the friendship of God? What would we be like if we were to come to God with the same trust and openness? What pain or struggle would we share? What questions would we ask? What demands would we make? How often do we refuse to enter into the tent of our own heart? How seldom do we enter this interior holy of holies? How are you being invited to trust the companionship of God this day?

"Show me your ways." Moses pleads, "Consider too that this nation is your people." God's response is the balm that quiets all uncertainties and impatient seeking: "My presence will go with you, and I will give you rest."

Whatever burden, doubt, or concern you carry within you this day, see if you can allow yourself to enter into the same intimate trust that Moses shared with God. See if you can speak the truth of your experience, and then see if you can hear in response what Moses heard, "My presence will go with you, and I will give you rest."

PRAYER: Holy Companion, open the doors of our hearts that your presence and rest might be with us this day. In Jesus' name we pray. Amen.

[‡]Codirector of the Youth Ministry and Spirituality Project at San Francisco Theological Seminary; member of St. Andrew's Presbyterian Church, Marin City, California.

If we are truthful, in each prayer we offer we want to receive the response from God given to Moses: "I will do the very thing that you have asked; for you have found favor in my sight."

No matter how advanced we are on the spiritual journey, we still carry within us the childlike desire to have a God that grants wishes. We want a genie in a bottle who will give us what we want. We live our faith like superstitious people—performing our religious rituals, presenting our best "spiritual" impersonation, and pointing to our good works in order to guarantee blessings. We then become disheartened and full of doubt when God does not grant us our desires. We become frustrated when we realize that God isn't interested in us in order to accomplish good things. Our disappointment deepens when we notice that God's deepest desire is just to be in loving relationship with us. "I know you by name," God says to Moses in response to his requests, as if the greatest of God's pleasures is to know us fully and openly.

Who knows you by name? Who knows you beneath the labels of class, ethnicity, job, and family? What is the true name by which God longs to call you? And what desires would you bring to God if you lived by this name?

PRAYER: Holy God, thank you for knowing us by name. Free us from all our impersonations. May we be our true selves before you and others this day. Amen.

Within each of our hearts burns a pure longing to see God. It lives behind our curiosity and wonder, within our hope and striving, beneath our grief and sorrow. It is a desire to make contact with real truth, real love, real peace. Most of the time we hide from this longing—it's too painful, disorienting, and impossible. Moses, however, chooses to speak it. "Show me your glory," he prays, and God responds in freedom. Like a nurturing mother God protects Moses' seeking heart, sheltering him in the cleft of a rock.

God provides shelter for our spiritual desire. Even as we misplace it on cultural trinkets and religious activity, God keeps our most sacred longings protected and safe. Even at this moment God's hand provides a refuge within each of us for our deepest yearnings. No matter how many times we've misused, ignored, and abandoned the search for the divine, God still waits patiently, protecting our heart in the cleft of God's hand, waiting to encounter us with mercy and graciousness.

How comforting to know that our desire for God is protected by God. And yet, what would we see if we were to open our eyes and look for God directly? What would it take to pray honestly, "Show us your glory"? What would we know, what would we be like if God granted this request?

PRAYER: Loving God, thank you for protecting our deepest desires for you. Give us the courage to look for you this day. In Jesus' name we pray. Amen.

We all know something of holiness—not as something we've possessed but as something we've entered. Every now and then we're stopped by the gaze of an infant, cleansed by the stillness of a mountain lake, or overwhelmed by a gentle act of kindness. And suddenly we find ourselves enfolded by a pure, real, and simple goodness. We're encountered by holiness and renewed by the life within life that's always fresh and new.

God is not worth our worship if God is not holy. Many forces in this world produce shock and awe. We meet powers that demand and force obedience, but none of these deserve or evoke true worship. We worship God because God is holy. We worship because this is the only truthful response—to fall on our knees, to sing praises, to extol and exalt the name of the source of all that is good, all that is just, all that is peace.

The presence of God's holiness draws us to worship. Our hearts cannot be held back, our knees weaken, our heads bow, and our tongues can only whisper, "Yes, yes."

PRAYER: Holy God, help us to turn from our preoccupation with self and truly worship you. In Jesus' name we pray. Amen.

We are all like the Pharisees who seek to trip up Jesus. In our prayer and biblical reflection we come to Jesus like lawyers looking for the hole in the argument, the inconsistency in character. We stand at a safe distance lobbing questions we hope will expose him as a fraud so that we might be free of him; so that we might shut our ears to his words, close our eyes to his actions, and assure ourselves that we really are quite well and good on our own.

But then Jesus speaks, responding to our craftiness with a quiet truth. He removes the distance and reveals the true source of our complicated questions with a simple reply: "Give to God the things that are God's." In an instant we're the ones exposed. Suddenly the tedious self-tyranny that rules within us crumbles, and we sense how lonely we've become. We stand naked, yet amazed, to find ourselves freed by this simple proposal: to let go of all that binds us, to give away all that is of no real value. We turn loose of our needy, self-protection and walk with open arms toward the One who claims us saying, "I belong to you. I belong to you."

PRAYER: Trusting God, help us to live into our poverty, giving away all that distracts us from you. Show us the ways in which we might offer you that which belongs to you. In Jesus' name we pray. Amen.

At his baptism Jesus hears God speak to him, "This is my Son, the Beloved, with whom I am well pleased" (Matt. 3:17). Maybe the primary difference between Jesus and others is that when he heard these words from God, he welcomed and believed them. He willingly received the love, presence, and power of God into the deepest part of his being. Jesus was a good receiver.

Many of us have heard of God's love for us. Yet how many of us really believe it, welcome it, and let it enter into us? What would happen if we allowed ourselves to be this vulnerable?

Paul gives thanks for the Thessalonians because they are good receivers. They know hospitality. "In spite of persecution," Paul writes, "you received the word with joy." They open themselves and welcome the power and presence of God, just as Paul did, just as Jesus did. So deeply do they receive the good news that they became "imitators of the Lord," imitators of freedom.

What are you receiving this day? What way of life are you imitating? What words of life are waiting to be welcomed within the depths of your being? How might this shape the person you're becoming?

PRAYER: Loving God, help us to receive what you want to give us this day. May we welcome you and your word into the depths of our being so that we might be friends and imitators of our Lord and brother, Jesus the Christ. Amen.

Preach the gospel, and if necessary use words."This was the hope of Saint Francis, that he might embody the message of Jesus Christ in such a way that there would be no need for words. In today's world this is hard to imagine. We have become overly reliant on words. We're overburdened with information, talking heads, and seducing billboards. The church is no different; our worship services and education and outreach programs are crowded with words.

What most impresses Paul about the Thessalonians is that the "word" of the Lord, the power and presence of God, has "sounded forth" from them by their example, their hospitality, their transformed lives and newfound patience. The good news Jesus brings is not a "belief" statement that we assent to; it's a reality, a presence, a way of life that we wait for, turn toward, welcome, enter into, and receive. The Christian life is to be lived, not just believed; it is meant to permeate the very marrow of our bones and to alter the way in which we live and breathe.

How do you carry the grace and peace of God within you? How are you being invited to live into the way of Jesus? How might the word of the Lord "sound forth" from you this day?

PRAYER: Loving God, may your way of life seep into the very depth of our being so that all those we meet might know your living power, simply by the way we live. In Jesus' name we pray. Amen.

Letting God Be God

October 17–23, 2005 • Dan R. Dick[‡]

MONDAY, OCTOBER 17 • Read Deuteronomy 34:1-8

Forty years in the wilds of the desert lands, leading a sometimes difficult and obstinate people, dealing with both the spiritual and mundane needs of hundreds—this is the reality of Moses as he crests Pisgah and looks upon the land promised to his descendants. So much work, so much responsibility, and yet the ultimate reward belongs not to Moses but to those who will come after him. After all the sacrifice and sweat, Moses will never enter the Promised Land.

Where is the justice in such an ending? How can God deny this reward to such a faithful servant? The very question points to an answer—Moses' reward lies not in the destination but in the integrity with which he serves God and God's people. Moses' motivation is not to win the prize, but to do what God called him to do.

What does it mean to serve God both faithfully and humbly? First, it means that our goal is not the destination but each moment of the journey. Wherever God leads us is where we most need to be. Second, it requires that we shed the cultural shackles that cause us to ask, "What's in it for me?" And third, it asks us to care more for the needs of others than we do for our own. Ultimately, our life of faithful service simply isn't about us.

It may seem unfair that God denies Moses the privilege of leading the nation into its new home, but we do well to remember that this in no way means Moses fails in his purpose. He succeeds in modeling for all time the powerful leadership of a true servant of God.

PRAYER: Gracious God, keep my focus on the journey and its integrity so that I don't worry about the destination. Amen.

[‡]Research Coordinator for the General Board of Discipleship, Nashville, Tennessee.

Pleasing God

People often define heaven as a place free from cares, strife, and woes—a place where nothing bad ever happens and everyone treats others with kindness and respect. Perhaps heaven will be just this way, but until then we live in a reality where not everyone is happy.

We need never confuse being Christian with being nice. While love, charity, kindness, and forgiveness are hallmarks of the Christian life, so too are honesty, integrity, accountability, and justice. Many times, when living up to our Christian values, we may not be nice. Telling the truth in love, holding people responsible for their actions, and challenging prejudicial beliefs and actions are all necessities of building authentic Christian community.

This message lies at the heart of Paul's message to the people of Thessalonica when he instructs the Christian leaders to write and speak, "not to please mortals, but to please God who tests our hearts." Telling hard truths and holding people accountable to their promises often made the early apostles unpopular, but they could do no less. The call upon their lives came not from a desire to be popular but from a desire to serve God.

One significant sign of Christian maturity comes when we realize that our faith is not merely for our own benefit but for the benefit of others as part of God's larger plan. We are not insignificant; rather, we are part of something larger, something greater than ourselves.

No Christian life is lived without sacrifice and times of discomfort. True faithfulness requires that we be ready to speak the truth in love, to challenge unkind or hurtful words and actions, and to hold people accountable to the highest standards of Christian community.

PRAYER: Grant me strength, O Lord, to seek first to please you in all things. Grant me courage to speak the truth in love. Help me to care so deeply for others that I can do no less than be honest and faithful. Amen.

Letting God be God

There is much current debate between theology and science about the reality of a creator God. Some voices from the scientific community criticize the lack of evidence for God, and often choose archaic images of a grandfatherly figure in white robes with a flowing beard to show how ludicrous the concept of a creator really is. Often, religious opponents to scientific explanations rely on images every bit as archaic to defend that just such a God can do anything *He* wants to! To make their points, both sides of the argument depend on a God who is much too small.

The psalmist regularly directs attention beyond the constraints of human knowledge with poetic language that paints the majesty of God. God is greater than any concept, yet we attempt to conceptualize nonetheless. What does God look like? Is God one thing, many things, or all things? Is God a part of all that is, greater than all that is, or all that is? Is God a part of time; does God transcend time; or does God exist in the eternal now? All big questions, and the only way we can answer them is to make God smaller, manageable, and like us, so that we might begin to better understand God.

The psalmist knows something that we sometimes forget— our understanding of God does not reside solely in our minds but in our very hearts and souls. What we cannot grasp with our minds we may touch with our hearts and connect briefly with our souls. God is greater than our best attempts to make God our size. Did a grandfatherly man in white launch all that is and that ever will be in all possible ways in all possible places? I doubt it, but that doesn't mean God didn't do it! It is not so vital that we fully comprehend God as much as experience God in all the ways we can.

PRAYER: Forgive my need to limit you, O God, as I struggle to "know" what in my heart I believe. Amen.

Keep it simple

How many balls can you juggle without dropping any? A few exceptional people can juggle seven balls at a time, while many can juggle three balls comfortably. The vast majority of people can juggle two balls without dropping them, though a few folks don't want to take chances so they focus on just one ball. It is a truth of human nature that we can focus well on only one or two things at any time. Why then do we fill our lives with so many competing demands, struggling to keep all the balls in the air? The physical act of juggling is a wonderful object lesson for the rest of our lives: don't take on more than we can safely handle.

This is the essence of Jesus' teaching of the greatest commandment. Challenged by a lawyer to declare which of all God's commandments is primary, Jesus instead sums up the whole of God's expectations for humankind by offering, "You shall love the Lord your God with all your heart, and with all your soul, and with all your mind. This is the first and greatest commandment. And a second is like it: You shall love your neighbor as yourself."

Two "balls," if you will, that we juggle as Christian disciples—to love God and neighbor. Two balls that demand our full attention, lest we drop one. Two simple (but not easy) rules that should govern our whole lives and the relationships we form with God and neighbor. Christian community is often split apart over issues that have nothing to do with loving God or loving neighbor. We take up the ball of judgment or the ball of accusation or the ball of moralism—balls beyond our capabilities to keep in the air—that cause us to drop the balls of love for God and neighbor. What a relief to let go of all the other demands, distractions, and lesser concerns to faithfully and comfortably juggle God's love!

PRAYER: Make me a juggler of love and grace, O Lord—a true fool for Christ. Help me to forsake concern with lesser things that cause me to judge others rather than love them. Amen.

Satisfaction

The root of the word *satisfaction* finds its meaning in the concept of sufficiency, having enough. The psalmist offers a beautiful conclusion to Psalm 90 by asking God not for wealth, abundance, or power but for "enough." The author does not ask God to take away all pain and struggle but asks for as many days of gladness as of affliction. The author does not ask for all responsibility and toil to be removed but that God's favor might strengthen God's servants for their tasks and prosper the works of their hands. What a simple request but a serious challenge to our modern culture's values.

Messages surround and cry out to us that our satisfaction rests on the acquisition of more things. Cars can make us happy. Clothes can make us happy. Homes and boats and jobs can make us happy. The "good life" requires fine food, expensive drink, jewelry, gadgets, and the right brand logo. Sufficiency is a concept held prisoner by the modern mantra that there is "never enough."

Worldly values teach us that we must compete to receive all the blessings of the good life. But this definition of the good life implies a scarcity mentality that says that there is not enough to go around. The psalmist offers a countercultural message: there is an abundance of God's good gifts, and there is more than enough to go around, if we will only be satisfied with "enough."

When we focus on building our relationships with God and neighbor, we find that we have little time to desire more than we need. Our satisfaction comes not in the acquisition of more things but in the quality of time spent growing in faithful community. We do not need more, and, in fact, we find that we do not want more. Finding satisfaction in what we have already received frees us from the relentless pursuit of what we lack.

PRAYER: O Lord, help me to be satisfied and not always wish for that which I do not have. Help me to celebrate and share the blessings I have received. Amen.

A job well done

Never since has there arisen a prophet in Israel like Moses, whom the LORD knew face to face." What makes Moses such a great man? Of all the men and women of faith in the Hebrew scriptures, why does Moses warrant such high praise? Is it for the signs and wonders, the glorious miracles and works of power? Is it for his courage and determination in the face of insurmountable obstacles? Is it his intelligence and wisdom, tried, tested, and perfected through a life of leadership?

More than any other factor, Moses' greatness lay in his obedience to God. All the power, all the signs and wonders, all the courage found its root in Moses' humble and obedient faith in God. Certainly, Moses' human failings got in the way from time to time, but never did Moses lose his conviction that he was a mere servant to a higher power. All that Moses did, he did because God was working through him.

As it was for Moses, it is for us today. While we live in a culture that values independence and autonomy, our faith demands that we acknowledge the true source of all wisdom, power, and achievement—God. The true meaning of the concept of stewardship is that we manage wisely and well that which belongs to God. Our ability for success in this world is ultimately measured by how well we honor God through the use of our minds, hearts, gifts, and talents. Little else matters. Moses knew this, and he so ordered his life that at the very end, he was honored, praised, and remembered as a mighty and righteous man.

Moses provides a model for us; all of us, using what we have been given by God, can be obedient to God and receive the final blessing: "Well done, good and faithful servant."

PRAYER: Help me, gracious God, to be an obedient and faithful steward of all your magnificent gifts. Remind me of Moses, and inspire me to love you as he did and to serve you with his level of trust. Amen.

The final answer

What a wonderful scene. Critics come before Jesus to discredit him and prove once and for all that he is nothing but a pretender. In a lull in the discourse, Jesus asks them a question, "What do you think of the Messiah? Whose son is he?" Automatically they respond, "The son of David," and Jesus knows he has entrapped them in their own snare. Those who want to reject Jesus based on his "common birth," those who ascribe to the Messiah the qualities of kingship, those who want to make salvation about power rather than wisdom—all are blinded to the possibility that Jesus just might be who he says he is. But even David himself acquiesced to the idea that one born into his bloodline, a common birth, would be the Lord, the Messiah, the very Son of God. From their own mouths, the learned teachers of the day professed a belief that the Son of God, the Messiah, would come from the human lineage of David. In short, they confessed the possibility that Jesus was the Messiah!

The question echoes through the centuries and is asked of us today: "What do you think of the Messiah? Whose son is he?" Our theological heritage offers us the best thinking and spiritual knowledge of the age—Jesus was both a human being and the Christ. Born into our reality, Jesus was the incarnation of God. For us he symbolizes the struggle to be fully human and to aspire to the highest ideals and practices God desires of us. Jesus is both example and friend—a model of what we can become and greater than our wildest dreams. Jesus is Lord of our hearts, our minds, and our lives—no question about it.

PRAYER: Gracious and mighty God, help me in my unbelief. Whenever the seeds of doubt begin to take root in my soul, remind me of who you are—both the human Jesus who walked the path before us and the incarnate Lord, God among us. Amen.

God Calls and Cares for Leaders

October 24–30, 2005 • Fritz Mutti[‡]

MONDAY, OCTOBER 24 • Read Psalm 107:1-7

God delivers anguished and frightened people from trouble. God gathers lost and wandering people into safe places. God cares for hungry and thirsty people with bread and drink.

My friends in the neighborhood thought it would be fun to head down Fairview Road to the river bridge at the Collins farm south of town. There were perhaps six or eight of us, ranging in age from four to ten. Someone asked if we should tell our mothers, but our leader said we would be back before they missed us. Wrong!

"Do you know where Fritz is?" Dr. Kirk asked my mother. "Across the street playing," she answered. "Well, I saw him on his tricycle going south on Fairview Road," he replied. "Just thought you would like to know."

Mom was glad to know. She got in the car and caught up with us just as we had started our trek back to town. "Hi, Mom. Am I glad to see you," I said. "I am hot, and I'm thirsty and hungry. Thanks for coming to take me back to town." "Well," she said. "Since you didn't tell me where you were going, you are going to ride your tricycle back home. I will follow along in the car to make sure you get there safely."

When Israel wandered away from God's will and purpose, God found the Israelites and brought them home. Like a mother who practices requiring love, God redeems them from trouble and leads them "by a straight road."

SUGGESTION FOR MEDITATION: Recall a time when you wandered into trouble. How did you pray to God in that difficult time? How did you experience God's steadfast love in that circumstance?

[‡]Retired United Methodist bishop, living in Topeka, Kansas.

The psalm writer forces us to see the demand as well as the gift of life for God's people. According to verses 33 and 34, when the people lead evil lives, God "turns rivers into a desert, springs of water into thirsty ground." When the people rebel against the Holy One, God turns "a fruitful land into a salty waste."

What a contrast these ancient verses provide to popular religion in the United States. Among the lessons we learn growing up in American culture are these: God wants us to take care of ourselves. If we stumble, God will always be there to pick us up. In truth, our trust that God will meet our needs first requires our acknowledgment that only God can meet our needs.

The psalmist forces us to confront the demand of a righteous God. When that happens, then God "turns a desert into pools of water, a parched land into springs of water." When we comprehend God's steadfast love and wonderful works in a more profound way, then God's deeds warrant our praise. There is no despair so deep, no trouble so agonizing, no fear so paralyzing that God cannot deliver us and set us on a straight path once again. These verses bear witness to the sovereignty of God in every aspect of life.

Phillip Watson, one of my seminary professors, caught the meaning of this psalm when he wrote a book titled *Let God Be God*. In that study of Martin Luther's thought, Watson reminded his readers again and again that God is creator and ruler of everything. Meant to live in obedient relationship to God's supreme power, "let the redeemed of the Lord say so" (v. 2).

PRAYER: Only you are God, sovereign ruler of nature. Come into my life. Take control of all that I am. Make me an instrument of your will. Amen.

God Calls and Cares for Leaders 311

Clearly, Joshua is elevated to the role of primary leadership because God wills it. "The LORD says to Joshua, 'This day I will begin to exalt you in the sight of all Israel.'"

There is more here than a mere transition in leadership. Joshua stands in the line of command, of course, but it is not a foregone conclusion that he will be exalted to the same status as Moses. Scripture attests, however, that God calls Joshua to the task and endues him with the qualities needed to fulfill the responsibility.

Then Joshua speaks to the people. Filled with the spirit of wisdom, Joshua says to the Israelites, "Draw near and hear the words of the LORD your God." He lays out the plan for the crossing of the Jordan River and promises that God will be with them, assuring the mission's success. He speaks the truth with conviction and authority. The people can believe that among them is "the living God who without fail" will deliver them.

In these troubled times at the beginning of the twenty-first century, people still need leaders. Many leaders see themselves as the fulfillment of that longing. Some report having completed spiritual gifts inventories that clearly indicate their gifts of leadership. How will we know unless we can see in them signs of God's call? How will we know without being inspired by their vision of the future? How will we know their leadership ability without seeing the results?

SUGGESTION FOR MEDITATION: **What gifts for leadership have you been given? Is God calling you to some special role of leadership? How will you respond to God's invitation?**

PRAYER: **Today, O Lord, I pray for the gift of discernment, that I might know my own abilities and respond with willingness and faith. Amen.**

Yesterday we focused on Joshua's leadership. Today we observe the faithfulness of the people. After the priests carry the ark into the flowing river, they cross over to a location near Jericho.

Scholars note that the description of the event has a ritual quality to it. It appears to be a worshipful remembrance of the joyful obedience with which the people receive God's gift of a land of promise, as well as a commemoration of the river's waters ceasing to flow as they crossed. The Israelites choose twelve men to retrieve stones from the river bed and carry them to the place where the people will camp after crossing the river. There they pile up the stones as a memorial.

On several occasions, I have led services of consecration in new church buildings. Once a congregation gathered at the old building to begin the worship service. A hymn was sung and prayers were offered; then the people walked from the old site to the new building. Outside the new facility, we paused to sing another hymn and offer a prayer of blessing. We assembled inside where worship continued with scripture reading, a sermon, and the offering. Then we moved from one piece of furniture to another. At each place, words of consecration were offered and the altar table, the pulpit, the baptismal font, and the lectern were set aside for all the days ahead when the people would gather to worship, praise God, and offer themselves for witness and service.

Those who would serve God faithfully need acts of crossing over rivers and piling memorial stones in order to live in connection with God.

SUGGESTION FOR MEDITATION: **Recall a special time when you crossed from an old way of being connected to God to a new way of following God's call. How were you changed? What new patterns developed in your life?**

PRAYER: **Take my hand, precious Lord, and lead me through every change toward a final faith home. Amen.**

Hard work leads to good character and excellent results. Paul reminds the Thessalonians of his hard work among them. His disciplined effort is tied to his deep affection for the people whom he serves. Comparing himself to a loving father, Paul urges and encourages the Thessalonians by "pleading that you lead a life worthy of God."

As the bishop of Kansas, I preached in many United Methodist churches of the area. On those occasions, I encouraged the people, urging them to lead lives that measured up to God's claim on their lives.

I did not think of myself as a parent dealing with children, but the image intrigues me. During worship children often came to the chancel for a time of sharing and learning. In some places there were many children. In others only a few came to greet the pastor or lay leader. It was always a heart-warming time enjoyed by all.

After worship church leaders and I sometimes drove around the village or neighborhood where the church was located. Often we saw children, and most of the children we saw had not attended the worship service. Perhaps they had gone to another church. We estimated that at least one-half of the children received ministry from no church. In every community the children of the poor seemed most neglected by the church.

Is our mission a ministry of loving like good parents? Perhaps yes. But like Paul, we come to understand that those with whom we share the word of God must accept it "not as a human word but as what it really is, God's word." Our work is to bring God's word to God's children. God, the one true parent, will handle the rest.

PRAYER: Loving God, heavenly parent, strengthen us for the hard work of living in your kingdom. Amen.

Jesus instructed the crowds and his disciples to follow the teachings of the scribes and Pharisees. But he added, "Do not do as they do, for they do not practice what they preach.

The death-dealing virus called HIV/AIDS started its global sweep a quarter of a century ago. In the beginning no one knew what caused the deaths. Fear raged rampant in many communities. Judgment and condemnation characterized the typical response in much of the religious community.

In December 1988, our middle son, Fred, broke the news to us that he was infected with the killer virus. A few months later our oldest son, Tim, informed us that he also was HIV positive. Together our family struggled to live with HIV/AIDS until their deaths in 1990 and 1991.

How grateful we are that the church communion that nurtures us declares: "Churches should be places of openness and caring for persons with AIDS and their loved ones. The church should work to overcome attitudinal and behavioral barriers in church and community that prohibit the acceptance of persons who have AIDS and their loved ones."

From the time our sons became ill, our chief source of support was a loving and caring church that rejected the TV preachers' judgment that AIDS was sent from God to punish bad people. Local congregations surrounded us with prayers and encouragement. They sustained us through every dark day and helped us rise above the heartache.

More than forty million people in our world today live with AIDS. They are sons and daughters of other anguished parents. They are mothers and fathers of children who will have to care for themselves. They are friends and neighbors.

PRAYER: God of all, I am sorry for turning away when someone stretched out a hand and asked for help. I am sorry that I was afraid to touch someone infected with HIV. I am sorry that I do not speak up for those who suffer. Forgive me, I pray. Amen.

One day as Jesus walked along the Sea of Galilee, he saw two brothers, Simon and Andrew, fishermen who practiced their vocation by casting nets into the water. "Follow me," Jesus said to them, and at once they left their nets and went with him. They became his disciples and learned from him that they were to be humble servants of the poor, the sick, and the lost.

My call to pastoral ministry came gradually. My parents saw to it that I attended church school and worship on a regular basis. They helped me learn some basic prayers and urged me to participate in the youth fellowship. Those experiences helped prepare me for the call when it came.

At age forty-two, my father was diagnosed with amyotrophic lateral sclerosis. As this terrible disease attacked his nervous system, depleted his muscular strength, took away his ability to speak, and finally snuffed out his life, I asked many questions about the meaning of life. I felt that God was pushing me toward a response of faith, that Christ was calling me to a life of service and humility.

Jesus teaches all of us who would follow him that the chief mark by which our faithfulness will be judged is humble service. Though we may become priests or teachers, we remain students of the "one teacher." Though we may become parents, we remain children of the "one Father." "The greatest among you," Jesus said, "will be your servant. All who exalt themselves will be humbled, and all who humble themselves will be exalted."

SUGGESTION FOR MEDITATION: Make a list of the most important values in your life. Where does service to others fall on your list? Is humility on that list?

PRAYER: Lord Jesus Christ, take my life and use it for humble service. Amen.

Choices: Wise and Foolish

October 31–November 6, 2005 • *Fred D. Smith*[‡]

MONDAY, OCTOBER 31 • Read Joshua 24:14-25

Joshua, a holy man and a man of war, gives the gathered people of Israel a choice. This choice represents a basic freedom that touches the deepest level of both our humanity and our divinity.

The Lord has placed in each of us a spark of the divine, free will, which finds its truest expression in the human ability to choose an object of love freely. Without that freedom, there is no loyalty. Questioning the people's faithfulness to the God who has brought them out of slavery and seen them safely to the land of promise, Joshua asks them to declare their loyalty: "Choose this day whom you will serve." He challenges them to keep the faith.

God who created us in God's image endowed us with free will and therefore with the capacity to be true to our promises. No greater decision exists than our choice of the god to whom we will pledge our love and devotion. Joshua offers the Israelites the God of their deliverance or the gods of their captivity—blessing or curse, life or death. The greater the decision, the greater the consequences. The Lord "is a jealous God," Joshua warns, who "will not forgive your transgressions or your sins."

Because God takes our choices seriously, choosing God requires our loyalty. The pledge of our life and love to God and our steadfast desire to keep that promise are evidence of the divine love and faithfulness to us.

PRAYER: Lord, in a world vying for my loyalty, help me choose, of my own free will, the God of my salvation. Give me the strength to keep the faith. Amen.

[‡]Associate Professor of Christian Education and Youth Ministry, Pittsburgh Theological Seminary; pastor, Fellowship United Methodist Church; living in Pittsburgh, Pennsylvania.

ALL SAINTS' DAY

These are they who have come out of the great ordeal; they have washed their robes and made them white in the blood of the Lamb." These are the ones who chose with single-minded determination to remain loyal to the God of their choice even in times of trial and tribulation. They chose faithfulness even in the face of death.

At Columbine High School, reports indicate that several youth before being shot down professed Christ to their assailants. They were faithful until the point of death. Shortly after the Columbine massacre, youth-oriented computer chatrooms were abuzz as the youth asked one another if they could die for their faith. "These are they...." Apparently some students did exactly that as they faced death on school grounds.

It is one thing to choose God after the defeat of your enemies. It is quite another thing to choose God in the face of certain defeat and suffering. Few of us have to make that decision at the point where our very lives hang in the balance. Yet, everyday we face smaller challenges to faith, and we fail. When we look at ourselves in the mirror of God's eyes, we realize that our righteousness is but filthy rags.

Can we then choose God? "They have washed their robes . . . in the blood of the Lamb." If someone asked the elder who you are, what would his answer be?

PRAYER: Lord, help me to face with courage and determination the challenges you place before me. Amen.

After entering the Promised Land, the people of Israel gather at Shechem, where Joshua leads them in the renewal of their covenant with the God who has protected them during their journey through the wilderness. Joshua begins the ceremony with a history lesson and concludes by confronting the people with the choice of a holy God.

For us holiness has little meaning that approximates the reverence for holy things in the Hebrew Bible, where holiness is like a force—protective of God and destructive of the irreverent. In the ancient Hebrew world, to approach the holy was fraught with danger. Moses was warned not to look on God's face at risk of his life. To look at or touch the ark of the covenant was to risk death.

Likewise, to choose a holy God is fraught with danger if we do not keep our promise to serve God faithfully. Joshua is not sure the Israelites can keep their word. If they cannot accept the responsibility of loyalty that accompanies the choice of a holy God, their zealous God, who "led [Abraham] through all the land of Canaan and made his offspring many," can and may do them harm.

Today we would never regard a baptismal pledge or confirmation in such a harsh light. Yet the book of James affirms that "God yearns jealously for the spirit that [God] has made to dwell in us" (4:5). Every day we choose in many ways to be present before or absent from God. And each time we allow other gods to rule our lives, we do ourselves spiritual harm. As Joshua explained to the Israelites, "You are witnesses against yourselves" (24:22).

SUGGESTION FOR MEDITATION: Consider the choices you make about serving God. On Sunday morning do you assemble with the faithful or do you shop, play golf, watch football or clean house? Which God have you chosen?

The early church expected a speedy return of Christ. The apostles approached their work with a sense of urgency and expectancy; they expected to be present at Jesus' return. Jesus himself had said, "Truly I tell you, this generation will not pass away until all these things have taken place" (Matt. 24:34). However, as the years passed, many died before seeing Jesus coming on a cloud. Those who remain begin to question the parousia (the second coming of Christ), an event integral to the faith for which they had suffered so much.

Their understanding and belief in Christ's immediate return impacted how they chose to live—and must now influence how they were to face death. They had chosen to live in preparedness for the return of Christ. How would they face death now that Jesus seems to tarry in the heavens? How do their lives differ from those of other people?

Paul writes to offer consolation related to the death of the believers in the community and to offer hope. Though death is is a common experience of all humanity, the hope of resurrection and being joined with Christ is a uniquely Christian hope. For Christians, the death and resurrection of Jesus Christ marked the end of the "old age" and the beginning of a "new age." In the present (old) age, the fear of death and the grave is the controlling ethical ethos that rules the hearts of human beings. Paul asks that those who continue to live choose the hope of eternal life over the fear of death.

The hope of the parousia is not only a future hope but a present reality. It is not only for the dead in Christ, but also for the living in Christ. It is the reality of a new age dawning in which love and eternal life will replace the old age of the fear of death and the grave.

PRAYER: O God, we affirm that whether we are living or dying, we belong to you. May it be so. Amen.

A wedding feast was an important event in early Palestine. Rabbinic students and rabbis were permitted to put down their scrolls of the law, and people were excused from solemn religious duties to attend a wedding. The wedding celebration often lasted for days. Jesus performed his first miracle at a wedding feast.

The parable of the ten bridesmaids reflects on choices related to preparedness for the coming kingdom of God. The bridegroom is Christ, and the bridesmaids are Christians who eagerly await his return. All have lamps with oil; all sleep; all await the coming of the bridegroom.

The parable calls five of the bridesmaids wise and five of them foolish. Why? Because from all outward appearances all ten seem ready, yet the five foolish bridesmaids are not prepared for the delay of the bridegroom. Their readiness hinges on events going as *they* plan, according to their timetable. The wise bridesmaids carry flasks of oil with them and so find themselves ready despite the bridegroom's delay. Clearly the story conveys a sense that some actions and readiness can simply come too late. Despite a mad dash to buy oil, the foolish bridesmaids get to the wedding banquet too late—"the door was shut."

Wise and foolish—choices related to preparedness. A wise choice is to anticipate a delay in the coming of the bridegroom; a foolish choice is to assume no delay. What does that mean for us? Like the bridesmaids, we know neither the day nor time of Jesus' return. Like many, we may wonder if Christ will return at all. We too may choose to be wise or foolish.

SUGGESTION FOR MEDITATION: We choose to be prepared or not to be prepared for the coming of Christ. How does one make such a choice?

God has chosen to call us God's children. My wife is adopted. She has often reflected on the time when she found out that her parents were not her birth parents. What she remembers with warmth and reassurance are her adopted father's words to her: "We love you all the more because we chose you." Being chosen evidences an even greater love, because it is a love freely given. What manner of love has God lavished on us that we are called children of God? Even as adopted children we are expected to take on the character and characteristics of God.

It does not matter if we are born of parents through childbirth or adopted. Developing parental characteristics comes with familiarity, which grows out of spending time together and struggling together. To be like God the Father we must come to know God through prayer, praise, and study of the word.

We know God is pure. To be pure in the New Testament means in many instances "singleness of heart." We love God with all our hearts, strength, minds, and our very souls; likewise, we love our neighbor. Any other aim in life denies the claim that we are the children of God. Just as God has chosen us, now we must choose God. Jesus Christ offers us the image of God in all its purity. Christ single-mindedly devoted himself to do the will of God, and God is love.

SUGGESTION FOR MEDITATION: Jesus gave a new commandment: to love one another as he loved us. If God is love, and we are children of God, then we too must love.

What will we choose to tell our children about God? Many young people today know little or nothing about their parents' faith or family history. The made-for-television movie *Roots* many years ago set off a tidal wave of people who began to research their genealogies. People want to know their roots—the sacred stories and holy histories told by those who love them. What have our ancestors told us? What are the dark sayings of old that are uttered in parables? Once our children listened to stories from loved ones who had something to tell. Now they hear tales from those who have something to sell.

In our society children listen to stories told by large conglomerates whose motivation is conspicuous consumption. The new altar before which we kneel is the television and the silver screen. Here the family gathers to hear mighty works of multinational corporations that deliver to us all we can desire and more. Our ancestors shared family stories and legends, their version of historical events. Today we choose to leave that task to others. In what or in whom will our children hope?

The choice is ours, says the psalmist. We play a large role in our children's choices. Will we open our mouths in parables? Will we utter dark sayings of old? Will we hide from our children and the coming generations the glorious deeds of the Lord and the mighty wonders God has done in our lives? How can our children choose to serve a God of whom they have never heard?

SUGGESTION FOR MEDITATION: When have your children or your community's children heard the stories of how God has been present with their family, their race or ethnic group or nation?

Fear of the Lord

November 7–13, 2005 • James J. Baker[‡]

MONDAY, NOVEMBER 7 • Read Psalm 76

You should have been there—it was awesome!" In this day and age that sentence could describe just about anything—a weekend, a concert. Listening to our talk, you'd think we were constantly having awesome experiences. But are we? What does it mean to be awed anyway?

Speaking to God, the psalmist declares, "You indeed are awesome!" Such praise arises out of the experience of God whose power has been shown in the disaster that befell warriors and weapons around Salem (an ancient name for Jerusalem). The specific historical incident behind this particular song of praise is not the point; the nature of the One behind the events is. God is glorious, "more majestic than the everlasting mountains." God is awesome, uttering judgments that cause the earth to fear and be still. "You indeed are awesome," sings the psalmist, and we might hear these words as implying that a lot of things are not awesome.

"From the heavens you uttered judgment; the earth feared and was still." The key word in this psalm is *feared*, for fear is the beginning of a sense of true awe. A weekend's activities or a good concert may be exciting or stimulating. They may pull us out of our humdrum lives and give a sense of transcendence. But they neither prompt a healthy fear or reveal a larger reality that is the origin and purpose of life for all the earth.

Awe isn't just an experience we add to our list of things that happen to us over the weekend and then talk about at work on Monday. It is a life-changing experience that stakes a claim and provides a sense of call that cannot be shaken.

SUGGESTION FOR MEDITATION: What do you stand in awe of? What interventions in your life have made a claim upon you and given you a healthy sense of fear?

[‡]Senior pastor, Westminster Presbyterian Church, Charlottesville, Virginia.

The Bible says that the fear of the Lord is the beginning of knowledge (Prov. 1:7), but the wrong kind of fear may produce a misunderstanding of who God is. There is difference between a healthy sense of fear that produces awe and an unhealthy fear that constricts life. Because the one-talent servant in the parable has an unhealthy fear, he leads a constricted life.

Perceptions determine actions. Once we have gotten it in our heads that persons will respond according to a particular pattern, we begin to see them acting that way. That is the message of the parable of the talents: the way we allow perceptions to determine actions, particularly a fearful stance toward life and its Source.

After the talents have been distributed and the master returns from a journey, an accounting takes place, and the servants report on their actions. The one-talent servant who buried his talent in the ground justifies his action by telling his master, "I knew that you were a harsh man, . . . so I was afraid, and I went and hid your talent in the ground." "I knew . . . ," the servant says. His perception determined his actions. But is that servant correct? Does the servant really know the master?

We find it tempting to offer excuses for this poor servant who had only one talent; yet one talent represented the wage of an ordinary worker for fifteen years in first-century Palestine. The problem, therefore, is not a lack of funds given to this servant; the problem is the servant's lack of trust in the master. The servant fears taking a risk, a fear that grows out of a misperception of the master who gave so much.

Perceptions determine actions. An unhealthy fear of life and its Source produces fearful servants.

SUGGESTION FOR MEDITATION: How do your perceptions of others predetermine your actions toward them? In what ways do your perceptions of God limit the way you respond toward God?

Our perception of another can determine our relationship with that individual. The relationship described in the parable of the talents is one of servant and master, a relationship found also in the psalm. In the parable there is a breakdown in the trust between the one-talent servant and the master, while in the psalm "the eyes of servants look to the hand of their master, as the eyes of a maid to the hand of her mistress." The fearful servant led a severely limited life, while in the psalm the master is perceived as merciful. What accounts for this difference?

Our psalm is fourth in a collection of psalms used by pilgrims on their way to Jerusalem. From a variety of places, pilgrims journeyed to the Temple, joining with others in search of God's mercy. It was a movement from isolation to community as seen in the shift from singular to plural in the opening verses of the psalm. "To you *I* lift up *my* eyes" (emphasis added) becomes a group affirmation that "*our* eyes look to the LORD *our* God" (emphasis added). For the psalmist, the move from individual perception of God to a group experience brings individuals to trust.

When we are weak and mistaken in our perception of God, the corrective may come through community with others. Our self-alienating tendencies need the corrective that can come in communal life. This psalm reminds us that we can fall prey to our individual misconceptions. The love of others can bring us out of our isolation. All fall short of the glory of God; in community with others, we often find the faith to sustain us in our times of doubt and misperceptions of God.

PRAYER: O God, to know you is eternal life; to serve you is perfect freedom. Give us greater trust in you that we might have greater life and freedom. Amen.

The book of Judges contains some of the R-rated material of the Hebrew Bible. The book organizes stories of political intrigue and assassination, lies and deception, rape and murder around a repetitive pattern: Israel does evil, God sends an enemy; Israel cries in distress, God sends a judge or deliverer; Israel again does evil, and the cycle is repeated. Our reading brings us in at the beginning of one of these cycles: "The Israelites again did what was evil in the sight of the LORD." What purpose do such stories serve for the life of faith?

We find the answer in the opening words of the passage and the organizing principle of the whole book. The people are constantly tempted to write God out of their lives. Israel is portrayed as having nothing by which to measure or determine its actions. As the author of Judges puts it several times, "all the people did what was right in their own eyes" (17:6; 21:25). That is the painful admission with which the story of Deborah begins: the people do what is right in their own eyes with no reference point outside of themselves for their actions.

Our world may not be as brutal in its actions as the world of this portion of the Bible (though that is debatable), but surely we see an undeniable parallel when it comes to the standards we apply to what we do. People still decide what actions to take based on what is good only for themselves. Leaders still explain decisions with arguments that contain their own justifications. All people continue to do what is right in their own eyes. Like the ancient Israelites, we need a judge and deliverer.

PRAYER: Eternal God, judge and save us, for we cannot judge and save ourselves. Break into the cycle of self-justification; and in your mercy, restore us to life in Christ. Amen.

FRIDAY, NOVEMBER 11 • Read 1 Thessalonians 5:1-11

Some of us handle uncertainty better than others, but all of us eventually weary of living in the dark. A period of unemployment, an unresolved relationship—we want answers, and we usually want them now.

The people the epistle writer addresses want answers. They feel the need to know how things are going to shake down, how things will be resolved. Yet the best information offered is not about *when* but *how*, and even that has its limitations. The day of the Lord (Christ's second coming) will come "like a thief in the night," which indicates that had they known when all would come to an end, that knowledge would change the present nature of life itself.

Some things cannot be known, though that does not keep us from trying. It also does not dissuade people from preying upon our anxiety. People make calculations, sell books based on those calculations, and pretend to have the answers. The warning to the early Christians is a warning to present-day believers: do not fall prey either to your anxieties or to those who might trade on them.

And do not think that you are completely in the dark. "You, beloved, are not in darkness, . . . for you are all children of light and children of the day." Even though you do not know the resolution, you know something of the values by which the true measure of life is taken. You do not know when the end is coming, but you do know the nature of the One who determines what is eternal. In this knowledge find your strength for living every day. And in true community with others, "encourage one another and build up each other, as indeed you are doing."

SUGGESTION FOR MEDITATION: When do you find yourself anxious to know when and how things will turn out? Does the anxiety you generate at these times propel you further from God or open you up to a frank confession of your need of God?

328   *Fear of the Lord*

As followers of Christ we know to look for "the first" at the end of the line, not elbowing their way to the front. As a result we may find it difficult to say what the rewards of the life of faith are. We are not supposed to be in it for the rewards. There are, however, some rewards; the parable of the talents gives us permission to admit that. When the householder returns and does an accounting with his servants, some receive a reward while the one-talent servant receives no reward. In fact, that risk-aversive individual suffers one of the favorite punishments meted out in Matthew's Gospel: being thrown into the outer darkness.

In negative terms, one might say that the desire to avoid that outer darkness motivates the faithful servants of God, but that would be an inadequate explanation. The other servants take risks before they know of any threat.

We find the key to understanding the motives of the "good and faithful servants" (RSV) in the words of acclamation: "Enter into the joy of your master." There is a joy that comes in taking faith seriously, joy in serving God. A life that is small and constricted will focus solely upon the rewards that can be measured by worldly standards. But a life lived with a sense of abandon for the sake of Christ leads to rewards beyond worldly measure.

The story is told of a newspaper reporter who watched a Catholic nun mop the gangrenous wounds of a Chinese soldier. "I wouldn't do that for a million dollars," the reporter said. "Neither would I," she replied quietly and went on mopping.

PRAYER: O God, to know you is eternal life, to serve you is perfect freedom. Free us from a preoccupation with ourselves that we might find life and freedom in you. Amen.

SUNDAY, NOVEMBER 13 • Read 1 Thessalonians 5:1-11;
Matthew 25:14-30

In 1789 the Speaker of the Connecticut legislature, Colonel Davenport, was imposed upon by his fellow legislators to suspend the session of that body due to a predicted eclipse of the sun. People felt certain it marked the end of the world and the return of Christ, and therefore all earthly activities ought to cease. Colonel Davenport remained unconvinced. "The day of Judgment is either approaching or it is not," he said. "If it is not, there is no cause for adjournment. But if it is, I choose to be found doing my duty."

Today's readings contain biblical warrant for the counsel given by the colonel. A day of reckoning is the backdrop against which each text stands, and in both instances the appropriate response is not the cessation of labor but its continuation. The faithful servants in the parable merit reward for having taken action, not refraining from it. Indeed, the overly cautious servant receives reprimand. In the case of the Thessalonians, the counsel is even more direct. The writer of the epistle urges them to remain awake to the times and simply continue what they have been doing—encouraging and building up one another.

How reassuring for the Thessalonians to hear that they need not make radical adjustments in their actions to avoid some disastrous final reckoning! They do not need to recalibrate their course in order to satisfy a fear-inducing God. They are already faithful.

Fear of God, properly understood, is the beginning of knowledge and the key to a rewarding life of faith.

PRAYER: Almighty God, in all the changes and chances of this world, grant us a calm spirit that our lives may be lived in true joy through service to you. Amen.

A Hole in the Soul

November 14–20, 2005 • Larry Hollon[‡]

MONDAY, NOVEMBER 14 • Read Ezekiel 34:11–16

In the small discussion group the conversation had turned from light banter to serious reflection. At some point one member of the group, unable to define her burden in traditional faith language, said simply, "I feel as if I've got a hole in my soul."

Those words cut to the quick. Others felt the hole as well. It was as if an inarticulate groan had been put in words. The inner fears were given voice: *I feel alone, apart, not connected. I feel disconnected from God, from others, even from family.*

Modern society promises us meaning it cannot deliver. Somehow, the attractions and the material goods of the consumer culture cannot fill this hole we feel. After all the shopping, we still feel there must be something more; and we yearn to fill the hole.

We desire deep connection, to live a life that is meaningful to ourselves and to others, to find our spiritual center and live with purpose. Apparently, this concern is not born in our time alone. The scripture speaks to us of sheep scattered and wandering as if no one will seek them out and lead them through the thick darkness and clouded days to their own land.

But Ezekiel writes that God says, "I myself will search for my sheep." We are not alone. We belong to God and to one another. God seeks to connect with us so that we may bind our wounds, heal our souls, and feed on justice.

PRAYER: We yearn to find you, O God, and be connected to you and others for a life of goodness and purpose. We are your sheep; come to us and lead us to good pasture and refreshing water. Amen.

[‡]General Secretary, United Methodist Communications, Nashville, Tennessee.

Sometimes we view vulnerability as weakness, but it is not. Our son, Matthew, was born with a life-threatening condition that resulted in multiple vulnerabilities to his health, which may have caused some to see him as weak. He struggled every day. He was like a lamb butted about and sometimes ravaged by staggering health challenges.

But Matthew was never weak. He was, in fact, the strongest person I've ever known. He lived with such verve and zest that it seemed his spirit fairly danced through the days. In every challenge he sought a way through with his indomitable spirit.

Perhaps you know someone who by all outward appearances the world might see as weak and vulnerable but inside is strong and power-filled. I suspect that we are never closer to God or more able to call upon God's strong presence, than when we are most vulnerable. For in our vulnerability we discover our own limits and reach out to God for strength. In our weakness we can claim God's power.

It is a remarkable thing that when we feel at our weakest, we are closest to God. Perhaps it is because we align ourselves with the source of our creation and in coming closer to the Creator Spirit, we find strength beyond human vulnerability. When we turn to God with this understanding, we hear God say, "I will be your God. I will covenant with you. I will nurture you, and I will give you peace."

PRAYER: O God, when we feel vulnerable, assure us with your strength. Thank you for those strong people in our lives who reveal the strength of your presence in gentle, life-enriching ways, even overcoming great challenges to illuminate your strength. Amen.

A young man in our congregation loves to sing. When his choir sings he rocks with the up-tempo songs and sways with the slow. He is outgoing and energetic. Watching him sing is an invitation to an expressive act of praise and thanksgiving.

I can't carry a tune, so I'm reticent to sing out for that reason alone. But this young man reminds me that the psalmist doesn't ask us to sing in perfect pitch; he asks us to make a joyful noise to the Lord. This young man, born with the condition known as Down syndrome, embodies with gladness the call to worship of the psalmist. Every time I see him and hear him sing, I am reminded that our offerings must be given without reserve. We are asked to give our best, but we are not asked to be perfect. This is a liberating idea for me because my reticence can hinder me from reaching into the joyfulness and playfulness of life that I believe God would have us understand and live.

We have so much more to be grateful for than to feel sad about. No matter our circumstances we have much for which to be thankful. My young friend reminds me of this through his exuberant singing, which is his gift to me.

To make a joyful noise to the Lord requires that we come before God in an attitude of celebration, aware of the goodness of the life we are given. My friend reminds me that I can't think my way into this spirit of joy; sometimes I just have to let go and do it.

PRAYER: Dear God, we come into your presence with joy and thanksgiving for the good life you give us. Keep us mindful of this wonderful gift, and help us to live in grateful thanksgiving. Amen.

The young boy stood before the city council and spoke in a strong voice, punctuated by nervous stuttering. A street child, one of hundreds of children who survive on the streets of São Paulo, Brazil, without benefit of parental care, he was pleading for protection from city authorities following the murder of seven children by vigilantes.

The room quieted as he recounted the times his hot lunch, provided by a church organization, had been stolen by local police officers. He spoke of being beaten. He lived under a bridge with several other boys, who were often rousted out in the middle of the night.

As the boy recounted these injustices his voice did not waver. He seemed to gain strength as he concluded his remarks. His last words seemed strange to me at first. He said he dreamed of the day when a street child could go into a restaurant and be served like any other person.

But it didn't seem strange when the young boy said at last, "We are God's children too." He knows he is God's child even if no one else claims him. That's a profound awareness born of sitting on the curb and watching rich folk entering the restaurant and knowing that he would be quickly rushed outside were he to try and enter.

In a world of injustice that denies human dignity, the psalmist's words ring with prophetic challenge:

> Know that the LORD is God.
>> It is he that made us, and we are his;
> we are his people, and the sheep of his pasture.

PRAYER: O God, each of us is yours. Lead us to right the injustice that causes some of us to be left outside. Set us afire with the commitment to include all your children at the table. In Jesus' name we pray. Amen.

As I handed him a release form to sign giving me permission to use video footage of him, a young man in a Job Corps training center suddenly looked crestfallen. He said, "Sir, I can't sign this." I was concerned since he was one of the principal demonstrators of a skill highlighted in the video. After some careful probing he said, "I don't have a home address."

Tagged with the label "homeless" at some point in his life, this young man had learned that it meant "excluded," and he was excluding himself now. I assured him that his address at the center was good enough for me, and his face brightened. He rejoined the teasing banter that floated through the room about his becoming a celebrity.

The world has many ways to exclude us: race, gender, age, class, physical condition, and many others. But the writer of the epistle reminds us that in Christ we find out who we are and what we live for. The love of God made manifest in Jesus Christ is inclusive, and we never need feel that we are left outside of that love, for it is never withdrawn.

The epistle writer says that we experience this love above every power, dominion, and name; and, it's not only in this age but also in the age to come. We are claimed now and forever by a loving God who does not ask for our home address but says, "Come home to me."

PRAYER: O God of the excluded, we thank you for your inclusive love that claims us and holds us within your reach now and forever. Amen.

Before I went to Luuq, Somalia, I was told it is godforsaken country. It's hot, dry, and far from the amenities of electricity and running water. I met two Muslim physicians, both volunteers. It was dangerous work. Land mines litter much of the region. A humanitarian aid worker had driven onto a mine and sustained severe injuries.

I stood in the small hospital, really open-air cinder block rooms bereft of even rudimentary supplies, as a doctor treated a terribly burned young woman whose hut had caught fire from a phosphorous bomb she had hidden for a rebel group.

In a room across the hall lay the injured humanitarian worker. The physician spoke softly. He touched the young woman with great tenderness to swab her wounds.

As in so many places, death and destruction rained down far too easily here, a place it was said that even God had forgotten. But in the midst of terror and pain—between a peacemaker and a guerrilla—I watch this man of medicine offering life and bringing wholeness. I hear compassion in his voice, and I see his hands offer healing touch. I felt that I stood in the presence of God. It's funny how you find God when you least expect it and in the most unlikely of places.

PRAYER: O God, we never know where we will find you or in whose face you will appear to us. Keep us mindful, therefore, that you are present in every place, even those places we've been told you have forsaken. Help us see your steadfast love in every face and every place. Amen.

REIGN OF CHRIST SUNDAY

Timmie lived down the street from us. His family was poor, and Timmie was rambunctious and sometimes like an unguided missile. He brought me an old bicycle tire to repair, and we knelt down beside it as I worked. Timmie rattled on offering me tall tales, and I listened and grunted appropriately at the right time.

But Timmie caught me off guard when he asked, "How come you're so nice to me?"

I wasn't prepared for that question. I stammered, "Well, why wouldn't I be nice to you?"

"Well," he said, "most people ain't very nice to me."

I think about Timmie often. No child should wonder why someone is being nice to him or her. But I wonder how many times I've looked into a face and failed to see God reflected back to me, or how many of my passing glances have communicated the message that I didn't have time or that the person wasn't important to me or that I didn't want to bother?

While God is always present, we may not always recognize or be aware of God. Jesus said as much when he said, "Just as you did it to one of the least of these who are members of my family, you did it to me."

So the challenge is not to bring God into our circumstances but to nurture the vision to apprehend the God who is already there. And we perceive God among the least, the most vulnerable, the forgotten, and the excluded. This is where we find God. These are the faces of God.

PRAYER: O God, we have overlooked you, forgotten you, excluded you, and denied you. Forgive our lack of vision and restore our sight so that we can see your presence in our world in every beautiful face. Amen.

To Know and Be Known

November 21–27, 2005 • Jan L. Richardson[‡]

MONDAY, NOVEMBER 21 • Read Isaiah 64:1-9

O that you would tear open the heavens and come down," Isaiah cries. The prophet's plea is a fitting prayer as we prepare to cross into the season of Advent. Soon we will begin the weeks of preparation for the celebration of the God who became flesh and walked among us. In our hymns and in our prayers, we will echo Isaiah's cry, "Come down!"

But sometimes, even as I join my voice to the prayer for God to become immanent, personal, real, I find myself wondering, *What am I doing, asking for the living God to become known to me?* I resonate with Annie Dillard's question in her book *Teaching a Stone to Talk*: "Does anyone have the foggiest idea what sort of power we so blithely invoke?" She goes on to observe, "It is madness to wear ladies' straw hats and velvet hats to church; we should all be wearing crash helmets. Ushers should issue life preservers and signal flares; they should lash us to our pews. For the sleeping god may wake someday and take offense, or the waking god may draw us out to where we can never return."

Yet we cry out to know this God. The coming season reminds us that God dwells in mystery and majesty that can overwhelm us, yes; but this God also came to dwell with us and still seeks to make a home among us. These Advent days invite us to acknowledge our longing, our yearning for the divine, to lean toward the horizon where God appears, to wait for God's coming—and to discover that God is there in our midst, waiting for us.

PRAYER: God of mystery, how do you want me to know you in this season? Bless me with courage to open my eyes to you. Amen.

[‡]United Methodist minister, artist, writer, spiritual director; serves as Visiting Artist, First United Methodist Church, Winter Park, Florida.

The author of this portion of the book of Isaiah most likely wrote these words during the period following the Israelites' return from their exile in Babylon. Having made their way back to their homeland, what would their lives, their community, their relationship with God look like now? They wrestle with a sense of God's absence even as they acknowledge their guilt and give voice to their hope.

"You have hidden your face from us," the writer says to God. His accusation haunts me, as does God's response in the following chapter: "I was ready to be sought out by those who did not ask, to be found by those who did not seek me" (65:1). It wasn't that God had hidden God's face; the people had hidden theirs.

Even as Advent invites us to celebrate the God revealed to us, the season also invites us to reveal ourselves to the divine, to "unhide" ourselves, to turn our faces Godward. This may be the more difficult invitation. In my own life I tend to respond with a dance of desire and resistance: "Come closer," I say; but sometimes, "Leave me be."

I encounter this dance particularly in my work as an artist and writer. In the place where images and words are born, I come to know God and myself deeply and clearly. But some days—sometimes weeks or months—I resist being in that place, allowing a litany of distractions to keep me from that creative space.

I have learned, though, that that's part of my dance. The distance eventually quickens my hunger to return to the work that God has called me to do, to turn my face to the Holy One who waits there, the God who wants to know and be known, the One who always welcomes the exiles home.

PRAYER: God of the exile, how do you want to know me in this season? Bless me with the desire to turn my face toward you. Amen.

Psalm 80 is a communal lament during a time of devastation. Its poetry resonates with the verses we have read from Isaiah; the community struggles with a sense of God's absence and anger and yet its members still cry out to God to turn toward them, to come into their midst, to restore and heal them.

I find myself continually struck by the psalm writers' willingness to bring the entire range of their emotions into God's presence. The sweep of the psalms reminds us that no feeling is foreign to God, no sorrow or anger we cannot offer to the divine, no question God would prefer we leave unasked.

The psalms challenge me to ponder how well I am doing this work of bringing my whole self to God as I pursue my own spiritual practices. Yet the fact that the psalms were created for communal worship presses me to ask further: How does this happen in community, this business of "unhiding" ourselves? How does our worship invite us to enter the terrain that the psalmists explored, to bring not only our joys and praises into the sanctuary but also our laments and anger and the parts of ourselves we would rather leave at the door?

In the congregation where I serve as Visiting Artist, I help lead a contemplative service where we seek to live with these questions. We invite the scriptures to ask us about our lives and engage the questions in silence as well as in conversation. We prayerfully enter the emotional range of the psalms. The musician can offer a song that includes the words, "Thank you, God, for not taking my life today; I could tell it was on your mind." We hold one another's celebrations as well as our sorrows, and we gather in a circle for Communion that Christ may feed us through one another, face-to-face.

PRAYER: God of community, how do you want me to be with your people in this season? Bless me with discernment to know when to open myself to others. Amen.

THANKSGIVING DAY IN THE UNITED STATES

In the small town in Florida where I grew up, most of the residents gather for a noontime feast on Thanksgiving Day. The town that is home to about a hundred people swells on this day, with relatives and friends adding their presence to the reunion and their sumptuous dishes to the long tables that stretch out beneath the gazebo in the community park. I have been able to make it back for this feast each year, grateful to reconnect with this landscape that shaped my soul and to offer thanks for this town that has been home to five generations of Richardsons.

Practices of communal thanksgiving help us guard against the kind of forgetting that the writer of Deuteronomy exhorts his hearers not to engage in. He reminds the people of Israel that the God who was with them in the wilderness is the same God who will be present with them in the Promised Land. The writer knows how coming into abundance can insulate us from the One on whom our lives depend. A state of plenty can lull us into thinking we have accumulated our blessings solely by our own power, that we are entitled to them, that they will always be present.

In our communities and in our personal lives, cultivating thanksgiving as a regular practice, as a ritual, helps us resist that kind of forgetfulness. By its nature, ritual beckons us to engage even when we may not feel like it, to practice turning our hearts toward God. As individuals and as communities, having a habit of giving thanks helps us remember that in whatever circumstances we find ourselves—in the Promised Land or in the wilderness—our sustenance comes from the same source.

PRAYER: God of blessing, how shall I thank you for all the ways you make yourself known? Bless me with a generous heart that I may share with others what you have given me. Amen.

My favorite time of day is, well, night. I have long had a certain level of comfort with being in shadows, literally and figuratively; a willingness to live with questions and uncertainty.

I encounter God in the darkness in ways that I don't in the daylight, ways that challenge me to know the Holy beyond what I can see with my eyes or know with my intellect. Particularly in the season of Advent, which unfolds in the darkest time of the year here in the Northern Hemisphere, I'm grateful for the passage in Isaiah 45 where God says, "I will give you the treasures of darkness and riches hidden in secret places" (v. 3).

Yet I am struck by the psalmist's prayer that we hear again today: "Let your face shine." Three times in this psalm he offers this prayer, a plea for restoration and salvation.

"Let your face shine." This prayer echoes throughout the Hebrew scriptures, with prophets and priests, as well as psalmists, asking that God become known to the people in this way, to bless them with the light of the divine presence. Such imagery resonates through the Christian scriptures too. In just a few weeks, as we gather to celebrate Christmas, we will hear the powerful words of the prologue to John's Gospel, in which he proclaims that "the life was the light of all people. The light shines in the darkness, and the darkness did not overcome it."

As much as I love mystery, I find myself wondering how it would be to pray the psalmist's prayer in this season. What place in my life is God longing to illuminate? In the dark Advent days ahead, what part of the mystery is God ready to solve?

PRAYER: God of darkness and of daylight, what part of my life do you long to illuminate? Let your face shine through me, that I may bear your light to the world. Amen.

I spent much of high school getting ready for college, much of college getting ready for seminary, much of seminary getting ready for my first pastoral appointment. When that appointment came, and I landed at my first church, I came to a screeching halt. After so many years of keeping my gaze on the horizon, preparing for the next thing, what did I do now? How did I learn to make a home where I was, to work without knowing where I would be next—and when?

This need to make meaning out of my current situation gave me a taste of what the disciples struggled with. Jesus' words in this passage are a response to a question they have posed about what is to come—and when. Jesus tries to prepare them for the events that will precede his return to earth, but he resists answering the when question. As he says in verse 32, not even he knows. Some things really are meant to be a mystery.

After I came to my screeching halt in that first appointment, I began to develop practices that helped me become more present to where I was, which is the essence of Jesus' response to the disciples: not to give them all the answers but to give them practices to help them do the work at hand. Stay alert, beware, stay awake, pray. Jesus knew these practices would shift their focus from "What will *it* look like when you come again?" to "What will *we* look like when you come again?"

Advent—whose Latin root means "arrival"—invites us to ponder Christ's second coming. It keeps our eyes on the horizon, and rightly so. But it also reminds us that Christ has called us to be his body in this present time, to share in the working out of his reign here and now.

PRAYER: God who was and is and is to come, how shall I prepare for you? Bless me with vision, that I may be part of your work in the world even now. Amen.

FIRST SUNDAY OF ADVENT

The second coming of Christ is on Paul's mind too. In this letter to the church at Corinth, Paul offers words to his friends who await the revealing of Christ. The Greek word he uses for revealing is *apokalypsis*, from which we get the word *apocalypse*. Though this word has popularly come to refer to a destructive ending of impressive magnitude, at its root it simply means "revelation."

Although Paul is not unconcerned with what the days to come will look like, he seeks to draw his audience's attention to the present. To a church beset with divisions, Paul offers a reminder that they have everything they need to be the body of Christ now. As they wait for Christ, their waiting does not need to be idle. There is work to do.

The word *apocalypse* has bridal connotations, as is evident in the book of Revelation, also known as the Apocalypse to John. Such bridal imagery speaks to how deeply God longs for us, how intimately God wants to be with us. As I have begun to prepare for my own marriage, the art of waiting as an active state has become particularly real for me. There is so much to do—and I'm not even talking about the details of the wedding itself but the soul work that Gary and I do alone and together as we seek to know and be known.

This causes me to circle back to Monday's question: do I want that? Do I want to reveal myself that radically to someone else—to another human being, to God? Do I really want to lay bare the landscape of my soul for another to see?

As we stand on the threshold of this Advent season, my answer is yes. Yes to revelation, yes to knowing and being known, yes to the work of being the body of Christ in this and every season.

PRAYER: God of all seasons, bless me with wisdom in the waiting. In Advent and beyond, help me to risk knowing you even as I am known. Amen.

Get Ready for God

November 28–December 4, 2005 • Will Willimon[‡]

MONDAY, NOVEMBER 28 • Read Isaiah 40:1–11

Messiah opens on a somber chord, then the orchestra moves upward toward a clear, tenor voice: "Comfort ye, comfort ye my people . . . the voice of him that crieth in the wilderness: Prepare ye the way of the Lord, make straight in the desert a highway for our God."

Last Sunday Isaiah spoke for a people in the wilderness; in exile, lost, orphaned. "Thou hast hidden thy face from us" (Isa. 64:7), they cry. Into this forlorn, self-deprecating exilic gloom, the preacher proclaims "a highway for our God. Every valley shall be lifted up, and every mountain and hill be made low."

It's the announcement of a divine highway construction program, a straight road through the wilderness, the lostness, from Babylonian exile back home. Ordinarily, the way back from Babylonia to Israel followed the Fertile Crescent, going out of the way to avoid the desert wilderness. But this road is "straight in the desert."

Notice the good news that this is God's highway into the wilderness. Isaiah speaks about what God will do, where God is going: God dragging Israel along, coaxing Israel down the straight road home. We have demonstrated in our twists and turns through the millennia that we cannot, of our own will, get back to God. Thus Isaiah's Advent good news: God gets to us. So the question today is not, What am I looking for? or What would it take for me get me on the way back home? The question is, What road is God building toward me today?

PRAYER: Lord, come toward my wilderness in order that you might bring me home. Then give me the grace to see your advent in my life. Amen.

[‡]Dean of the Chapel and Professor of Christian Ministry, Duke University, Durham, North Carolina.

Christmas is homecoming. Already many families prepare to receive long lost relatives and friends who will be back home for Christmas. Look out on any mid-to-late-December congregation, and one sees familiar faces of kids home from college, wise relatives from the East bearing gifts. Welcome home.

And always I think, there are the "exiles" come back to church. We preachers sometimes make wisecracks about these lost sheep who wander back in from the cold at Christmastime. Attendance picks up in December; by Christmas Eve, the place is packed. Where have they been all year? we want to know. See you again on Easter! we say.

But why not homecoming now? Have you been in "exile"? What voice, what recently smoothed way (Isa. 40:1-11) has beckoned you back? Advent is the good news that our sense of separation, the loneliness that pervades our age, the boundaries between us, the amnesia, and the alienation are all being overcome by the God who says in Christ, "Good news! Come home."

The psalmist describes a great homecoming. To the lost the Lord speaks forgiveness and peace so that they may turn toward home. Steadfast love meets faithfulness; righteousness and peace kiss. Every good thing is rejoined, reunited, back home.

What voice calls you home—those words spoken not to you, but you heard them as if spoken only for you? That face from the past? That vaguely felt, but gnawing, sense of yearning? That echo evoked from deep in the soul's memory upon hearing again a carol not heard since childhood? That coincidence that might not have been merely coincidental?

"Come home, come home; you who are weary come home!" we sing.

Wilderness is that place, which is no place. Exile is that time when we are far from where we are created to be. Home is that place where we are at last where we ought to be.

PRAYER: Lord, let me hear what you will speak; and let me turn toward you with my whole heart. Amen.

As a preacher, I've always felt pride and some consternation as well that Mark's Gospel begins with a preacher, John the baptizer. Luke's Gospel begins with angels whispering in Mary's ear. But Mark has no angels, no shepherds keeping watch over their flocks by night, no wise men following a star, no animals at a straw-stuffed manger. Mark does not care about these Yuletide theatrical touches. For Mark, the good news of Jesus Christ begins in the wilderness with an old-fashioned preacher named John.

John was the first real prophet in Israel in at least three hundred years. And John sounded and looked like a prophet, with his strange look and wild words. While Matthew and Luke give us the gist of John's sermons, Mark simply says that John was "a messenger ahead of you." The Gospel of John introduces him as "a voice" (1:23).

John is therefore a reminder: you can't know about Jesus if someone doesn't tell you. The good news of Jesus Christ always begins as news, as something told to us, a message delivered by a messenger. The messenger may be an angel whispering in Mary's ear, a parent telling a child a bedtime Bible story, or a peculiar prophet standing knee-deep in a river. As Paul says, faith is always an acoustical affair (Rom. 10:17).

As a preacher, I'll now let you in on my deep discomfort with John the Baptist—John never preached from a pulpit and didn't go near a church. Those who insisted on staying hunkered down in the church missed John's message. Only those who willingly risked going out to the wilderness heard John's good news. What does that tell you?

PRAYER: Lord, come on out to our wilderness. Speak to us, use any means you have to get through to us, and then help us to hear you. Amen.

Thursday, December 1 • Read 2 Peter 3:8-15a

Here is one of the most unflattering descriptions of God in all scripture: God's coming among us is like a thief. God "like a thief"?

I know someone who had her home burglarized—treasured heirlooms ripped off, her space violated. "That thief ruined my home," she said, "and destroyed my sense of safety." God coming "like a thief"? It's not a very nice thing to say about God.

And worst of all, true.

I know two people who at midlife have been struck down by terminal illness. One is embittered, alienated, consumed by self-pity and, "Why me?" I can understand how suddenly staring death in the face might lead to bitterness.

Yet the other, while in much sadness, receives friends, treasures memories, gathers her grandchildren, and prepares for her departure.

The difference between them, I believe, is preparation. The first was a sometime church visitor and dropout of two Bible study groups. The other person was every Sunday in her place, in church, a constant student of the scriptures, someone who took her discipleship seriously.

Second Peter warns us to be ready for God as if God were a thief. Live each day as if it were our last. Hold possessions lightly, as if they were about to be pried from us. When it comes time to be faithful, will we have a faith to draw upon?

The soothing rhythm of the everyday can easily lull us into complacency. Yet one day there will be that "day of the Lord," the day that shall be the end of all days, that day when what we should have done or would have done will be at an end and we shall stand before God, not as we intended to be, but as we are.

Be prepared.

PRAYER: Lord, enable me to live this day as if it were my first day with you for all eternity. Amen.

Years ago, then Chrysler president, Lee Iacocca, began his commencement address at Duke by saying to the students, "I'm the only thing standing between you and your diploma!"

If we are to reach the Christ child at Bethlehem, we must first get by John. John admits that he is not the way but rather is the one who prepares and points to the way. How? By "proclaiming a baptism of repentance for the forgiveness of sins."

The Savior who comes may take us "Just as I Am," as we sing in the old hymn; but this Lord will not leave us just as we are. From the first he demands change, turning, conversion. Many of us say we want Jesus to come to us, to give us what we want, to help us through the challenges of this life.

John implies that we can't have Jesus without his transforming us, not giving us what we want but rather changing us into what he wants. We can't meet Jesus, says John, without being willing to change.

If I were honest, I ought to put a big sign over the front door of our church: DON'T RISK COMING IN HERE IF YOU DO NOT WANT TO RISK CHANGE!

PRAYER: Lord, you are coming. How do you want me to change in order to be ready to receive you? Amen.

When you hear Mark or Isaiah mention "wilderness," think of that shadowy, terrible place where Israel wandered in its long Exodus. Getting free from Pharaoh was not the toughest Exodus task. Between Egyptian slavery and freedom in the Promised Land lay homeless, desolate wilderness. Get out of your head the fuzzy modern notion of "wilderness" among the back-to-nature folks in their cozy cabins in the woods, as well as the granola visions of hiking in the Adirondacks on vacation. Wilderness for Israel was a place of wild beasts, temptation, sin, and bewildered wandering. It took Israel forty years of wandering the wilderness to find its way home.

And that's where Mark says the story of Jesus begins— wilderness. If we are to meet and be met by Jesus, it must be in the wilderness, that trackless wasteland where people sometimes wander, stumble, and lose their way.

I reckon every one of us has some idea where wilderness lies. The poet T. S. Eliot said that wilderness was not a geographical location; it was a corner of every heart. Wilderness may be your address right now. If it is, then Mark says that's good news because it's an excellent place to meet Messiah.

If we only listen for the Christ in comfortable contentment and ordered serenity or seated on a soft pew in church, then we might not hear the voice. Yet when we are far from home, lost, stumbling, then, for God's sake, listen.

The good news is that the story of God with us begins in the wilderness. Anybody who has never been in a wilderness may have trouble hearing that voice. Any church that's afraid to go out to the wilderness and look for the lost has no part of that voice. Wilderness is where we are most apt to hear God's voice.

PRAYER: O God, this day, while I wander the wilderness, help me to listen. Amen.

SECOND SUNDAY OF ADVENT

Dan Wakefield, in his popular book *Returning*, describes how he wandered away from God, allowing his life as an adult to become chaotic and confused. Then,

> I cannot pinpoint any particular time when I suddenly believed in God again. I only know that such belief came to seem as natural as for all but a few stray moments of twenty-five or more years before it had been inconceivable. . . . Was this what they called 'conversion? . . . That's what my own experience felt like—as if I'd been walking in one direction and then, in response to some inner pull, I turned.

Wakefield had returned.

From the wilderness John the Baptist calls out, quoting Isaiah, "Prepare the way of the Lord, make his paths straight." Mark tells us that this was, "The beginning of the good news of Jesus." The beginning of good news is the announcement by a voice "crying in the wilderness" that a lost people can return. By using the words of the prophet Isaiah, words that everyone had known since childhood, John calls Israel to remember and to return.

Recent studies suggest that many in my generation are returning to the church. Having wandered away, having tried several versions of "spirituality," having tried to be faithful alone, they are returning.

PRAYER: Lord, make me someone's reminder, someone's welcome back home, someone's invitation to return to you. Amen.

Song in a Minor Key

December 5–11, 2005 • Diane Luton Blum[‡]

MONDAY, DECEMBER 5 • Read Psalm 126

As you read Psalm 126, listen for the prayerful celebration of God's companionship with Israel and its people. This song about their dreams and the realization of their dreams is set in what musicians would call a minor key. The song beckons us, in the presence of God, to lift up our dreams as well as our hungers to see them become a reality. As we enter this song, become attentive to the plaintive notes that echo experiences in your life that sound a haunting minor key. Wait with these as you become aware of God's promise to accompany Israel and to accompany our present journeys.

Since childhood, my favorite Christmas song has been an Appalachian carol of lament, a prayer of questioning that simultaneously evokes deep praise and thanksgiving to God. It is set in a minor key. I have come to realize that part of the song's attraction for me is its emotional honesty about the coming of Christ: all is not already well because Christ is born, rather, Christ is born and we are still irritable, hostile, and crabby.

Listen to the yearning in your soul, and that of your community for wholeness, health, well-being, and peace—not just in heaven but now, on earth. Celebrate this longing and the shalom of God for which we hunger. The members of a beloved congregation close each worship service by singing an Israeli folk tune. They sing of *shalom*, the Hebrew word for God's gift of holy wholeness. They offer this vision of God's wholeness, sung in a minor key, for one another and for the world.

SUGGESTION FOR MEDITATION: Let the memory of what God has done for you in the past awaken your dreams for the ways God will provide in the present and in the future for your life.

[‡]Clergy member, Tennessee Annual Conference, The United Methodist Church; living in Nashville, Tennessee.

Christians can delight in reading this passage when we discover that Jesus studied, meditated, and preached from this portion of the Holy Scriptures within his own community of faith, particularly as he announced his self-understanding and initiated his ministry in Luke 4. Isaiah 61 poetically invites us into a living vision of God's shalom on earth, as in heaven: good news for those impoverished by the forces that can steal life's necessities, healing for broken hearts, freedom from the jails that we or others construct around our lives, forgiveness and amazing grace for the consequences of human sin.

Meditation on this vision changes our perception of the poverty, prisons, grief, and brokenness of our world. Dwell with these word pictures; expect them to make a home within you; let them spark acts of love that lead us to become people of God's shalom. Scholars say that the prophetic voice of Isaiah in chapter 61 is indeed a voice crying in a wilderness of exile, displacement, economic and social upheaval. The visionary song of God's shalom offers a place of centering peace and hope.

As you pray these verses, name and envision the points of deprivation, imprisonment, and sin that break your heart. Become aware of God's tender compassion for our world's brokenness into which the word of God becomes flesh in Jesus. In honest awareness of our broken world and broken selves, listen for God's passionate intent that we become whole, both as individuals and as a human community. Like Jesus, we are called to allow the holy texts of our faith tradition to name our ministry and shape our life together.

SUGGESTION FOR MEDITATION: Meditate upon one arena of brokenness from the verses of this text. Imagine God seeking, through the word of your life, to bring or to be good news for that human need. Let God prompt you to make a plan for faithful living this week of Advent.

Jesus echoes the blessings and praise of Isaiah 61 when he shares the "beatitudes" (see Matthew 5:3-11) in the Sermon on the Mount. Try praying each of these passages from Isaiah and Matthew that invite us to rejoice and be glad in circumstances that most of us would prefer to avoid. Isaiah 61:8-11 celebrates God's passion for justice, for right relationships of fairness and sharing, for communities of cooperation. How does this vision compare with the community in which you dwell? How does your faith community provide a glimpse of this eternal covenant?

In my city this year there are more young persons in public schools but fewer funds than last year to operate our educational system. Health-care expenses frighten many elderly, ill, or uninsured persons. Fear and anxiety abound in an otherwise wealthy part of God's world. How I long for the worries that shadow our community to be dispelled by a fairer sharing of common resources and wealth. Our longing for a different, peace-filled reality reflects the divine passion for justice and righteousness.

Read verse 10 and consider the reasons for the prophet's rejoicing. The world around this person is not yet a realization of God's shalom. The reasons for rejoicing come from the willingness to let God's loving and saving power be the center of his life. Clothed in God's mercy, decked out in God's fairness, and adorned with God's life-giving compassion, this faithful person joyfully invites you and me to live near the heart of God. When we routinely bring ourselves into God's presence, we find ourselves freer to relinquish the corrosive power of worry and fear. In God's presence we can be joyful despite awareness of the daily news of our broken world. Called into God's heart to holy wholeness, we are restored daily to be agents of shalom in this Advent season.

SUGGESTION FOR PRAYER: Begin your prayer time with intercession for painful facts you face today in the world. Now turn to God with trust and pray or sing for joy that God's saving grace is still born anew within and among us.

Paul urges the Christians of Thessalonica to lead a distinctive life of inner joy, peace, and gratitude that can readily surface in joyful, prayerful, and grateful action and relationships. As a young adult I studied this passage with dismay—surely Paul is exaggerating! Listen to the whole passage. Paul is quite serious. His own life story evidences this kind of joy, prayer, and gratitude. I have heard stories of God's people shining with holy wholeness in the dark nights of suffering, oppression, and death. This is not inevitable; it is a choice. I pray that we can be part of the continuing witness to this kind of faith.

Verses 19-22 remind us that we do not rejoice, pray, or give thanks out of ignorance but in careful living. We take care not to "throw cold water" on the work of the Holy Spirit. We watch to discern which spirit is at work among us. A trusted church leader once noted that if the *Holy* Spirit lifts you up, it won't put you back down in the same place. The new place will be marked by your growth in love, hope, joy, and justice. If it is God's good work, honor it and hold it fast. If it proves to bring harm, mislead, or diminish, Paul calls us to abstain and let it go.

A mark of God's holy wholeness is what we call integrity of life. Growth in the Holy Spirit leads to increasing unity between thought and action, inner motive and outward expression of faith. We give thanks not just when things seem to be going our way but when circumstances become threatening. By living a prayerful, attentive life in God's presence, we take joy from our conviction that God's saving grace will keep us in the valleys shadowed by death as well as in the green pastures of life. With Jesus, as he spoke and lived the beatitudes, we can rejoice and be glad in all things.

SUGGESTION FOR PRAYER: In your time of prayer, offer God an inventory of all the good to which you would hold fast and the evil you are willing to release or forego. Let God guide your decisions and actions from this inventory today.

The God of peace in the New Testament is one and the same God of shalom we meet in the prophecy of the Old Testament. This holy God's concern centers not just on our souls but also on our bodies, on our hearts as well as our minds, on our intentions and our actions. Walking in attentive prayerfulness with God in *all* parts of our lives calls us into wholeness and health. In a world that allows us to compartmentalize various pieces of our lives, God beckons us to become one in body, soul, and spirit, and one with God's purposes in the creation.

Consider the care of your body. How have you attended to your health and to the divine gift of dynamic energy that comes from emotional, physical, mental, and spiritual wholeness? Offer God praise for your physical well-being by caring for your needs for good nutrition, movement, and rest. God's shalom includes and extends to the stewardship of our bodied lives.

Over several years I shared in a Covenant Discipleship group with five other Christians in our congregation. We carefully drew up a covenant to which we held ourselves and one another accountable. We sought to grow through acts of mercy and justice, devotion, and worship. We included in our covenant a remembrance that it is God who is at work in us.

We are "not our own." We are held in God's saving grace by faith, not by our achievements or good works. God's love became very real for me as we prayed together and honored the work of God in our bodies, spirits, and souls. I no longer serve in that congregation, but I keep my copy of our group's covenant with me in my daily calendar. I give thanks for these faithful friends even though circumstances keep us apart. As I offered a stranger the gift of compassionate listening this week, my heart could hear their loving support to hold fast to what is good.

SUGGESTION FOR MEDITATION: Consider the memory of a faithful friend. Now reflect on God's faithfulness that transcends all human effort. Ask God to grant you peace in body, soul, and spirit. Open yourself to receive this gift of shalom.

Read verses 1-18 and then, in the context of this sweeping vision of the incarnation of God's word of love, meet John, the one who baptizes and preaches at the Jordan River. Every grand project has an "advance" team, a pioneer, a road builder. So John comes to bear witness to the light of Christ. Awake and attentive to God's movement among humankind, John does not miss his moment, his cue. He walks out on God's stage so that others will not miss the light of Christ, so that other hearts can prepare for and receive God's love made flesh.

Every Advent, we hear John's story. Willing to wait in the wilderness, willing to live unencumbered by luxuries and diversions, willing to call others to prepare for God's coming, John's voice still speaks among us. Advent is an ideal time to give up some unnecessary luxury in order to prepare our hearts and lives to make room for Christ's coming. Removing clutter from our homes and our habits can counter the pressures of holiday expectations. John is one of those unvarnished pioneers who can help us get ready.

As a follower of Christ I was relieved to learn that God calls me *not* to be a judge for others but to be a witness to God's light in Christ, redeeming grace, and resurrection power. In this season of Advent God invites us to let go of the clutter in our relationships that comes from judging others. We can then make room for witnessing to the light of Christ by word and deed.

God can use our unique identities, flawed and limited as we may be, to give testimony to the incarnation of divine love. We become transparent to that love and light and offer faithful witness with honesty, humility, and integrity. We see these characteristics in John and pray that these traits take root and grow to fullness in our lives and ministry.

SUGGESTION FOR MEDITATION: Reflect on the integrity of your witness to the light of Christ. What keeps this Light from shining through your life? Pray for courage to relinquish one of these obstacles today.

SUNDAY, DECEMBER 11 • Read John 1:19-28

THIRD SUNDAY OF ADVENT

The religious leaders quiz John. They seem to have an agenda, a preconception about who John is. John answers their questions with holy wholeness, with openness and clarity, without apology or hedging.

John tells them that he is not the Messiah or Elijah or the prophet. John leads us to a courageous assessment of who we are, and who we are not. How hard it can be to resist the desires of others who would prefer to impose on us an identity that meets their needs in that moment. We pigeonhole others or we allow others to pigeonhole us. Yet labeling one another prevents us from knowing and being known in the wholeness of our identity as God's children.

John, in the tradition of holy wholeness, identifies himself with God's purposes: his unique mission and selfhood, planted by God for this moment in human history. John reveals his deep roots in the tradition of God's shalom as a road builder for the Word made flesh as it moves into our hearts and lives.

A wise church leader once advised a group of younger pastors to be prepared to step aside "if you know you are not the one called by God for a particular task." By "making way," the one God *has* called can come forward; our support can provide the road upon which that person travels.

The baptismal work of John sets the stage for what God will do in Jesus and in the baptismal life of the church. Church leaders who carry out the rite of Christian baptism set the stage for divine work in the life of the baptized person. The whole church makes ready a road for God to travel directly within the life of the person who is invited to die and rise with Christ. The God of shalom calls all of us to holy wholeness.

SUGGESTION FOR REFLECTION: Consider who God is calling you to be. Now reflect on who you are not called to be at this time in God's plan. May God grant you courage to be exactly who you are and who you need to be in your ministry with Christ.

Good News!

December 12–18, 2005 • *Michael Willett Newheart*[‡]

MONDAY, DECEMBER 12 • Read 2 Samuel 7:1-11, 16

Today's passage is pivotal in this section of Hebrew scripture, often referred to by scholars as "the Deuteronomic history." The central character in the Deuteronomic history is David, and here in 2 Samuel 7 the Lord promises an eternal dynasty to David. The crucial word in this passage is *house*, which means alternatively "dynasty" or "temple." David intends to build a "house" for the ark of God, that is, a temple. But the Lord says to David (through the prophet Nathan) that the Lord will build him a house, that is, a dynasty.

While David is promised an everlasting throne, the power behind that throne is the Lord God. According to this passage, God has given David rest from his enemies, brought the people of Israel out of Egypt, and taken David from pasture to prince. And more is to come: God will make for David a great name, appoint a place for Israel where they will be at peace, and make David a house which will be forever.

Swiss theologian Karl Barth said that we are to read with the Bible in one hand and the newspaper in the other. I cannot read about ancient Israel without thinking about the present violence in the Middle East. As I write this week's meditations, a Palestinian suicide bomber in Haifa, Israel, killed nineteen and wounded fifty, and Israeli forces killed six Palestinians in a Gaza refugee camp. Alas, the peace promised to David and Israel has yet to come to pass!

SUGGESTION FOR MEDITATION: Read today's passage and then read an article in today's newspaper about the Middle East. Close your eyes in prayer, and imagine peace in the Middle East. What might you do to enflesh that imagining?

[‡]Associate Professor of New Testament, Howard University School of Divinity; member, Adelphi Friends Meeting (Quaker); living in Berwyn Heights, Maryland.

Nathan performs an important role in this story. This is his first appearance in the Bible, and he is simply introduced as "the prophet." We read nothing of his background or origin. He obviously has an intimate relationship with the king because it is to him that David notes the seeming contradiction between the king living in a cedar house and the ark residing in a tent. Initially it seems that Nathan encourages David to build a house for the ark, for he says, "Go, do all that you have in mind; for the LORD is with you."

A prophet, however, does not speak on his own authority but only on the basis of "the word of the LORD." So that night the word of the Lord comes (presumably in a "night vision" or dream). Nathan is instructed to tell this word to "my servant David" with the introduction, "Thus says the LORD." What the Lord says comes in two parts. First, God has not wanted a house to live in. Second, God says that the Lord will build a house (and a kingdom and a throne, all of which are synonymous) for David that will last forever.

This is obviously good news for David, and he responds with a prayer of thanksgiving (7:18-29). Later on, however, when Nathan makes his second appearance (12:1-15), he does not bear glad tidings. Rather, he condemns the king in no uncertain terms: "Why have you despised the word of the LORD, to do what is evil in his sight? You have struck down Uriah the Hittite with the sword, and have taken his wife to be your wife" (12:9). He is no fair-weather prophet!

SUGGESTION FOR MEDITATION: **Who are the prophets in our day? What are they saying to those in power? In what ways do you serve as a prophet?**

Our reading today comes from the first part of a rather long psalm that is actually a royal lament, occasioned by some major defeat (see Psalm 89:38-45). The first four verses, however, sound out the psalmist's praise to the Lord for choosing David as king. We may further divide this section of the psalm into two sub-sections. In verses 1 and 2 the psalmist addresses God through singing, proclaiming, and declaring the steadfast love and faithfulness of the Lord. (Notice how "steadfast love" appears in the first and third lines, and "faithfulness" appears in the second and fourth lines.) In verses 3 and 4 God addresses the psalmist, referring to the covenant with God's chosen servant David. Verse 4 essentially restates the promise made to David in 2 Samuel 7:16, which we have considered the last two days: God will establish (that is, build) David's descendants (that is, throne) forever (that is, for all generations).

A strange note appears after verse 4 in the New Revised Standard Version, the Hebrew word *selah*. Translators have left it untranslated because of their uncertainty as to what it means. We read *selah* again in this psalm after verses 37, 45, and 48. It appears throughout the Psalter. Since it appears at the end of a short section within a psalm, it may be an instruction for the reader or a place for readers to rest, but that is only a guess.

Let us "rest" there. Read Psalm 89:1-4 aloud a number of times using various tones and differing volumes. Then be quiet and allow the words to reverberate within your soul. Be aware of any images that arise. Simply rest in the steadfast love and faithfulness of the Lord. After you've taken some time in meditation, write down whatever came for you. What does resting in the steadfast love and faithfulness of the Lord mean for you?

PRAYER: O God, as I go about my responsibilities of the day, may I ever rest in your steadfast love and faithfulness. Amen.

Our passage today begins the second major section of this psalm. In the first major section (89:1–18), the psalmist praises the Lord. In this second section (89:19–37), the psalmist gives us a poetic version of 2 Samuel 7:4–17. The psalmist mentions throughout the psalm God's "steadfast love" and "faithfulness" (see verses 24, 28, 33, 49). God has shown steadfast love and faithfulness by defeating David's enemies (vv. 10, 22–23; also 2 Sam. 7:1, 9); God's hand and arm have been with David. Indeed, God rules the sea and has given that power over to David (vv. 9, 25).

The psalmist says that God has spoken to David in a vision. (Nothing is said about the vision appearing to Nathan, as in 2 Samuel 7:4.) And the Lord is said to have anointed David. (No mention is made of Samuel, as in 1 Samuel 16:13.) The Hebrew word for "anointed" is *mashiah*, from which we get the English word "messiah." David is God's messiah, and as such, he is to call God "Father." God has made him "the firstborn" (v. 27). In the word of the Lord delivered by Nathan, God says of David's off-spring, "I will be a father to him, and he shall be a son to me" (2 Sam. 7:14). The king will be an anointed son of God. We find the same combination of anointing and divine sonship in Psalm 2, in which the king, the Lord's anointed (2:2), tells of the Lord's decree, in which the Lord says, "You are my son; today I have begotten you" (2:7).

We are all sons and daughters of God, anointed not for violence but for peace.

Suggestion for prayer: In prayer, imagine yourself as a son or daughter of God, anointed for peace. What qualities do you embody? How do you feel? What activities do you picture yourself involved in?

Here Paul offers his closing benediction to his magisterial letter to the Romans. He picks up words from the beginning. Compare these verses with the salutation in 1:1-7. In both places Paul talks about the gospel, first referring to it as "the gospel of God" (1:1) and "the gospel concerning his Son" (1:3) and then as "my gospel and the proclamation of Jesus Christ" (16:25). Paul also notes that this gospel was first promised through "prophets in the holy scriptures" (1:2) and through "the prophetic writings" (16:26). Now it is proclaimed to the Gentiles (1:5; 16:26). And among the Gentiles Paul wants to bring about "the obedience of faith" (1:5; 16:26).

This week's first four meditations have focused on God's blessing of the king of Israel. Here, however, in the ministry of Paul, the blessing extends to the Gentiles, that is, non-Jews. Indeed, Paul often refers to himself as an "apostle to the Gentiles." For Paul God's plan all along included this expansion of inclusion, which has been kept secret until now, when the "mystery" has been revealed. Paul speaks about this mystery in 11:25; he says that part of Israel has been hardened "until the full number of the Gentiles has come in." And then all Israel will be saved.

It is all pretty mysterious. God's mercies now extend to the Gentiles. Who are the Gentiles in our day? Who are the people we consider to be outside divine blessing? Perhaps they are people of a different race, social class, religion, or sexual orientation? What are the Gentile parts of ourselves? What aspects of our humanity do we exclude from the divine presence?

Suggestion for meditation: In prayer, imagine all people and all parts of yourself being accepted by God. What would that look like, feel like? How would you behave differently?

Of the four Gospels, only Matthew and Luke narrate the birth of Jesus (Matt. 1–2; Luke 1–2), and only Luke narrates the birth of John the Baptist as well as that of Jesus. Indeed, their stories are paired. First the angel Gabriel goes to tell Zechariah of the coming birth of John, and then Gabriel goes to tell Mary of the coming birth of Jesus (Luke 1:8-20, 26-38). Next the birth of John is narrated (1:57-80), then the birth of Jesus (2:1-20). At each point Jesus is greater. John is born to an elderly couple, Jesus to a virgin. At John's birth his father "sings" a hymnlike prophecy, at Jesus' birth the heavenly host sings. Compare what the angel Gabriel says to Zechariah about John (1:13-17) and what he says to Mary about Jesus (1:31-35). Both will be great. John will be great because he will turn many of the people of Israel to the Lord, thus preparing the people for the Lord. Jesus, however, will be great, because he will be called Son of the Most High God, and God will give him David's throne upon which he will rule forever. The language here reflects what we have already read in 2 Samuel 7 and in Psalm 89. The promise made to David is now extended to Jesus.

These stories tell of unexpected births that broke the cycle of violence and oppression that surrounded the first-century Jew (and Gentile). In Mary's hymn (often called the Magnificat), she praises God for bringing down the powerful, lifting up the lowly, filling the hungry, and sending away the rich (1:52-53). Zechariah blesses God for redeeming the people through a "mighty savior . . . in the house of his servant David."

SUGGESTION FOR MEDITATION: In what ways is something new being born in you and around you? How is the Holy Spirit coming upon you and overshadowing you?

FOURTH SUNDAY OF ADVENT

The angel of the Lord, Gabriel, visits two people here in Luke 1. First he visits Zechariah while he performs his priestly service in the Temple (1:8–20), then he visits Mary in Nazareth of Galilee (1:26–38). Both visits seem to follow a pattern: the angel appears, and the person is terrified or perplexed. The angel then says not to be afraid (calling Zechariah and Mary by name) and then gives them a reason why. Zechariah is not to be afraid, for his prayer has been heard; his wife will bear him a son, whom he is to name John. Mary is not to be afraid, for she has found favor with God (thus her being greeted by the angel Gabriel as "favored one") so that she will bear a son, whom she is to name Jesus. Both are then given a sign of the truth of the angel's message: for Zechariah it is his muteness; for Mary it is her cousin Elizabeth's pregnancy. This pattern continues in the angel's appearance to the shepherds in Luke 2:8-12: they are terrified. The angel tells them not to be afraid, for he tells them "good news of great joy," the birth of a Savior, Christ the Lord. He then gives them a sign: they will find a child wrapped in bands of cloth and lying in a manger.

The word *angel* literally means "messenger," and Gabriel the angel of the Lord performs that function well in the first two chapters of Luke. He gives to Zechariah, Mary, and the shepherds the message of the births of special individuals.

When has an angel appeared to you? What was the angel's message? In what ways does God communicate messages to you? What have those messages been recently?

PRAYER: God of great news, as I go about my activities this Advent season, make me receptive to your message, in whatever form it might take. Amen.

Apocalypse Now

December 19–25, 2005 • Patrick J. Nugent[‡]

MONDAY, DECEMBER 19 • Read Isaiah 9:2-7

Christmas is deadeningly familiar. The lectionary readings, however, confront us with an eschatological Christmas, the event by which God chooses to turn the world upside down, breaking into the world, shattering its history. The Incarnation is apocalyptic: it dramatically reveals God's nature and will for the world.

About twelve hours' drive from where I live, the district of Lira, Uganda, is in quiet but bloody siege. Members of the "Lord's Resistance Army" have been terrorizing the rural areas around the town, killing, raping, pillaging, and drafting children into their murderous armies. Closer to where I live, the barren district around the refugee camps in Kakuma, Kenya, was in an uproar not long ago when two young Sudanese refugees beheaded a local Turkana woman as she sat selling her wares. Revenge followed, then counterrevenge, then an exacerbating government intervention.

"Every boot of the tramping warrior in battle tumult and every garment rolled in blood" (RSV): in peaceful places these words sound garish. Not far from me, they are daily bread.

Christmas is an apocalypse *now*, the eschatological will of God revealed in the midst of the violence of history. Christmas is not about fuzzy donkeys nuzzling a cute baby; it is about God crashing into history with joyfully absurd power—"for unto us a child is born"—to burn crushing boots and bloody garments. God-become-flesh points the direction of salvation history against the flow of our self-destructive history. Babies overturning generals—the promise of a world turned upside down.

SUGGESTION FOR MEDITATION: In what darkness do I dwell? From where do I await a great light?

[‡]Member of the Religious Society of Friends (Quakers); principal of Friends Theological College, Kaimosi, Kenya.

How beautiful upon the mountains are the feet of the messenger who announces peace"—Isaiah's answer to the psalmist, "I lift up my eyes to the hills. From whence does my help come?" (Ps. 121:1, RSV). These verses too are eschatological: in Africa, in Latin America, in the Philippines, the hills are often hiding places of bandits, nurseries of war. To look to the hills for the bearers of peace is to resist the threat of violence with a radical and desperate hope in the Prince of Peace.

In Nairobi, the lavishly spreading estates of the wealthy, the diplomats, the politicians, the business tycoons are guarded day and night by watchmen who receive less than fifty dollars a month in pay. Some wear policelike uniforms; others wear whatever they can find. These guards usually live in one of the city's sprawling slums and are likely financially responsible for a wife and children in Nairobi and unemployed family members at home in the rural area. They guard the palaces but live in what Isaiah calls the "waste places" (RSV). Isaiah asks me to imagine the day when these watchmen—and indeed all of creation—break into song, lifting up their voices. Somehow, it is they who will see "eye to eye . . . the return of the LORD to Zion" (RSV). The singing is no accident. Today in churches and fellowships small and large across Africa, a week of labor and suffering, joy and celebration is punctuated by vibrant, sometimes ear-splitting song—lavish and spreading, musically palatial. It is the song of an entire people shouting out their unquenchable hope in the gospel of peace and the tidings of salvation.

Christmas is apocalypse now, not back then and not far in the future. "Sing to the LORD a new song," now, already. "Let the sea roar"—the song of creation itself ushers in the hope of peoples and the power of the Incarnation *now*.

SUGGESTION FOR MEDITATION: God's love is steadfast, and all the ends of the earth have already seen God's victory. Where? How?

Praising God is too familiar. Cutting-edge Protestants have grown bored of it, and hip evangelicals dress it up in amplified commercial music. Praising God becomes a euphemism for thanking God for fulfilling my wish list, a projection of my desire, and a monument to the idolatrous sources of my satisfaction.

But those who praised God in the Hebrew Bible, for whom the psalmist speaks, praised God out of their poverty and their precariousness. Praise is a strategy of resistance against suffering and meaninglessness, shouted out with joy against the great darkness in which we walk. Psalms 96 and 98 proclaim a revolution of praise, declaring against darkness and suffering that a light is beginning to dawn and praising its divine source before we see its effects.

Praise is pointless, and that is the point. Praise differs from thanksgiving because it has little to do with what God has done for us. The point of praise is to turn us completely outside of ourselves, a response of love and wonder to our lover, simply for who God is, not for what God does. Yet by turning us out of ourselves, praise also opens our eyes to what God is already doing.

In a startlingly similar way, the Incarnation turned God out of God's self and toward us, pouring out anew to shatter our history by mingling the heavenly and the fleshly. God chooses to share our condition and to join in our singing against the void, our praise of the dawning morning of peace and deliverance. Jesus lives as one of us, beginning his journey as a baby in the condition of insignificant vulnerability that most of us share but which threatens some far more than others. Jesus takes our nature to orient us toward the dawn, to lead all the universe in the song of praise that ushers in the New Creation and shatters the idols that woo us.

SUGGESTION FOR MEDITATION: Do I trust enough in the coming victory of the Prince of Peace that I can raise a song of praise to him, a song powerful enough to cast down my idols of darkness?

The song of praise with which we greet the New Creation is a song of the whole universe. The creation groans with birth pangs, yet shouts and claps its hands at the coming of God's apocalypse in Jesus.

The song of praise in the face of darkness that turns us outward toward our Source, also turns us inward. In Jesus, God's victory comes; but he comes first as a vulnerable baby, not as a general or emperor, because the divine revolution in history begins in small, vulnerable places, none of them smaller or more vulnerable than the wounded and alienated heart. The victory of God in creation is also the victory of God's goodness in my own heart, dawning in the darkness of my inward confusion and chaos. The letter to Titus reminds us that the grace of God, appearing for the salvation of all humanity, begins its revolution in the way I myself live in the world. I can sing the song of praise only if the universal revolution first appears as a revolution in my conduct toward others, just as the great eschatological revolution of love begins in the birth of a baby without a home, an insignificant person in a troubled place.

Yet, as the letter tells us, this revolution is not a revolution of efforts, tactics, and strategies but a revolution of grace, a revolution of God's wanton love. The love that drove the divine to incarnation drives the divine with the thirst to save, to deliver, to reconcile persons to God's self, one at a time and the whole world with us. The world may be a place of violence and despair, yet in it are lives lived in the song of praise, empowered by God's power, the very power of the Incarnation that enfleshes itself in our attempts to counter violence and despair with lives charged with love—"sober, upright, godly lives in this world, awaiting our blessed hope" (RSV). And hope does not fail.

PRAYER: **God of never-ending hope, renew our spirits in a song of praise. Amen.**

If the weight of God's revolution seems to rest squarely on our conduct, John reminds us that the necessary grace and power begin in us. The light Isaiah promised begins dawning in the human heart. This light, enlightening everyone, is the power of God raised against cosmic darkness, a protean underground resistance—hard to see but everywhere. If we are skeptical of God's cosmic victory, John reminds us that the Light gives us power. God dispels the darkness by a sheer abundance of love. This Light breeds a revolutionary intimacy, a power transforming our hearts so that God may transform the world.

Our intimacy with God begins in God's intimacy with us. The Word became flesh, took on the complexity of body, mind, soul, will, love, knowledge, ignorance, and limitation. That makes us not just beings of spirit but fully enfleshed creatures—a complicated mess that God joyfully declared as good the moment of its creation.

This is the radical mystery of Christian faith. The take-it-or-leave-it proposition is not the Resurrection or the miracles but the apocalyptic fact that God truly became so fully human that Jesus could suffer death at the hands of the powers of this world. Once we accept that, the Resurrection simply becomes God's own victorious contribution to the great song of praise we are all called to sing in the midst of the darkness.

"We have beheld his glory" (RSV). God who becomes flesh is also the Word of power and wisdom through which the universe is created. Jesus, the Light of grace and truth, enlightens every heart.

SUGGESTION FOR MEDITATION: We already behold the glory of the Resurrection in the Light that shines, draws, pleads, calls us to join in the cosmic hymn of praise which the watchmen rise to sing in the midst of their watching, which the crushed spirits rise to sing in the waste places of Jerusalem.

CHRISTMAS EVE

If light and power seem abstract, Hebrews reminds us of the gospel fact: God speaks to us in person, through a person. The human Jesus is not only God-bearing flesh but the fullest revelation of who God is and what God is like. Isaiah and the psalmist talk about God's victory and God's power over the tramping boots and blood-soaked garments, leaving us with the impression that the feet bearing the tidings of peace will be mighty by human measure.

The Christmas narratives subvert this expectation. The disciples of Jesus expected a political savior not because they were misguided but because they were miserable. The conditions faced by children and parents in Lira and pastoralists in Turkana are not unlike the lives of Jesus' disciples under Roman colonial occupation. Judas Iscariot may have been the most disappointed of the disciples, betraying Jesus not to sell him out but to provoke him to reveal his hidden glory.

But Hebrews reminds us that the Jesus we see is the God we get. Jesus shows us plainly who God is and what God is like, demonstrating God's power and victory in his own acts of compassion and freedom. The God who upholds the universe by a word of power is revealed precisely in the visible person of Jesus, born an infant in filth, living poor and homeless, healing people's infirmities, sharing their oppression, dying because of the weight of human sin. These are the deeds that uphold the universe and bring the tidings of peace, then and now. "You are the same, and your years will never end." The Jesus of the Gospels is the one who sits at the right hand of God. His revolutionary deeds of love subject the forces of dehumanization and destruction as a stool beneath his feet. "We do not yet see everything in subjection to him. But we see Jesus" (Heb. 2:8-9).

SUGGESTION FOR MEDITATION: **When I look for the glory of God, what do I look for?**

CHRISTMAS DAY

The angels joined creation's song of praise, crying "Glory!" But the glory of God they behold is so far from obvious that only a cosmic light show can lead the shepherds. Where I live, shepherds (cowherds, goatherds) are everywhere. They are among the poorest of the poor, often young boys of six or eight. Likely Luke's shepherds were almost as vulnerable as the baby Jesus, and probably not much older. Shepherds live in the outdoors, defenseless against wild animals and cruel humans. Announcing the birth of the vulnerable, endangered Messiah, the angels come first to vulnerable, endangered children. Somehow, they better understand the manger-hid Glory and Peace, because their expectations are simpler and their vision less clouded.

American babies are surrounded by a fortress of technological protection. In the pastoralist, refugee, and village cultures of Kenya, babies are often born under the most precarious of conditions. Immediately after the child's birth, parents prepare themselves for the possibility that the child may die early. In the last year I have preached at the funerals of two children under the age of two. Each time, the parents have said, "It is sad, but it is a normal part of life." A lot of pain is buried beneath those words.

Jesus' parents were not quite refugees, but close—alone, in a filthy place, far from home and family, on the edge and on the margins. The young shepherds were probably more hindrance than help. Were Jesus' parents already preparing to say, "It is sad, but normal"? Apocalypse, revelation—now. "He reflects the glory of God and bears the very stamp of [God's] nature, upholding the universe by his word of power" (Heb. 1:3, RSV).

PRAYER: Come, Lord Jesus, renew the hearts of your faithful. Kindle in them the fire of your love. Send forth your Spirit, and they shall be created, and you shall renew the face of the earth. Amen.

The Mystery of Christ

December 26–31, 2005 • *Jennifer Grove Bryan*[‡]

MONDAY, DECEMBER 26 • **Read Luke 2:22-40;
Isaiah 61:10–62:3**

During the past few weeks of Advent, for what were you waiting? What were your expectations? How did you spend your days leading up to the celebration of Jesus' birth?

During the first century in Jerusalem, then ruled by Rome and governed by the despised Herod, two of Israel's faithful were "looking for the redemption of Israel." They watched eagerly for God's presence in their bleak situation.

Though circumstances defied the likelihood that "the consolation of Israel" was at hand, devout Simeon and pious, elderly Anna, both of whom served in the Temple. They prayed, fasted, and watched. These two believed God's words through the prophet Isaiah—that Jerusalem would be restored as God's "crown of beauty" for all nations to take notice.

Though they went about their daily business, Simeon and Anna nevertheless waited and longed for God's "light for revelation to the Gentiles, and for glory to your people Israel." Had they not been steeped in the prophecy, had they not been ardently disciplined and steadfast in hope, would either have recognized God at work? Instead, gazing into baby Jesus' face, each praises God and expresses faith that in this newborn, the Savior has come! Israel's Messiah has arrived, according to God's word!

Led by God's Spirit, both of these saints see the link between Jesus and Jerusalem's renewal. The world's salvation, Israel's glory, has just been born to Joseph and Mary of Nazareth. To what word of God do you cling? How will you convey that?

PRAYER: Lord God, help me to dwell in your word and act upon it in faith. Amen.

[‡]Candidate for ordination as deacon in The United Methodist Church; member of Lenexa United Methodist Church, Lenexa, Kansas.

Joseph and Mary surely found the Holy Spirit's revelation regarding their newborn staggering. Was it even possible that God had chosen to come to Israel in this manner—let alone in *their* child? Yet they move forward in trust, clinging to the angel's words.

Mary and Joseph bring Jesus. Obeying the Jewish religious customs following a baby's birth, they bring their offerings to consecrate Jesus in the Temple. Their son is circumcised on the eighth day, according to the law, and they name him Jesus, as the angel Gabriel has directed, well before his conception.

In the Jerusalem temple the new parents receive confirmation about Jesus. The prophetic praise from Anna and the jubilant song of Simeon acclaim their son as God's agent of salvation, the One for whom Israel's faithful long, although many will oppose him. Sadly, it remains so today.

We often forget that Advent not only recalls the fulfillment of God's promised Messiah in the vulnerable babe but also anticipates a second coming of Jesus in resplendent magnificence, not to be missed! The eyes of all will be opened "and every tongue [will] confess that Jesus Christ is Lord, to the glory of God the Father" (Phil. 2:11, RSV). Are we living accordingly? When we pray, "Thy kingdom come," are we expectantly working toward it with God's help? Like Simeon and Anna, like Joseph and Mary, we too choose how we go about our daily lives.

Mysterious as it seemed, Mary and Joseph nevertheless obeyed God's instruction, believing that their child "will reign over the house of Jacob forever" (Luke 1:33). Like Simeon and Anna, Mary and Joseph act on God's word.

PRAYER: Gracious God, help me to trust and obey. Amen.

Given a vision of Israel's vindication while many mourn the loss of Jerusalem, the holy city and God's symbolic dwelling place, Isaiah issues prophetic words of hope to those exiled in Babylon. Though called to be a light to surrounding nations, Israel's kings have turned from seeking divine guidance, ignored God's prophets, and relied on political alliances to protect them.

People of the land began to live like the other nations instead of revealing a lifestyle shaped by God's word and law. Around 586 BCE the city's political and religious leaders were utterly disgraced and humiliated by capture and taken into exile far from Jerusalem.

The Babylonian conquerors took all the bronze, silver, and gold from the Temple; Nebuchadnezzar's siege completely desecrated the city. The Babylonians carried off the city's best and brightest as prisoners, almost five thousand people (Jer. 52:30), and killed King Zedekiah's sons in front of him just before they gouged out the king's eyes. There was little comfort left to the Israelites when they remembered Jerusalem.

Then comes Isaiah's encouragement, comfort, hope! Jerusalem, devastated and reminiscent of shame, will become Zion, the new Jerusalem, shining forth God's salvation! God will make it happen, Isaiah says, just as a garden produces mature plants from tiny seeds.

When the time is right—according to God's schedule—Jerusalem will be renewed. All will recognize God's power, sovereignty, and righteousness. Anna and Simeon saw the seed. Are you watching for promised produce to spring forth from the divine gardener's hand?

PRAYER: Eternal and sovereign God, may it be so. Our Lord, come. Amen.

Praise God! There is no other appropriate response. Heavenly beings and earthly creatures: let everything and everyone, visible and invisible, shout praise to the God of all creation! The Lord's righteousness and sovereignty make ready the redemption of all creation—animate and inanimate. For God "has raised up a horn for his people, praise for all his faithful."

Arising from the coronation of one of Israel's kings (v. 14), this psalm highlights the strength God gives Israel in an anointed ruler. The land sings in jubilation that God has appointed one who will rule the chosen people according to God's law and relying on God's instruction. We know from scripture, however, that the law and prophets did not procure for Israel the righteousness God desired. Even King David, a man after God's own heart, fell far short of this role.

Psalm 78 is a litany of God's history with the chosen people Israel. Verse 68 speaks of God's love for "Mount Zion," an eternal throne where God will reign among the faithful. The temple in Jerusalem not only announced to the Israelites that the favor and presence of God was with them, but also it shouted to Ancient Near Eastern cultures surrounding them that Yahweh's people were not defenseless. They were not without the world's sovereign ruler in their very midst. The One whose mighty arm has not shriveled provides for and protects them.

Though Israel's earthly kings often failed to represent God's will, this word will be fulfilled nevertheless by the son born to Joseph and Mary. Jesus, the eternal priest, prophet, and king, will return victoriously one day; all of life will rejoice in Zion's renewal. Am I watching, waiting, and working accordingly?

PRAYER: Creator God, inspire me to cocreate with you until Jesus returns. Amen.

Renewed! Rescued! Pardoned! Delivered! Redeemed from sin and death! By whatever term that resonates with you today, hear the good news: in Christ we have been released from slavery to legalistic demands and given God's grace and glorious adoption!

Claimed as children under a covenant of care begun in Jesus, we are now his spiritual heirs. Rather than being slaves to a law that failed to bring about the sinlessness it intended, we receive God's goodness through Jesus' total obedience to God. Jesus' life completely satisfies the law. This is what the apostle Paul declares as he writes to believers in Galatia.

Since Paul's preaching to them, the Galatians have turned from the gospel "that is, in Christ God was reconciling the world to himself, not counting their trespasses against them" (2 Cor. 5:19). In Jesus, God accomplishes the ideal Israel could not attain by striving to keep the Mosaic law: righteousness.

The time of Advent repeatedly reminds us of prophetic promises given ages before Jesus' birth that assure the faithful of God's redemption, restoration, renewal, and return of righteousness. What Paul distinguishes for the Galatians is that faith in Jesus Christ provides access to this undeserved mercy!

God sent Jesus to do for us what legalism cannot do. The letter of the law does not necessarily yield the Spirit from which the law came. Christ's spirit with us now, *in* us at our adoption as heirs, motivates us to live in proactive love of God and of neighbor.

We are heirs of Jesus, and through him we trust God for our renewal and transformation. Thanks be to God!

PRAYER: Generous Holy Spirit, take my life and let it be consecrated to you. Amen.

The kingdom of God has come in Christ. Like the baby Jesus, it still exists in an immature state on this earth. The seed will grow, however, and when the glorified Christ returns, "the Lord GOD will cause righteousness and praise to spring up before all the nations" (Isa. 61:11). We affirm that God's kingdom on earth begun with the baby Jesus—God incarnate—ushered in a new age, a new covenant. Now we live with Christ's spirit among us, present with us; we depend upon God's mercy, not humanity's striving.

No longer does a symbolic temple or a priestly cult have claims upon us, for Jesus is *the way* God now draws broken humanity to restoration. Paul clearly states that Jesus' coming is not happenstance. On the contrary, Jesus' arrival on earth is specifically designated. The long-awaited Messiah, the Anointed One who pleases God appropriately in humanity's stead, appears purposefully when the sovereign Lord of all history determines "the fullness of time had come" (Gal. 4:4).

Those who trust in Jesus to do for them what they cannot do for themselves are now God's chosen, Paul declares. Salvation comes through God's goodness to those in Christ! While the law still serves as a useful guide, it no longer serves as master. Instead, Jesus is Lord by God's design, and all who recognize this cry out, "Abba! Father!" for we realize that we are truly God's children.

Our adoption comes through faith in Jesus Christ and is generated by the power of the Holy Spirit. Paul tells the Galatians that Israel's ancient legalistic code no longer holds tyranny over God's own. Heirs of Jesus are no longer slaves. We live without fear and in freedom because Christ has set us free indeed!

PRAYER: Creator God, your grace supplies. Jesus saves. The Holy Spirit enables. Abba! Father! Amen.

The Revised Common Lectionary[‡] for 2005
Year A – Advent / Christmas Year B
(Disciplines Edition)

January 1–2
New Year's Day
Ecclesiastes 3:1-13
Psalm 8
Revelation 21:1-6a
Matthew 25:31-46

EPIPHANY, January 6
(or first Sunday of January)
Isaiah 60:1-6
Psalm 72:1-7, 10-14
Ephesians 3:1-12
Matthew 2:1-12

January 3–9
BAPTISM OF THE LORD
Isaiah 42:1-9
Psalm 29
Acts 10:34-43
Matthew 3:13-17

January 10–16
Isaiah 49:1-7
Psalm 40:1-11
1 Corinthians 1:1-9
John 1:29-42

January 17–23
Isaiah 9:1-4
Psalm 27:1, 4-9
1 Corinthians 1:10-18
Matthew 4:12-23

January 24–30
Micah 6:1-8
Psalm 15
1 Corinthians 1:18-31
Matthew 5:1-12

January 31–February 6
THE TRANSFIGURATION
Exodus 24:12-18
Psalm 99
2 Peter 1:16-21
Matthew 17:1-9

February 9
ASH WEDNESDAY
Joel 2:1-2, 12-17
Psalm 51:1-17
2 Corinthians 5:20b–6:10
Matthew 6:1-6, 16-21

February 7–13
FIRST SUNDAY IN LENT
Genesis 2:15-17; 3:1-7
Psalm 32
Romans 5:12-19
Matthew 4:1-11

February 14–20
SECOND SUNDAY IN LENT
Genesis 12:1-4a
Psalm 121
Romans 4:1-5, 13-17
John 3:1-17

February 21–27
THIRD SUNDAY IN LENT
Exodus 17:1-7
Psalm 95
Romans 5:1-11
John 4:5-42

February 28–March 6
FOURTH SUNDAY IN LENT
1 Samuel 16:1-13
Psalm 23
Ephesians 5:8-14
John 9:1-41

March 7–13
FIFTH SUNDAY IN LENT
Ezekiel 37:1-14
Psalm 130
Romans 8:6-11
John 11:1-45

March 14–20
PASSION/PALM SUNDAY

> *Liturgy of the Palms*
> Matthew 21:1-11
> Psalm 118:1-2, 19-29
>
> *Liturgy of the Passion*
> Isaiah 50:4-9a
> Psalm 31:9-16
> Philippians 2:5-11
> Matthew 26:14–27:66
> (*or* Matthew 27:11-54)

March 21–27
HOLY WEEK

> **Monday, March 21**
> Isaiah 42:1-9
> Psalm 36:5-11
> Hebrews 9:11-15
> John 12:1-11
>
> **Tuesday, March 22**
> Isaiah 49:1-7
> Psalm 71:1-14
> 1 Corinthians 1:18-31
> John 12:20-36
>
> **Wednesday, March 23**
> Isaiah 50:4-9a
> Psalm 70
> Hebrews 12:1-3
> John 13:21-32

Maundy Thursday, March 24
Exodus 12:1-14
Psalm 116:1-4, 12-19
1 Corinthians 11:23-26
John 13:1-17, 31b-35

Good Friday, March 25
Isaiah 52:13–53:12
Psalm 22
Hebrews 10:16-25
John 18:1–19:42

Easter Vigil, March 26
Exodus 14:10-31
Psalm 136
Romans 6:3-11
Matthew 28:1-10

March 27
EASTER DAY
Psalm 118:1-2, 14-24
Acts 10:34-43 (*or* Colossians 3:1-4)
John 20:1-18 (*or* Matthew 28:1-10)

March 28–April 3
Acts 2:14a, 22-32
Psalm 16
1 Peter 1:3-9
John 20:19-31

April 4–10
Acts 2:14a, 36-41
Psalm 116:1-4, 12-19
1 Peter 1:17-23
Luke 24:13-35

April 11–17
Acts 2:42-47
Psalm 23
1 Peter 2:19-25
John 10:1-10

April 18–24
Acts 7:55-60
Psalm 31:1-5, 15-16
1 Peter 2:2-10
John 14:1-14

April 25–May 1
Acts 17:22-31
Psalm 66:8-20
1 Peter 3:13-22
John 14:15-21

Ascension Day—May 5
(These readings may be used for Sunday, May 8.)
Acts 1:1-11
Psalm 47 (*or* Psalm 93)
Ephesians 1:15-23
Luke 24:44-53

May 2–8
Acts 1:6-14
Psalm 68:1-10, 32-35
1 Peter 4:12-14; 5:6-11
John 17:1-11

May 9–15
PENTECOST
Psalm 104:24-34, 35b
Acts 2:1-21
1 Corinthians 12:3b-13
John 7:37–39

May 16–22
TRINITY SUNDAY
Genesis 1:1–2:4a
Psalm 8
2 Corinthians 13:11-13
Matthew 28:16-20

May 23–29
Genesis 6:11-22; 7:24;
   8:14-19
Psalm 46
Romans 1:16-17; 3:22b-31
Matthew 7:21-29

May 30–June 5
Genesis 12:1-9
Psalm 33:1-12
Romans 4:13-25
Matthew 9:9-13, 18-26

June 6–12
Genesis 18:1-15; (21:1-7)
Psalm 116:1-2, 12-19
Romans 5:1-8
Matthew 9:35–10:23

June 13–19
Genesis 21:8-21
Psalm 86:1-10, 16-17 (*or* Psalm 17)
Romans 6:1b-11
Matthew 10:24-39

June 20–26
Genesis 22:1-14
Psalm 13
Romans 6:12-23
Matthew 10:40-42

June 27–July 3
Genesis 24:34-38, 42-49,
   58-67
Psalm 45:10-17 (*or* Psalm 72)
Romans 7:15-25a
Matthew 11:16-19, 25-30

July 4–10
Genesis 25:19-34
Psalm 119:105-112 (*or* Psalm 25)
Romans 8:1-11
Matthew 13:1-9, 18-23

July 11–17
Genesis 28:10-19a
Psalm 139:1-12, 23-24
Romans 8:12-25
Matthew 13:24-30, 36-43

July 18–24
Genesis 29:15-28
Psalm 105:1-11, 45*b*
Romans 8:26-39
Matthew 13:31-33, 44-52

July 25–31
Genesis 32:22-31
Psalm 17:1-7, 15
Romans 9:1-5
Matthew 14:13-21

August 1–7
Genesis 37:1-4, 12-28
Psalm 105:1-6, 16-22, 45b
Romans 10:5-15
Matthew 14:22-33

August 8–14
Genesis 45:1-15
Psalm 133
Romans 11:1-2*a*, 29-32
Matthew 15:10-28

August 15–21
Exodus 1:8–2:10
Psalm 124
Romans 12:1-8
Matthew 16:13-20

August 22–28
Exodus 3:1-15
Psalm 105:1-6, 23-26, 45*c*
Romans 12:9-21
Matthew 16:21-28

August 29–September 4
Exodus 12:1-14
Psalm 149 (*or* Psalm 148)
Romans 13:8-14
Matthew 18:15-20

September 5–11
Exodus 14:19-31
Psalm 114 (*or* Exodus
  15:1*b*–11, 20-21)
Romans 14:1-12
Matthew 18:21-35

September 12–18
Exodus 16:2-15
Psalm 105:1-6, 37-45 (*or* Psalm 78)
Philippians 1:21-30
Matthew 20:1-16

September 19–25
Exodus 17:1-7
Psalm 78:1-4, 12-16
Philippians 2:1-13
Matthew 21:23-32

September 26–October 2
Exodus 20:1-4, 7-9, 12-20
Psalm 19
Philippians 3:4*b*-14
Matthew 21:33-46

October 3–9
Exodus 32:1-14
Psalm 106:1-6, 19-23
Philippians 4:1-9
Matthew 22:1-14

**Thanksgiving Day
(Canada)—October 10**
Deuteronomy 8:7-18
Psalm 65
2 Corinthians 9:6-15
Luke 17:11-19

October 10–16
Exodus 33:12-23
Psalm 99
1 Thessalonians 1:1-10
Matthew 22:15-22

October 17–23
Deuteronomy 34:1-12
Psalm 90:1-6, 13-17
1 Thessalonians 2:1-8
Matthew 22:34-46

October 24–30
Joshua 3:7-17
Psalm 107:1-7, 33-37
1 Thessalonians 2:9-13
Matthew 23:1-12

All Saints Day—
November 1
(May be used for Sunday, November 6.)
Revelation 7:9-17
Psalm 34:1-10, 22
1 John 3:1-3
Matthew 5:1-12

October 31–November 6
Joshua 24:1-3a, 14-25
Psalm 78:1-7
1 Thessalonians 4:13-18
Matthew 25:1-13

November 7–13
Judges 4:1-7
Psalm 123 (*or* Psalm 76)
1 Thessalonians 5:1-11
Matthew 25:14-30

November 14–20
REIGN OF CHRIST SUNDAY
Ezekiel 34:11-16, 20-24
Psalm 100
Ephesians 1:15-23
Matthew 25:31-46

November 21–27
FIRST SUNDAY OF ADVENT
Isaiah 64:1-9
Psalm 80:1-7, 17-19
1 Corinthians 1:3-9
Mark 13:24-37

Thanksgiving Day (USA)—
November 24
Deuteronomy 8:7-18
Psalm 65
2 Corinthians 9:6-15
Luke 17:11-19

November 28–December 4
SECOND SUNDAY OF ADVENT
Isaiah 40:1-11
Psalm 85:1-2, 8-13
2 Peter 3:8-15a
Mark 1:1-8

December 5–11
THIRD SUNDAY OF ADVENT
Isaiah 61:1-4, 8-11
Psalm 126
1 Thessalonians 5:16-24
John 1:6-8, 19-28

December 12–18
FOURTH SUNDAY OF ADVENT
2 Samuel 7:1-11, 16
Psalm 89:1-4, 19-26
Romans 16:25-27
Luke 1:26-38

December 19–25
December 24
CHRISTMAS EVE
Isaiah 9:2-7
Psalm 96
Titus 2:11-14
Luke 2:1-20

December 25

Christmas Day

Isaiah 52:7-10

Psalm 98

Hebrews 1:1-12

John 1:1-14

December 26–January 1

First Sunday after Christmas Day

Isaiah 61:10–62:3

Psalm 148

Galatians 4:4-7

Luke 2:22-40

New Year's Day

Ecclesiastes 3:1-13

Psalm 8

Revelation 21:1-6a

Matthew 25:31-46

Epiphany, January 6 (or first Sunday of January)

Isaiah 60:1-6

Psalm 72:1-7, 10-14

Ephesians 3:1-12

Matthew 2:1-12